A Summer in Italy

Sean O'Faolain

A
SUMMER
IN
ITALY

THE DEVIN-ADAIR COMPANY
New York 1950

14.5
of 31

Contents

LIST OF ILLUSTRATIONS

NOTE OF ACKNOWLEDGMENT

Thanks are due to The Warburg Institute, University of London, and to Miss Enriqueta Harris for their courteous assistance in the selection of illustrations; also to the following for permission to use their copyright photographs: W. F. Mansell for Florence Cathedral, Siena Cathedral, and the Mosaics in the Cathedral, Isola di Torcello; to Valentino Bompiani for two votive paintings reproduced from *Italia*; and to the copyright owners of the photographs of the Palazzo Durazzo, Genoa, the church of S. Maria in Cosmedin, Rome, and the view of Camogli.

A Summer in Italy

A Summer in Italy

Entry

THE slowing train passed out of the dry moonlight into a vaulted, empty station glaring with electricity. I looked out of the carriage window down the blank perspective of platform. Outside the station I glimpsed the equally blank Piazza Carlo Felice through the first of those arches which form arcades along so many of the streets of Turin.

This hot summer night the arcades look histrionic. In the winter, when snow and rain whirl down these narrow streets from the Alps, those *portici* will be a welcome protection, and I was glad of them when the zenith broiled. Under the nearest of these arcades, against the lurid arc-lit grass of the Piazza, two young men are sitting at a table, eagerly conversing over their drinks. The Piazza is otherwise bare. In the empty courtyard of the station there is a lone carriage under its white-tasselled umbrella. It is twenty-five minutes to two o'clock in the morning; the warm summer morning; the warm summer morning of Turin.

As I climbed down the heat gushed into my face from the

platform as if there were red coals beneath it. Suddenly the platform was no longer empty. A small cheering group raced along it immediately they saw Eleonora Spinelli behind me in the doorway. There were four of them, all bareheaded; two women of about forty, a tiny tottering white-haired woman who might have been eighty, and a youth of about twenty; three generations. Such screams of joy and such gushes of tears! Such wailings, kissings and huggings! And then such a hysterical collapse into laughter, with all four pointing their fingers like swords at the little old grandmother, who was waving her wrinkled arms in the air and bawling like a baby. It was my first experience of a family reunion in Italy.

I had met Eleonora soon after I got aboard at Chambery, in Savoy; an appropriate enough place, for you already feel Italy under your fingers in Savoy. You see it and feel it in the heat and the siesta; the sallow skins and the dark eyes; the Italian servants; the Lombardy poplars along the Lac de Bourget; the tall houses with their cool, tiled loggias, and their wide Italianate eaves, and their closed shutters and their desiccated gardens; the risotto, the macaroni, the small tapering pomodori, the figs, the good coffee. The whole story of this borderland is half Italian; once part of the Kingdom of Sardinia; the duchy that gave Italy its first and last royal line; the duchy that made Turin a capital and has now left it such a pleasantly musty anachronism. Savoyards are passionately patriotic Frenchmen; yet Savoy was only welded back into France in 1860; a mere yesterday. There are many links. Turin was for many generations the university city of Savoy. One of its princes is buried over at Haute Combe.

I had been alone in the rather gloomy dining-car watching for the first foothills of the Alps when she staggered in. I saw a woman in her fifties, entirely in black; sallow, greying, lined, heavy-lidded, tired, tough. She flopped to a table at my left and looked around her in disgust. Then in the unmistakable accents of the adopted country of so many Italians she said:

'You Yank?'

'No.'

'Spik French?'

The car is French as far as Modane.

'Yes.'

'Come over and sit with me.'

I humoured her; besides, I was curious. I had barely joined her before her life-story cascaded in hideous Americanese. Forty years in the United States. Coming back now to see her old mother. A widow of a year's standing whose first husband had been a Czech who could speak no English. In love with an Irishman who runs a hot-dog stand on the highway out of Yonkers. I read his love-letters. Hot. I was shown his photographs. Not so. She showed me her Travellers' Cheques, her passport, her body-belt thick with dollars about her bare golden midriff, her nylons and her birthmark on her thigh. She talked and talked and talked of Manhattan and Yonkers; of her rich sisters in Turin; of the millions of lire she was going to spend on her poor relations; and 'Santa Maria Vergine,' she wept, 'after forty years, won't my poor old mom cry when she sees me!' Was I a Catholic? She nearly tore my shirt off to see if I was wearing a holy medal, as most Italian Catholic men do.

'Jesus! French Customs are sons of bitches you gotta stick to me I gotta wadda five thousand Lucky Strikes and all them dollars.' (Slapping her amber belly again.)

And look at her hair. 'No, look into it!' shoving her grey-black head under my nose—wouldn't the first thing she did be to have it waved when she got to Turin? It would like hell!

Then back to New York, the busy days and the neon-lit nights of the Yonkers roadhouse. And all this while the mountain peaks of the Mont Cenis wheeled in slow majesty among the clouds and dusk was in the valleys.

I wanted dearly to know what her life had been like as a child in Turin; and what she had felt when leaving Italy as a little emigrant. It was all gone from her, all forgotten, all overlain by the strain and grind of America, and it became plain to me that all this wild babbling was an effort to spew forty years of exile in order to be ready and in tune for her mother, her sisters, her lost childhood. I could see that she was terrified of their judgment. She clung to me like a woman making her death-bed confession.

The point in her mad onrush of words where I realised this was when she described to me, in that long empty car, with coy zany laughter, over the cognac—and at that moment we swung over a ravine that was ghostly with spume and held the night in its depths—how her 'Irish' had gone down on his two knees and begged and implored her to marry him before she left for Italy. In many ways I tried to find out from her why she refused to marry him. She only made more hideously coy faces, just like a young girl keeping a secret lover up her sleeve.

'I said, "You wait, Pat, you wait a bit, I marry you when I come back, maybe!" *Dio! Dio!* He curse me and he kiss me.'

She slapped me drunkenly on the shoulder, and smiled sadly, her tawny eyelids drooping, her weary, middle-aged, bistre eyelids, vastly pleased, exhausted and tormented by it all.

' "No," I say to my Irish, "not yet, soon maybe!" But, "Hell," he say, "you meet some damn wop in Italy and you never come back to me!" '

She laughed loudly. But her eyes on the snow of the mountaintips were troubled by something far older and far younger than the New World.

At Modane she became American all over again. She would not allow me to leave her side for a second. At first I thought this was because she had such a cartload of stuff to smuggle through the Customs, but it was merely that she wanted me to help her make a phone call to Turin. (She had rung Turin three times since she left Paris. 'Coming nearer! Coming nearer!')

Those Modane customs men were devils. Every third traveller was taken by men and women searchers into special booths and came out buttoning. I saw one *douanier* open a man's shoe-heels with a screwdriver. We were there for hours.

She was expertly competent with them. She played the part of the lunatic female—without much difficulty; the one type *douaniers* hate to handle—the woman mad with the exhaustion of life and of travel and the desire to see her poor old momma in Turin after all these years. She attacked their conventions with proffered bundles of dollars which they pushed aside with trembling, furious hands. She waved two hundred and fifty contraband Lucky Strikes at them. They were too scandalised to speak. She winked. She pleaded. She swore.

'Take 'em! Jesus, take 'em! I give 'em to you! Why don't you take 'em? I got *lots* more. After forty years! You fixa dissa for me? Back to see my poor old mom! *Dio mio!* Why don't you let me go? *Let me go!'*

When they asked her how much money she was importing she spat at them.

'What the hell you care? I spend it in Italy. I brought it from America. Santa Maria! I go back after forty years to my poor old mother. Sons of bitches! Here, five dollars. Take it! Curse of Jesus, my own money? You talka da bullshit!'

'You talka da patois,' he said good-humouredly, and knowing he had lost the battle he waved her away in disgust. Droves of porters fell on her like harpies.

'Forty years,' they said and looked at her in awe.

Forty years in the Land of Milk and Honey!

She bestowed cigarettes right and left. She kissed one of them. She bellowed with laughter, proud of her skill in handling men. A few miles farther on and two hours later, at Bardonecchia, the Italian post, she girded herself to go through it all over again. But the Italians were welcoming, and much more easy-going and human than the French, and I had peace because the Italian checker, a thin, handsome, half-starved young man, discovered her. He wooed her all the way to Turin to let him change her American money.

In joy of being with an Italian boy, talking in Italian, in Italian pity for his big eyes and his thin face and his big family —his life-story as usual came out in the first ten minutes—she would have liked to let him profit by her; but she was also much too sceptically Italian to give way to sentimental feelings, so she compromised by giving him a present of five dollars, a windfall to him. He earned them. The nearer we came to Turin the more overwrought she became. We had to soothe her like a frightened mare. By the time we drew into that hot, overlighted station at twenty-five minutes to two she was a wreck.

I escaped from her and her emotional family by promising to come to lunch to-morrow, and drove off under the white umbrella of the carrozza down the perspective of the Via Roma, arcaded from end to end, down to the Piazza Carlo Felice, where some vast equestrian statue presents its backside to all entrants from the railway station. The fountain in the park of the Piazza played softly. The grass was lurid in the electric light. The cafés were deserted. The midsummer heat was enveloping.

The hotel's tiled floors were cool, the bath was heaven, and I began to fall asleep, naked, thinking: 'Eleonora is going through it now. They'll be drinking every known drink until the dawn, and her babble will never stop. They'll look at her, and at one another, not understanding in the least what has happened to her in those forty years. And she won't calm for weeks, until, some evening by the riverside, alone, or when she kneels in the dusk of one of the churches, all the old things that have been waiting for her as patiently as Time will open the wells inside her and she will cry herself back into . . .' Into what? I wondered sleepily, and sleepily wondered what might be her devouring maggot. 'O Eleonora, thou art sick, the invisible worm that rides in the night, in the howling storm . . .'

Turin

TURIN is one of those cities that was. It has its present life, industrial and prosperous. The outlying factories, railroads, immense American-style blocks of flats, the university, the suburban villas, the rich business-men gathering at night in the cafés tell you that. It is dusty with past tense, and this has a great charm. I know very little of its history beyond the fact that it was ruled by its own nobility ever since the Middle Ages and came later by marriage to the House of Savoy. This explains all those romantic statues of horsed and sworded and plumed dukes or princes which give it such a stage-set atmosphere of pretentious glory to-day, as well as the dignity and impressiveness of so much of its architecture. It is laid out in straight and striking lines and lines of parallel streets, tall, narrow, noisy, cool and shady. It must have had a great hey-day when it was capital of all Italy for five wonderful years in the 1860's.

The much-bombed Piazza San Carlo is a truly noble square. The arcades, once, so an old resident tells me, crowded with old bookstalls, are now packed with heaps of rubble. The statue I had seen the first night presenting its dark rump down the perspective of the Via Roma is to Emanuele Filiberto, one of its sixteenth-century ducal rulers. When one has glanced at it one has seen all the Emanueles or Victor Emanueles one wants to see. In the course of the summer I must have seen scores of those royal, ducal or princely horsemen who had fame thrust upon them. How many Italians, not to speak of strangers, could disentangle these alternating Carlos, Vittorios, Carlos, Vittorios, for that is how they came ever since the sixteenth century— with one intruding Francesco? I suppose the only one who means anything to most of us is Vittorio Emanuele II, who, with Cavour, accepted Italian unity, that accursed event, so

nobly achieved by Garibaldi, which has brought so much mis-
fortune to Italy, and, indeed, to the world, for it destroyed the
old local ways and gave Italy an inflated idea of its own political
destiny. No statue did I see to Vittorio Emanuele III who
abdicated in 1946. A brief, inglorious line with a faked-up
glory. The first, perhaps, because of the second. As local princes
these men had a function. Blown-out into royalty, the house of
Savoy could not carry so much dignity, like the vast Piazza
Vittorio Emanuele beside the Po—blank, bleak and big enough
to contain a small army. It is like so much in Turin, an anachronism from 'the great days'. Humble shops now hang up
tin bath-tubs and chamber-pots under the Roman arches, and
half the houses look like tenements. But Italy has one King on
her side, the sun. Unlike a woman she can afford to owe much
of her charm to her disintegration; to fading murals, peeling
plaster, and the exquisite delicacy of rotting pinks and bleached
corals. Colour is the chief joy of most cities in Italy, not struc-
ture or texture as with us in the North who have to rely on the
chisel and the quality of the stone for our effects and can grow
lyrical about green moonlight on granite or all the shades of
blue possible in limestone. There are as many hues in a pink
wall in Italy as there have been seasons to corrupt its matter.
An American entering Venice for the first time with a friend
of mine kept saying, in dismay: 'Why don't they clean this
place up?' He was confessing to a conventional notion of the
meaning of dirt.

The Piazza Vittorio Emanuele is not particularly colourful
but if it were bright with flat paint it would have no colour
at all. Behind it rises one of the most absurd structures in Europe, the Mole Antonelliana, built like the Eiffel Tower and
almost as tall, a fantastic tapering pagoda abruptly introducing
an oriental contrast into the heart of the Roman tradition. It is
so bizarre as to have a ridiculous and exciting kind of beauty of
its own.

Below this desert square flows the Po under its shattered
bridges, deep between walls, lavishly wide promenades to its

edges, an unmistakably Italian perspective of vine-streaked hills, gleaming villas, speared poplars, faded grass patches, trellised gardens, an abbey high up over all, all miasmic in the sun and heat; and below, in the golden water, brown with alpine mud, yet a limpid bath of light, bathing boys and girls, as golden as this river that moves slowly and powerfully across Italy to the Adriatic. Here in the far north is southern somnolence, a mesmeric and languorous dreaminess that keeps one for hours leaning over the warm parapets, or lying and dozing full length on them, peering through protective eye-lashes at the sunshot world.

Santa Christina and a Bookstall

IT takes an act of will to move. One day I began to climb Monte Cappuccini, on the far side, and when I had done it I stayed there for a long time staring back over the sea of red roofs at the snow-covered panorama of the Alps, soft as milk in the haze of morning heat.

It is easier to think than to stir. There returned to me up here a thought (not, I now feel, unconnected with Eleonora) that had first brushed my mind below in the Piazza San Carlo. This is the way it stole on me.

To enter this piazza from the Via Roma you pass directly under the walls of two churches that form a sort of fortified entrance to the square. I went into the one on the right, Santa Cristina, and said a brief prayer, as so many parishioners do in passing, even if it be no more than to touch the bleeding feet of a crucifix. Neither church is particularly graceful; as always each is dramatic, with the usual Virgin pierced by a dozen real swords and the usual general glittering gaudiness lighting the dusk. Just beyond it I paused at a paper-stall, as any northern traveller might, to buy a dozen papers and periodicals at random, and intending to read politics over my coffee found myself reading about love. Or, perhaps, I was reading about what we carelessly call love, saying as easily that we love our wives, the heat or whisky. I could not help thinking, as I looked from the bathing-beauties in the clerical paper *l'On Palmilio* to the only more luscious bathing-beauties of the anticlerical paper *Don Basilio* that during the last three weeks in Geneva and Savoy I had not seen a single bathing-beauty on a bookstall; this one was full of them; furthermore, that readers of any clerical paper, Irish, English or American, would be very surprised indeed to find a bathing-beauty grinning on the front page. But sooner or later, and sooner rather than later, one admits that *l'amore* is insistently in the air of Italy. Art, literature, history, conversation, posters, newspapers, advertising, all record the Italian's keen and frank admiration of the body. What other country would advertise a 'Grow More Wheat' campaign with a poster of cornfields, a farmer with a scythe and a reclining naked woman. How often have not young men, thinking me English, started conversations about English women, distastefully parodying a stiff wooden soldier—'Come una mummia ambulante!'—unconsciously forming with their hands curves of happier reminiscence. In this climate the body shows itself frankly. Now, as in the days of Boccaccio and Firenzuola, the Italian's love of beauty is chiefly by 'education of the eye.' You sleep naked; you work half-naked—we associate antique Rome with the toga, but its slaves must have displayed the torsos of Michelangelo's Adam, like the road-labourer of to-day, in trunks and paper cap, no more; often not even sandals. One is hourly eager to strip and swim, and it is a constant delight to watch little boys and girls gambolling like water-rats. One lies bare to the sun all day long on bathing-beaches where there are no sneaky winds like ours, crowded from sunrise to sunset with women and men chatting, drinking, reading or eating in semi-nudity.

This idle summer morning as I looked down at the body's glory in the golden river it seemed a fair question to ask: 'What do they do about it? After all, they are also a religious people?

Are these passionate creatures never troubled as the puritanical North is troubled?' To this their literature gives hardly a clue; not even Dante, who though he consigns the carnal to Hades is gentle enough with them to put them in the first circle. In all but a few Italian novelists, such as Fogazzaro, is there anything but a rampant delight in carnal love, and writers like D'Annunzio and Moravia never even hint at that reaction of the soul where *omne animale triste est*. They suggest a too simple paganism; they propose no conflict between Venus and the Virgin; or, I might say, between Santa Cristina at one side of the piazza and all those beauties of the bookstall on the other.

Venus and the Virgin

I TURNED and climbed the battered steps of the little church behind me and straightway met with one answer. In its grubby porch Saint Rita of Cascia smiled at a thousand mendicants. From floor to ceiling, on the walls, where a notice helplessly said *É vietato scrivere sui muri,* a multitude had scribbled their passionate prayers. Not an inch of space remained unscrawled by these barely literate worshippers of whom a great many would have seemed to D. H. Lawrence as frankly in heat. They had drawn intertwined hearts, spitted and pinned them together by arrows of love, written amorous prayers and such idle memorials to happy hours as *Affinchè sia segno della nostra felicità,* signed by Luigi and Bettina; though somebody had been unhappy in that affair, for Luigi's name was passionately obliterated and one Michele had put his name in its place; or perhaps Bettina had? A common prayer in this forest of prayers was *Chièdo la grazia di essere promesso.* Here a woman begged for the safe return of her beloved from the war. *Proteggi il mio Beppe. Fa che torni salvo.* She signed it with a trembling hand, Lotta, Maggio, 1943. Here a poor German begged, in German. Here a Nora had come up those steps and written the appealing prayer: *O Santa Rita fa che Mario mi voglia sempre bene come gli voglio io.* 'O Saint Rita, make Mario love me always as much as I love him.' (These scribbled prayers are a common feature in Italian churches. A few I have seen are gaily indecorous.)

What on earth would Lawrence have made of this medley of venery and sanctity? His *Twilight in Italy,* a veritable Pervigilium Veneris, broods heavily on the Italian worship of the phallus. To him it seemed that the Italian cult of Venus is a destructive thing; a worship of love not as part of creative divinity but as the whole of it, and therefore the worship of a killer not a creator, a suicide-complex. He did agree that the Italian does not worship Venus naughtily (I think of those Genevese night-clubs where what Calvinism denies by day is peeked at secretively by night); nor obscurely and nastily and fussily after the manner of Ibsen and Strindberg still farther north. The Italian rejoices in love unashamedly, so that even if Venus is his master she at least creates new life while she kills him.

A good deal of this is, I think, nonsense, though there is some truth in it; moral Ruskin would have said an enormous amount of truth. There is here something delicate and subtle and human that is beyond the understanding of the unremitting moralist, of the type of Savonarola, or of the inverted moralist, like Lawrence, sick of one orthodoxy and replacing it by another just as absolute. Could Lawrence, who, I think, thought rather too much as Renoir is said to have painted, have even faintly understood the sigh that passed through this porch like a summer wind when Nora lifted her love-clouded eyes to her saint? Would he have seen Nora only as proud for her Mario? Cannot the flesh and the spirit, the pity and the sorrow of love, nature and the supernatural, lie together in one passionate bodily embrace?

I do not understand how life can be divided as the moralists divide it. To the Italians who live life to the full, brimming it over, throwing their whole bodies and souls into everything they do, life must be an indivisible oneness; whereas we, of this forbidding North, who measure and strain, tuck God away in the Church and Venus away in the bed, and miserably and foolishly drain each part of life of the richness of the other. One is constantly meeting travellers who, because they do not accept this, are puzzled that Italians gossip in their churches, kiss behind a pillar, spit in the aisles, may even, as I have seen happen, wheel a bicycle in one door and out another. These observers are equally shocked by the sight of unshaven friars with faces like pirates, begging nuns in the capital of Christendom, gaudy and grubby dolls, tinsel bambinos, baby-Virgins and the like in lovely quattrocento churches cheek by jowl with exquisite sculpture; and when I say that I find these bambinos both horrible and funny, even this will probably shock; as if religion were not sometimes so funny that one must laugh at it with God.

(Autumn: an Italian friend has just read all this. I said, 'How wide of the mark is that?' He laughed and replied: 'To us religion is a family affair. You must have seen mothers nursing their babies in church. Why not? The Madonna is sometimes depicted giving the breast to *her* baby.[1] We are very familiar with God. You are very respectful.' As I was at it I asked about the half-empty churches of Italy. 'In Ireland,' I said, 'if one misses Sunday mass that is a *most* serious sin. What happens in Italy when you go to confession and say you have not been to mass for six months?' He replied: 'Our priests are indulgent. They would say, "That was wrong. Try to do better." This is not weakness on their part. They try to see the best in every sinner.' But I do not think my question interested my friend. His shrug seemed to say, 'What are you fussing about?' I was, to him, being niggling and finicky: with my talk of Sin I was chopping up life into cat's-meat.)

Surely, the keyword for the Italian is *esuberánte?* They adore superabundance, hailing it with that lavish gesture

---

[1] I think this is not so much Italian as medieval. There is a Madonna Allattante by Van Eyck.

which forms curves of approval for what Yeats called 'the bursting pod'. A people of such passionate intensity could never be moralists. Neither could they ever be merely sensualists. There is too much overflow of emotion, imagination and human sympathy for either. This is something that few historians—of the Italian Renaissance, for example, especially Burckhardt—recognise clearly enough; for although Burckhardt strives hard with his northern or Reformed conscience, it never really melts, and his views on the Italian character are discoloured by it. True, he stresses the imaginative influence; but he overstresses it, seeing the result in a 'subjective' religion which disintegrates all morality. What I have called the 'jumble' is, to him, a frightening lack of moral distinctions, so that instead of being pleased to find that even the most wicked men went to the sacraments and revered their priests as priests while mocking them as men, he sees this duality which is, at its lowest, surely better than single-minded wickedness, merely as a hideous dishonesty. It is this rigid attitude of Reformation historians which has fostered some of our more vulgar fantasies about Italian life; such as the servant-maid picture of the terrible puritanism of Savonarola and the as-terrible viciousness of the Borgian Pope. I call this a 'servant-maid' fantasy because it is too simple-minded to be true; as if a copulating hog or a savage Puritan could simultaneously have their warm love of children; the admiration of the most cultured men; an intense adoration of the Virgin Mary (it was Alexander VI who established the Angelus bell); a most discriminating taste (it was Savonarola who saved the Laurentain library); a great love for order, for both these men reformed religious orders, Savonarola his own in Tuscany, Alexander several in and out of Italy; and both had an eager missionary spirit—the Dominican's is freely admitted, and Alexander's plans roved as far as India and the two Americas. One cannot be simple about so exuberant, ambitious and passionate a race as this. To them Woman could never be merely either a Distraction or a Temptation. For them she is heaven and hell, the light of the world in her eyes and the light of damnation in her breasts, pride and pity, anguish and bliss. For them sacred and mortal love are love confederate, all rolled into one big, warm featherbed.

To them, I feel, Woman is not merely a necessity but a joy, as well as something between the unfailing joke and a Holy Terror. I recall a comical conversation, in Rome, between a young Frenchman and a young Italian. The Parisian was hollow-eyed, unshaven, half-asleep. 'Les femmes de Rome! Une semaine! Je suis mort.' The Italian was enchanted, but teased him for being unpatriotic. 'Allons! Pas meilleures que les femmes de France?' A shrug, a struggle, a weighting-up, a shuddering surrender. 'Plus chaudes!' The Italian youth laughed for five minutes.

I went back several times to that height of Monte Cappuccini, pleased to find the lovers and saints and heroes of Italy all clustered on one small hilltop. For there is here, also, a tiny museum belonging to the Italian Alpine Club to remind us of that active and enduring side of the Italian character which we too easily forget and which is a saga of bravery, brains and endless endurance. And how characteristic the variety of these displays, in minute illustration of the natural encyclopaedic curiosity of the Italian genius; examples of peasant art in the Alto Adige and the Trentino beside pictures and models to illustrate electrical development at high intensity in high altitudes; the trophies of explorers in Africa; examples of the botany and geology of the Alps; all part of an historical and scientific study that has been going on since the days of Garibaldi. One will be reminded of it in many unexpected places, as when the bust of some Alpine explorer looks rather incongruously over the Venetian lagoons, or lurks in the cool shadows of the Pincio. They keep us from forgetting that this great peninsula is vertebrate with one vast Apennine arm thrust up from the tip of Calabria to circle the mighty arena of the plains of Piedmont, Lombardy and Venetia, of which Milan is the centre, Venice the exit to the sea and Turin the door.

Italian Miracles

THE systematic traveller, unlike the casual traveller, has, I believe, more to record than to remember. The casual wanderer stays here, ambles there for each moment's pleasure, and afterwards when people ask him 'What did you do?' he cannot reply. The things that made him happy are too little, too evanescent, too personal to be named. I have no idea now why I wandered up so often to that restaurant on Monte Cappuccini. But over and over again I foresee that I shall have no idea about many such caprices that were, at the time, delightful to indulge. I used to read there, doze there, write there, not go down into the city until the late afternoon, when the swallows were whirling above the vine-trellis over my head. I was often the sole person to take lunch, usually ham with melon, a heap of *maccheroni napolitano,* tomatoes in olive oil, bread, butter, black olives and a white wine, for about 650 lire, then around seven shillings. Many boys and girls, or husbands and wives, also came there to pass a portion of the day, but they brought paper bags of bread and fruit, with, perhaps, a little meat or salami, and bought only the beer. I liked to spend the long afternoons in the public gardens along the river; they must be among the finest public gardens in Europe, bosky, natural, shaded by elms and chestnuts, with grass to the water's edge and lovely views down the river to the hilltop basilica of the Superga—a tiny Bois de Boulogne, an ideal refuge for nuzzling lovers, playing children, and idlers like myself. The nights I was content to spend, after some sight-seeing in the cool of the evening, drinking among the prattling, noisy crowds of the Piazza, talking with anybody who wanted to talk, listening to the band, letting time eat its tail at its own sweet will.

One quarter where I liked to wander particularly after dark

was the old quarter west of the Cathedral. The ground plan of Turin is unique among the cities of Europe. New York is the nearest city to Turin laid out in the same rectangular design. This is because the ancient nucleus of Turin, the colony called Julia Augusta Taurinorum, built its home in the shape of a classical rectangle, and the spreading city retained these lines down the centuries. Near the Cathedral is the main street of this Roman town, the Via Porta Palatina, ending in a Roman arch. It is now a lane in a near-slum. I adored it because it has the suppurating, pullulating, exciting, half-animal character of a ghetto, the sort of thing which sprouts so easily and uncontrollably in so many Italian cities, like a jungle. This quarter remains in my memory as a fantastic medley of rookeries clambering to the sky, with washing as colourful as banners drying over crapulous ruins that one does not know now whether to ascribe to bombs or decay; everybody living in everybody's else's pocket, as all Italians, who by nature hate privacy, love to do. As I wandered here of nights, overcome by pity for the poverty, and excited by the congestion of this den of almost pustular humanity, I often had the feeling that I was not in Turin at all, but back in New York, strolling around McDougall Street of like summer evenings where the same unprivacy spills out on the porches, squats on the pavements' edges, gossips along the balconies, and I would be brought back to Italy only by the heat, or by the drums of an arcade, or by the sight through a doorway of a swarthy group at a *trattoria* table playing cards, or by one of those melodramatic sworded statues with which the city swarms like Grand Opera, or by the sight of the Cathedral's outline against the sky.

The Cathedral, on the rim of this quarter, is a lonely and empty cave. Even on Sunday, at mass-time, I did not see more than a score of people gathered together at a side-altar; or in the chapel up the baroque stairs behind the high altar, where a second glittering altar stands high under the roof, divided by a great glass window from the nave below. It is in this upper chapel, lined with black marble, that they have

stored the shroud in which, so tradition says, Joseph of
Arimathea wrapped the body of Christ when He was laid in
the tomb. It was one of the things I had most wanted to see in
Turin. All one does see is a painter's reproduction, with the
marks of the limbs and the divine face startlingly outlined. The
actual shroud has been shown only twice in the last fifty
years, during the Anno Santo and for the marriage of
Prince Umberto. It is a long strip of fine linen, fourteen feet by
about three and a half. If we refer to the Catholic Encyclo-
pedia we find that it has denied the authenticity of the relic.
How old is the relic? It has had two main and relentless op-
ponents, the Abbé Chevalier and Father Thurston, S.J., both of
whom maintained that the linen was manufactured in the
fourteenth century, with Father Thurston adding that the design was probably painted on it originally without fraudulent
intent, merely as a pious picture. 'Practically everywhere—'
sighs one who believed in it utterly and fought passionately for
it—'practically everywhere in the English-speaking world the
precious relic of Turin is received as spurious. And why?
Chiefly because Father Thurston, following Canon Chevalier,
has for more than twenty years [this was written twenty years
ago] strenuously opposed its claim to authenticity and has ever
been on the alert to criticise anything that may be said in favour of that claim.[1] The arguments for and against have
been mainly historical. A modern Catholic writer, more de-
tached than most, has said, however: 'It is a question for
science . . . not for history. For the fate of Christ's garments,
for which the soldiers diced, and of His graveclothes, is not
historically attested. But absence of Historical proof is not disproof.[2]

It may be said that since it is agreed that there can be no
historical 'attestation' here, that last point does not greatly matter. But it does matter somewhat. If absence of historical proof
is not disproof, its absence surely ought to deter people from

[1] *The Holy Shroud.* P. A. Beecher, D.D. (Dublin, 1928).
[2] *The Burial of Christ.* Alfred O'Rahilly, D.LITT. (Cork, 1942).

making positive claims, unless there is some other very good reason for making such claims? Otherwise at any moment anybody might, let us say, produce the rope with which Judas hanged himself, and say that it should be accepted as genuine, since there is no historical disproof; he might, in this manner, produce anything at all, from the sword of Theodoric to Cain's jawbone. It may be said that tradition alone can claim where history is silent, and that tradition is to be respected—if it really is tradition and not myth or legend. But even there history must come into it. For history reaches back to the rise of the tradition, or at any rate to the date of its promulgation which history records. If that date is within not more than two hundred years of the event, and if the tradition has had universal acceptance—as, for example, in the case of Saint Peter's martyrdom (for which there is no contemporary documentary proof) —we may accept the tradition's accuracy. If the tradition arises more than two hundred years after the event, one will be wise, at least, to suspect a legend. The 'tradition' regarding the Holy Shroud of Turin arose at a very great remove from the Crucifixion.

One can very well appreciate the reluctance of the Catholic clergy to accept these pious relics officially. They must often wish that such questions never arose. The disputants wax hot and their disputes are not always intellectually impressive. When one of the controversialists in this matter declares triumphantly that 'there are no pigments' on the Turin linen the reader cannot be happy in the knowledge that the man who said so had never laid eyes on the linen at all; nor when he points to the photographs of the shroud and says 'See the clots of blood on the hair, see the marks of the scourge', and one looks and can see nothing at all but vague smudges.

But, as far as ocular 'proof' is concerned, one might as well stay at home as hope to find assurance from the actual sight of any one of the almost innumerable vessels of pious belief for which Italy is famous. I think, for example, of the elaborate and sometimes exquisite reliquaries in the ante-rooms of the

Medici Chapel in Florence, shelves upon shelves of gold and
silver-work, every one containing a relic of some holy person.
One might as well, as far as eyesight goes, be looking at the
ashes of a rabbit or the bones of a lemming. As I stared, so often
afterwards, in church after church, at similar saintly relics to
many of which miraculous cures have been attributed, I realised that all this is beyond reason. To the pure reason a miracle
is simply that which does not occur; that is to say, it is a denial
of what is presumed to be the fixed order of nature. Present any
rationalist sceptic with a record of an alleged miracle and he
will, no matter how impressive it is, instinctively seek for a
'natural' explanation; as he logically must, since anything which
occurs must by that very fact become part of nature, even if
only as a freak of nature. If he finds no natural explanation, he
will suspend judgment, and suspend it all his life rather than
accept the alternative.

I do not find fault with him for this. The people I do think
illogical are those who say: 'Why don't miracles occur to-day?'
—since even if they saw Lazarus walk out of the tomb they
would still look for 'explanations' in nature. Those who believe
in miracles believe in them because they believe in God. I have
never seen God, and I have never seen a miracle, but I believe
in both, and there is no rational way of proving either that I am
wrong or right. *Credo quia impossibile.* It is the cornerstone of
faith. Indeed, if I wanted to try to convert an unbeliever in
anything from Aspirin to mixed bathing, from ghosts to the
Holy Ghost, far from appealing to his reason I would assail the
whole tin-pot mechanism of reason whose processes are, ultimately, no stronger than an accumulation of probabilities, and
whose final conclusions, except in minute mathematical meas-
urements, are a presumption, a leap into the dark. The exceed-
ingly large number of Italians who believe in the miraculous
will never surprise an Irishman. Neither they nor we are ever
sure, in Yeats's phrase, of the earth beneath our footsoles. It
does not prevent, it may even induce, an accompanying protective scepticism and compensatory realism. It makes both races

poorer hands at politics than at the arts. It encourages steadier races to treat us as slightly dotty, as—if this mad world of the rationalists is 'sane'—I hope we are.

Eleonora Mavourneen

'WHAT does the visual surface tell me, anyway, about anything?' I mused as I came away that morning from the Cathedral shrine. How superficial the observations of every casual traveller must be! How rarely he enters to the hearth of life! Suddenly remembering Eleonora, I wandered off to lunch with her family, eager to pierce to one scrap of this intimate life of which I had hitherto been enjoying the façade.

She received me with joy. She was dottier than ever. She dragged me after her around the apartment, shuffling in her mules around the house, dragging open cupboards to show me her sister's ranked frocks, flinging open the wine-press to show me enough liquor to give an army the D.T.s, throwing open the windows to let me see all the blocks of flats she was about to purchase. Her family was at bay. They kept looking strangely at her and even more strangely at me. Once her sister said: 'She never stops!' The local radio played Rossini all the time ('Italians in Algeria'), and sometimes they all joined in the singing, and now one and now another of them would cry 'Listen!' to some favourite tune; or as the table was laid forks and knives would halt in their descent and beat time in the air. That afternoon, I found, they were all due to drive over to Bardonecchia to meet Eleonora's son *en route* from Paris. This was the first I had heard of him; an American soldier who could talk no Italian. We ate and ate, and they talked and talked, and Rossini played and played, and they plied me with drink after drink until my head swam with all the talk and drink and music; and then—the door-bell rang and they all jumped up screaming, because it was Eleonora's boy, who had taken an earlier train so as to be with her the sooner. This reunion was even more joyful and more anguished than the reunion the week before at the station. I found myself embracing them all in turn with tears pouring down my face.

For that one emotional moment I *was* beside the hearth of life. For a second the thought occurred to me: 'Stay in Turin. This is *it*. An Italian novel would radiate out from this room; their friends; their ambitions; their lives past and present.' But then I thought: 'It would take a lifetime!' Even as I sat there, alone at the table now; they had already gone from me. They were doing a ballet around the room, squabbling like Furies about something so involved in personalities of whom I knew nothing that I was suddenly a complete stranger again. I staggered up to go. They hardly noticed me going, hurling pressing invitations to supper over their shoulders as they fought their private war.

As I walked away I began to realise what a fool I had been about Eleonora. Of course she was coming back in search of something precious to herself; but, of course, she would never find it. Had I not seen Irish exiles coming back to Ireland in just the same hopeless search for the dreams they had dreamed on Broadway? Had I not myself written a novel called *Come Back to Erin* to show that you can never go back, and should never go back; that the heart is always exiling itself. She would quarrel and be quarrelled with all the time; ultimately hate and be hated; and go back to Yonkers, to everybody's relief. Suddenly, as I sat among the mobs in the Piazza Carlo Felice and ordered an *Americano* I remembered that at Bardonecchia, on the very threshold of home, she and I had got talking to an Italian-American, and he had said, bitterly: 'I been here three months, and gee, *will* I be glad to get home again!' She had not heard him. Later I was to meet several such exiles, and it was always the same story. And Carlo Levi's *Cristo si è Fermato a Eboli*[1] tells the same thing about the

---

[1] *Christ stopped at Eboli.* (Farrar, Straus & Co., Inc.)

Italians who came back to the mountains of Campania and spent the rest of their lives regretting it.

'The peasants who emigrate to America remain just what they always were; many stay there and their children become Americans, but the rest, those who come back twenty years later, are just the same as when they went away. In America they live apart, among themselves; for years they eat nothing but bread, just as they did in Gagliano, saving all their meagre earnings. They live next door to the earthly paradise, but they dare not enter.

'Then one day they come back to Italy, with the intention of staying only long enough to visit their family and friends. But someone offers to sell them a parcel of land, and they run into a girl whom they knew when they were children and decide to marry her. Before they are aware of it, six months have gone by, their re-entry permit has expired, and they have to stay at home. Soon they sink back into the poverty they lived in so many years ago, before they went away. Along with poverty they regain their agelong patience and resignation and all their former peasant habits; in short these "Americans" can in no way be distinguished from the rest, unless it be by deeper bitterness, and the regret that from time to time haunts them for their lost riches. Gagliano is full of these returned emigrants, who look on the day of their return as the unluckiest of their lives.'

Levi records several typical stories, such as this one:

' "Over there I had a shop of my own and four assistants," my barber told me. "In 1929 I came here for six months, but I got married and didn't go back. Now I've only this miserable hole in the wall, and I'm up against it." His hair was already gray at the temples and there was a mournful and solemn look about him.

'When the barber thought of old times his face grew dark and sad. What was left to him of the life of ease he had led on the other side? A little house at the upper end of the village, with an elaborately carved door and geranium pots on the balcony, a sickly wife, and poverty. "If only I hadn't come back!" '

Whether she stayed or whether she went any competent Italian writer could make a whole novel of *her* Coming Back to Erin. Was it well for her that her 'Irish' was waiting for her in Yonkers? What would she lose by going back to New York, or gain by merging, however uncomfortably, into Turin? It is a nice, if uneasy, problem in values.

Eden's Apple

THE arcades of Turin began to feel claustrophobic. The narrow, shaded streets are cool, but they are also close. The hustling 'busyness' is indifferent. The clattering amiability of the cafés is shutting-out. The traveller feels his own isolation. The spectacle, however splendid, does not suffice, and Turin is not quite splendid enough. He has no remedy but to add more spectacle, and one can have a surfeit of the spectacular. What was it I needed? Something still more congested? Still more pustular? Where life would overflow the *décor?* Genoa? Noise, docks, ships, sailors, slums, the open sea and the roads of the world? That was the ticket. In the cool of early morning, before the trams were tearing down the lean perspective of the Via Carlo Alberto, I saw Monte Cappuccini slowly melt away behind factory chimneys and the Po become a wide, shallow country river.

It was only when I came to write a last entry in my diary, at the summer's end, that I knew what I had fled from. I had simply done what every traveller does and has always done. For a while he loses himself in a strange place. Then, by degrees, the strangeness wears away, and instead of looking he begins to think, and thereby he finds himself again. Then he runs away. Every traveller should be what the old Irish priest called the local bad woman: 'A perambulating receptacle for lusht.' He should feed on sensation. The happiest travellers are the un-enquiring. Because they never ask they never regret, and, as Racine has very wisely observed, the only man who is really continent is the man who is without regrets. To ask is to know; to know is to sigh; to sigh is to desire. There are so many kinds of desire; for Woman, for Power, for Change, for Money, for Drink. My lust is for thinking; which is just as devouring and destructible as any of the others. Those put purity and sanity and love to flight. I do not know which Greek it was who said, or in what words exactly, but it is true that when dialectic comes in the door it puts poetry to flight through the window. How well I know it! How often I repeat for myself Keats's wish for a life of sensation rather than of thought. But if you are cursed, as I am, with a poor but enquiring brain, it is as hard to stop asking questions as it is for another man to stop wenching or drinking.

In my country this 'lusht' is fully recognised. They ostensibly ban books for what they call indecency. But you will not always find legs or breasts or beds in those 'indecent' books; you will find my kind of 'lusht'; you will find people asking what our censors consider to be dangerous, evil and imponderable questions, questions about God and Love and Sin and the Devil, and it is these that they like most of all to ban. Can it be that our Irish censors are on the side of pure Pleasure? Can it be that they are all Keatsians? Can it be that they believe that all life should be one long happy brainless Eden?

'And the serpent said unto the woman, Ye shall not surely die. For God doth know that in the day ye eateth thereof, then your eyes shall be opened, and ye shall be as gods, knowing good and evil. . . . And the eyes of them both were opened and they knew that they were naked.'

That was what I fled from. That was what poor old Eleonora Spinelli would in due course fly from, and spend the rest of her life in flight from it, though she has not got a brain at all. She would fly from the apple; from that in Italy which, in the midst of joy, provokes thought.

'Thinkin'—'said a Dublin Metropolitan policeman to me one day, holding up the traffic to say it, because I had explained to him that I 'thought' I could go such-and-such a way—'thinkin' never did any good to any wan. An' it ruined many a man's happiness.'

'Oh, come, now,' I protested, leaning out of the car. 'Whose happiness did it ever ruin?'

'Look at Tertullian!' he cried, waving on the traffic.

The Riviera

THE end east of Turin is level and rich, thanks to the Po and its sister rivers which carry down across the plains of Piedmont and Lombardy that fertile Alpine dust whose final spread lies underneath the lagoons about Chioggia and Venice.

Even so early in the morning the plain was soporific as a breathless sea. The poplars were as delicate and thin-stemmed as flowers. The vines, blue as dawn with sulphate spray, had a ghostly look. The roofs of the farmhouses, and their old brick walls, were wine-red, and the sky beyond, domed down to the level horizon, was an intense blue. This clarity of the Italian sky at morning is Dante's *bianca aspetto di cilestro,* that pale clearness of the air which he so loved to describe and which must be familiar to everybody from Italian painting. No sooner do we see this shadowless sky and bath of light, above and across these Lombard plains, than we long for a pink campanile to break its boundless reign; and when we do see a campanile we at once see a hundred familiar Italian paintings. But this is a thought which may come to us more forcibly when we step out of the sunlight into a gallery in Florence, or Venice, or Rome, and wonder, perhaps, why the painters have universally sieved the black-slashed light outside into a shadowless radiance; or, at most, permitted it only to cast not so much shadows as shades and those as delicate as at dawn. It is well, then, to remember these plains that are all one vast glow of unbroken light, those outlines of houses, trees, and horizon so clear and flawless, where light is an ambience as universal and as indivisible as the air, where shadow is swallowed up by the same sun that makes it.

The long roads were dusty. The clouds of dust behind a car took a long time to settle. By the time one cloud had settled another car raised another cloud to hide the plumed cornfields and the leafy reeds. Not that the mention of reeds must suggest moisture. These dry reeds are used as vine-props, or thrown over rude trellises to make a weak sun-pierced shadow, their withered leaves dangling like broken spearheads overhead. The only other trees I recognise are the sweet chestnuts and mulberries—these to feed the silkworms. Drouth is universal. The clay is cracked. The sun is king and tyrant. At Asti—oh, for a bottle of cool Asti Spumante! and the vendors selling nothing that morning but Cinzano!—we enter the valley of the Tanaro. I cannot remember where we crossed this stream that in winter will be a river. It was the first of the hundreds of blown bridges I saw that summer, a great fifteen-arched span. We slowed down, as so often on every journey after that, to sneak slowly across the trembling spiderlegs of the temporary wooden bridge high over the almost dry bed and parched stones.

The sun rose higher. The heat gathered force. At every halt people tumbled out like bags of apples and crushed in a laughing mob about the water-tap. I still had with me a bottle of the good red wine of Savoy, and I wrapped it in *Don Basilio,* soaked it in water, and hung it by string in the window to cool. Now and again I tilted it on my head. The scenery began to swim a little in its own miasma. Or maybe it was my own?

The train had started late and would arrive late. One accepts this. It was otherwise a good train: that is, it was by Italian standards not full. An Italian train is empty when by our standards it is packed. Nobody was standing on my toes. Nobody travelled on the roofs. The poor travellers sat in the open doors of the wagons, legs dangling. In one wagon a bunch of girls with chaplets of flowers in their hair sang like the angels in Botticelli's illustrations to the Vita Nuova. Or, perhaps, I should say it had been a good train to begin, for gradually the full train became still more full, and, as all Italian trains do, it went on filling and filling and yet was never, apparently, too full to take on more.

In this web of railways of northern Italy no train is merely carrying passengers to where it says it is going; it is a link in the web. Any laden traveller clambering aboard at, say, Alessandria may as easily be struggling south to Marseilles from Trieste, or on his way north to the Brenner from Sicily. A train marked westward to Ventimiglia may help you eastward to Pisa. A train marked to Innsbruck may be your ticket for Verona. At Milan the practised commercials clamber like steeplechasers from platform to platform in search of useful trains. Lone carriages in sidings, apparently going nowhere, fill up. Presently when 'your' train pulls in, those happy, knowing faces grin at you from the crowded windows. You fight to get aboard or get left behind. Officials walk away. At Genoa I once lost a finger-nail in a frenzied struggle to squeeze inside a door that, for jammed bodies, would not open once shut, nor, once open, close again. That day four of us travelled in the w.c. with the entire domestic furniture of a family of refugees wandering from somewhere in Istria to somewhere in Liguria. A bird-cage tumbled on our heads at every bend.

Genoa One

THE natural entry to Genoa is from the sea; as it is to Venice. One might, with a proper sense of origins, enter Venice from the island of Torcello; and with a romantic feeling for death enter Genoa from the lovely and lonely bay of San Fruttuoso behind Portofino, the burial-place of the Dorias, Genoa's last oligarchs. If you do not come that way, or from Marseilles, you come down from Torino, through this exciting mountainous region of La Bocchetta, whose ravines and mountain views vanish constantly and reappear abruptly behind the jagged hills.

The route has its own historical associations, as I find this sleepy afternoon. My first glimpse of Genoa was dramatic, or rather of one of its imposing back doors. I saw a great castle, or fortress, high up on the tip-top of a mountain peak pointed like a pyramid. I was wondering what this lone castle had defended, and how on earth anybody had ever reached it with carts of supplies and munitions, when, suddenly, on the tip-top of a neighbouring cone I saw an identical castle, as remote, as forbidding, and as inaccessible. Then, to my right, there appeared another peak and another castle! And yet another— and all about on every peak a fort, and, to my astonishment, I saw that these forts are linked by a mighty wall.

I went up a few days later by the funicular through the orchards behind the Piazza della Zecca to the Forte Castellaccio, one of the highest of these keeps that have protected Genoa on the landward side ever since the seventeenth century, and surveyed the Mediterranean proudly, from Savona to Portofino. I found then that this mighty wall is not a curtain-wall but a grassy rampart wide enough for thirty men to march abreast, and almost ten miles long. I might have guessed this had I be-thought myself earlier of my Uncle Toby, who would have driven Slop into ecstasies with talk of their bastions and revetments, their gorges and casemates. For the seventeenth century was a late date for fortifications, and cannonading would, by then, have made mere curtain-walls futile. Even bastions were no longer impregnable, as Garibaldi found when defending Rome, for all that the French first assailed it in the lunatic manner of the Crusaders. Later on Vauban would be extending even such defences as these with outer ravelins and spreading outworks as the range of guns became longer and longer. The zone of defence would go on spreading farther and farther to keep the guns at bay: until in our time the wheeled ravelins race madly through the fields and the last thing anybody wants to be forced to defend is a city.

These antique ramparts of Genoa are now pleasant evening walks; indestructible memorials to the centuries when Genoa was still a fighting city; though no longer the capital of an Oriental empire and the envy of every other city and state in Italy, as rich as Venice, her power reaching to Constantinople and the Levant. The weakness of the defences of Genoa was that they did not extend far enough. She fell not before cannons against her bastions, but, far away, where Venice defeated her fleet on the Adriatic and the Turks crumbled her eastern possessions one by one. When Napoleon annexed Genoa to France she was no longer the fabulous Genoa.

From up here one sees the unbroken seam of gentle foam along the two Italian Rivieras, spreading east and west of this greatest port of the Mediterranean: the Riviera di Ponente, or of the sunset, to the west, the Riviera di Levante, or of the rising sun, to the east. One can see the great winding Roman road to Gaul, the Via Aureliana, where the mountains crush it down to the shore, and all the villas of the wealthy Genovese.

If one is fortunate enough to have the entry to one of those Mediterranean villas or, better still, may command a yacht, Genoa will rise before the eye and the memory as a city of matchless beauty, all cream and pink and yellow as a tea-rose, or like old worn pearls, or bleached bones on a sun-baked shore.

one great shimmering mass of pastel colour circled in an amphitheatre of sunlight about the cup of the throbbing port.
(How Louis XIV must have envied it when his guns battered
it from the sea! In our day the guns that bombarded it did not
see it.)

At night, in the distance, it is entrancing. It can be superb
when one of those common August Mediterranean storms
rumbles thirstily for hours over the sea and flashes from the
mountains like wildfire about the head of Thor. One may lie,
then, on a *chaise longue* in an open verandah idly watching
the lizards on the ceiling stalk the cream-winged moths, tiny
pterodactyls, horribly fascinating, moving with panting gills,
heavily-winking eyes and infinite stealth towards the witless
wings, to snap like lightning; lie watching murder; timeless;
sipping "Vermut"; smoking Macedonias (or better); see the
lights of the fishing-fleet come out like floating stars on the dark
rose of the Mediterranean; hear the rumble of the cars on the
ancient road below the garden mingling with the rumble of
the dry storm; watch the great *lanterna* of Genoa flash at intervals; or stroll in the garden while this tideless Ligurian sea
laps lightly and lightly the cicadas chirrup, as they will all
night long. You pass fireflies whose tiny green head-lamps go on
and off, on and off, as if they were winking; silent floaters. It
is exquisite; and Genoa in the distance, all crowned with
lights, is exquisite beyond description.

Genoa Two

But if you are not so favoured
you walk the panting streets of a barbaric stews, raucous, sweating, stinking, villainous, jammed with the crews of ships from
every nation in the world. There is no sleep. The trams scream
as if they were being tortured. The trains rattle and shunt. Arc-
lights blaze along the docks. The rattling winches are never

still. Genoa is no tourist city, with polite café quarters, urbane piazzas, suave waiters in white aprons, leisurely Pernods, dainty ices, bands to entertain the ladies, quiet gossips over morning coffee, guides, carrozzas, gondoliers, vine-shaded restaurants, discreet gardens, long moonings over river-walls while the Arno or the Po or the Tiber whispers by. It is a devil-town; a seaman's whore. It is the best port in the Mediterranean for a sailor's money from Gib to Port Said. If you want to see life pullulating like an ant-heap go to Genoa.

One need only walk twenty paces from the railway station down the steep Via San Giovanni to be in the thick of a cosmopolitan swarm, jostling, shouldering, gabbling in a dozen tongues, of which the easiest to understand is not Genoese, a dialect containing bits of many tongues not excluding Spanish, and Turkish, and even Arabic, remnants of the old Saracenic influence. Only an expert could record this dialect. All I could catch was the habit of saying *Shuh* and *Shah* for *Signor* and *Signora*—as in Shah Giacoma; or instead of the common *scusa* the Frenchified *perdón;* and on the map I see a mountain called Al Rasel.

One might form here an acquaintance with a Chinese, an Irishman, an American, a Norwegian, an Egyptian. . . . I picked up a very pleasant man who proved to be a Swedish ship's engineer. I called him Carl and he called me John and we 'did' Genoa together. He was a charming man, I almost said boy, though he must be about thirty-five, he was so boyish in mind; slim, wiry, blonde, blue-eyed like a boy and as eager as a boy on a holiday. His home was in Gothenburg. When his ship had finished unloading he would go to London and cross by Harwich and the Hook to Sweden to see his wife and small daughter. For two years he had been working up and down the Mediterranean. Going about with him I felt like uncle and nephew, because my one big trouble was to keep him from spending money. Down here around the docks there are hundreds of tempting open-air vendors who use the earth for their counter, offer seamen everything from pin-up nudes to full rig-

outs, razor blades, mirrors, soaps, American cigarettes, boot-
laces, contraceptives, knives, combs—everything. Carl wanted
to buy everything he saw. Then at night he would pull something out of his pocket, a picture of Betty Grable in a bathing-
dress, or a china doll, or a tin ash-tray, and say, 'Why the hell I
buy that?'—and try to off-load it on me. He was the friend-
liest thing that ever walked on two legs. He attracted girls as a
flower attracts bees. We would sit to a table in a café and in ten
minutes he would have two girls opposite us. They never
stayed very long; it was a tribute to his gaiety that they ever
stayed more than half an hour; for he spoke no Italian and mine
was not up to it. He just laughed at them and they laughed at
him, and he would pull out a tin pocket-knife of a shaving-mug
and say, 'You take it', or show them his snaps of his wife and
kid. Besides, the American fleet was in that week and the girls
made straight for the dollars. It was comical to see them sitting
on American sailors' knees outside the big cafés on the Piazza
Deferrari, none of them able to speak any language but the universal language of lire and love, and the naval police in their
white tin helmets like chamber-pots racing madly around in
jeeps to overawe, warn or protect.

Carl, like all Swedes, was hyper-civilised in a material way.
Whenever he adverted to the poverty of Genoa he winced; and
it is not easy to avoid it. You have only to walk a hundred yards
down the reputable Via Balbi, so narrow there is hardly space
for a footpath—indeed, there is not an impressive street in
Genoa: no room—to be held up by the sight of a white cross on
an ominous black circle. It draws your eye to the notice: *'Out
of Bounds for all Allied Troops.'* You are looking down the
first of those forbidding canyons which criss-cross this part of
the town. To enter one of them is to be lost in five minutes.

The houses of these dim lanes are many storeys high; washing is slung from window to window; no sun ever touches the
ground except at the zenith; the sky above is a narrow blue
thread; a woman in one window could kiss a man across the
lane in another; one slight bend in those narrow passages makes

them seem to close inward like cul-de-sacs. We explored them
at random. We found that each entry opens into a warren of
others, all alike, all dark, twisting, turning, climbing over rubble, leaning and tottering, diving down steps and up steps, a
maze of what must be the worst slummery of all the slummer-
ies of the world, a rookery of palpitating poverty smelling like
its own corruption, an insidious, low, throaty smell beside which
gorgonzola or garlic is sweet as a rose; a goat-smell clinging to
the nostrils all day long, so potently that now, months after, I
can smell it still.

What oppressed me was not so much the sight of these warrens as the thought that they are wellnigh ageless. Ever since
the days of the Crusades nobles and bankers and shipowners
have lain in their villas or palaces and looked idly at these
lights that climb to heaven and go down to hell, and done nothing about the misery of it all. No wonder all this Riviera was a
stink of Fascism. The six-foot letters VIVA IL DUCE fade slowly
on the villa walls along the Aurelian road. The suburban resort
of Nervi was a virtual German H.Q. long before the war. One
does not need to make a social study of Genoa to feel that the
Italian middle-class is here at its most impervious, or to get the
smell of their ancient selfishness.

The city lies open before us like a book. It is not a great industrial centre, as Milan is, but it is not in Milan, but hereabouts,
for these striking contrasts of wealth and misery, that one
vividly recalls such sentences as Giolitti's warning, uttered as far
back as 1901: 'The Italian people are not naturally prone to
revolution. They tend, rather, by long tradition to rely on their
Government, and probably no race has, over the centuries, suffered with such resignation so many serious ills. An earnest
period of social justice, directed by the Government and the
ruling classes, would recall the masses to their ancient love for
our institutions.'

Or one may remember Count Sforza's judgement[1] some
forty-five years later: 'The industrialists who financed Mus-

[1] *L'Italie telle que je l'ai Vue.* Carlo Sforza (Grasset, p. 132).

solini and Fascism were not afraid of Bolshevism; they hated
Giolitti much more than Lenin, because Giolitti wanted to
establish clearly who profited most by the war and by how
much they profited; and they hated Sforza more than Trotsky
because Sforza was trying to establish a durable peace in the
Balkans, and if a certain peace would have been precious to
Italy it would not have been to the manufacturers of arma-
ments and guns.' (Even Mussolini himself at one time saw,
and said the same thing, that Fascism was 'too subservient to
private interests'.)

So, it is all very well for Italians to tell me, when I describe to
them my emotions on exploring these warrens of Genoa, that
once you are within the walls, behind the dirt, you may find in
a dressmaker's rooms, or a tailor's, a cosy interior and a simple
innocent life. I know enough about Irish lanes and slums and
the slums of London and America to believe it, and yet to be
unimpressed. Soldiers are not forbidden to go down among
rookeries which can be adequately described as containing cosy
and innocent interiors. I wonder how many of my Italian ac-
quaintances would take their purses with them down these
lanes at midnight? Though it is not the violence of these places
that one fears, but their exigencies, their attenuations of life,
their despairing pieties, their bitter resignations, their unconscious despairs that make them, in the end, the understandable
victims of demagogues mad with hate.

O lovely city! O monstrous city! Whose aureole delights the
distant eye while the lizards stalk the moths and the oleanders
swoon in the gardens at that hour when the palaces of the
doges and the bankers are shut, and in whose uncharted warrens of lofty leaning lanes a thousand lives may, at last, with the
end of the day, spread their petals and become masters of their
souls at the setting of the sun!

I do not intend to make more than one political remark in
these pages, and I make it now. I am writing these lines in
April 1948, before the elections whose results may affect Europe for several years to come. If I were to judge by Genoa

alone I would expect them to result in favour of Communism, and whether they do or not I will let the remark stand. It will be the fate the Italian middle-class deserves if Italy ever does go Red.

But does Europe deserve the Italian middle-classes? What can Europe do about them? What *is* Europe but millions of people like my friend Carl? He hated all the poverty he saw about him; but it was not his affair. He was a ship's engineer, from Gothenburg, eager to get back to his wife and child, an ordinary man, no politician. One night I said:

'What do you think of Genoa, Carl? Really, now?'

He said:

'I love Genoa. Best port in the world that I know. I tell you why. Good fun. Good food. Cheap. And much better than Marseilles. In Marseilles,' he said proudly, 'we unload in three days. In Genoa it take two weeks.'

And he did not see the force of what he had said! For what he meant, as he admitted when pressed, was that these Italian dockers simply have not the bodily energy of underfed Frenchmen. That judgement, so casually uttered, so unconsciously devastating, stuck in my mind for days as I wandered about the city enjoying, though with a little acid in the enjoyment now, the excitement of its bustling life.

Nepenthe

BUT, after all, Carl and I were on holiday, and as far as he was concerned I had asked him a holiday question and he was answering it in a holiday mood. Besides, is there not something deliquescent about the life of the sea, and of ships, and of ports, a happy power of reducing everything and everybody about them to their own formless element? Writers about the sea sooner or later fall into a languorous style, brood and ponder in monotones, as if mesmer-

ised by the great vacancy on which they live; and even when
the time comes to them, as now to me, to recapture the pleasures
of any one of the great ports which punctuate the monotony of
each voyage, there appears to be something equally and bliss-
fully elusive and bewildering about their endless rattle and
flicker. Are all seaside hours as nepenthean as the dazzle of
sun on water? Ask any seaman, as I used to ask Carl, to talk to
you about Port Said, Odessa, Amsterdam, Marseilles or Genoa,
and you will find, as I did with him, that these places mean
to him so many cosy corners of the world at the end of the
ocean's roads.

'Odessa?' said Carl, and laughed happily. 'That is the first
place I drink kirsch.'

Port Said? He pulled out his pipe.

'I buy that there, my best pipe I ever buy.'

Great ports leave little of their greatness in the memory. This
Genoa must have been even more mesmeric in the old days
when the hotels lined the quays and, as I read in old travel-
books, voyagers preferred the third storeys so as to lean on the
window-sills, above the traffic, and watch for hours the ships
come and go to a Yo-ho-ho and a capstan creak, and a pennant threading to or from the open sea through a forest of
gleaming pine and furled canvas.

There is no describing the joy of aimless wandering in the
sun about this restless harbour in the armpit of the Ligurian
Sea. I only realised when I had returned home among the red-
brick villas and the Victorian terraces, the rain and the fog, that
what I had enjoyed most was the gluttony of the eye; yet when
I asked myself on what specifically my eyes were glutted day
after day, I could recall only a jumble of sun and shadow on
passing faces and an indefinable sense of having been excited
and contented. I believe that of all the places I have been in
Italy I lost myself most thoroughly in that raucous city.

As I look back at it now, what do I see? I see the crammed
and babbling piazzas by day and night. They were vitally gay,
exciting and palpitating, at the time. I see the dockside Via

Carlo Alberto with its little seaman's shops, cambios, Bible Society rooms, whorehouses, taverns, eating-houses, ships' offices, all as noisy and as busy as a bazaar. It seemed a hub of life—at the time. Off it, through the Piazza Fossatello, I see the long and narrow Via Fossatello, a lane, not a street, hot and crammed as when a procession breaks up—the cheapest shopping quarter in all Italy—where Danes, Swedes, Americans, Italians, Levantines, Greeks, Chinese, and doubtless Irish and British sailors, seemed to wander all day long with their purchases in little paper bags, gutting the windows like greedy children. Carl spent ten thousand lire there in one afternoon. I still see myself buying a panama—the like not seen in these islands this ten years—for half a guinea; it made me look like a milord. Beside me a Chink in white uniform was trying on a blue felt with a little feather; it made him look like a pirate. Carl was wading in silk ties as glaring as Pacific fishes in a technicolour film. That street seemed to me to compass the whole Mediterranean—at the time. We watched an American liner casting off, while ashore and aboard people wailed as for a thousand Morts d'Arthur. Those emigrants seemed to us to epitomise all Europe's despair—at the time. I remember the wonderful meals we ate; cheap when it was some place Carl knew; dear when it was not, such as the *zuppa di pesce* at the Olivo on the Porto—down the Via San Lorenzo past the marbled zebra of the Cathedral; the *fritto misto* on the thirty-third floor of Genoa's one skyscraper, the Grattacielo; or in the 'Due Colonne' that succulent meal of *Scampi all' Americana,* to be matched only by the same dish in the Grappolo d'Uva in Venice, by the Rialto. They all seemed matchless—at the time. I see again and again those terrible lanes. I see the superb staircases and courtyards of the palaces on the Garibaldi, a dozen masterpieces of architecture in one brief hundred yards. But when I say all this I seem to recite what sounds, compared to the reality, a dream litany now.

A Mediterranean day is like a dream whose effect persists after its substance has been forgotten. The details that the traveller cannot recapture seem to him the most precious, though all he has left of them is a gleam; a midnight glitter; a blob or two of phosphorescence on the tide of his being which, if he could but put his hand in the waters of Lethe and cup them, would imprison the mystery and embalm the night. I think that what we remember is not half so important as what we half forget; for these are the moments that sink into our deepest being. Those lost idle hours of those lost idle days are what I ache for when I take up again the rotted net of memory, crumbled by the narcotic sun, and find that all that remains to me of that shoal of hours swum back into the depths of their own proper reality are a few shining fish-scales. These silvers on my finger-tip are among my dearest possessions; but a poor dish for my friends.

Dan O'Connell

THERE is a fatality, too, that dogs the casual traveller and which the dogged traveller escapes. I think of the things I intended to do and did not. In Turin I could not see the sudarium. In Rome I wanted to see the Colosseum by moonlight and the dawn from the Pincio, but the moon never rose for me and I never rose for the sun. I wanted to see the hotel where Corvo lived in Venice, but they had pulled it down. I wanted dearly to see the Baptistry doors in Florence, but they had covered them up. A friend in Verona had promised to introduce me to a charming contessa, but they had fallen out. I had the fancy to stand on the bridge where Dante met Beatrice in the famous picture, but, alas, it had fallen into the Arno. I wanted to kneel in Rome by the body of Saint Peter, but I found that several hundred archaeologists, historians and Popes had had the same wish for the last five hundred years. Here in Genoa I had wished to see the house where my compatriot Daniel O'Connell died. I did not find it, because it no longer exists, though as I circled about the spot where it used to be I trembled like a dog after game in a wood, and perhaps his ambience persists.

It was No. 12 Via Ponte Reale. You approach it from the Port, hard by the Palazzo di San Giorgio. It probably once faced the sea and was a ships' hotel. Or you can go to it from the town by working through a maze of streets west of the Piazza Fontane Marose, or the Piazza Deferrari, until you come to the Borsa, behind which it once stood. Thither, at two-o'clock in that still May morning of 1847, the Cardinal Archbishop of Genoa—an old man of eighty—came with his priests and altar-boys, toddling by taperlight through the silent streets, either from the Cathedral or the Church of Santa Maria nearer at hand, carrying the Viaticum to the dying and dreaming and half-crazy old man for whom all Genoa was praying. And it is a strange coincidence that with Saint Columbanus, who died here in Liguria, at Bobbio, and the Great O'Neill, Earl of Tyrone, who died in Rome, O'Connell was the third of the only three men of European size that Catholic Ireland gave to the world who died in Italy. O'Connell died here at night, around ten o'clock, when the port would have been calming and the people of the lanes coming out to breathe. His heart was cut out and put in a silver urn and sent to Rome. His body sailed out of the port for Ireland. These had been his last wishes before his soul sailed towards Death who can rarely have received 'a braver spirit or a more welcome shade'.

San Rocco

It is less easy to say why, although I must have gone into a dozen churches in Genoa, one which no guide-book mentions held me longest and thrice recalled me. It was by chance that I came on it, and any other casual traveller might as easily pass it by. In the afternoon, when folk are coming out of offices and returning home, climb in their tracks the long winding cobbled steps behind the railway and the docks, up and up, through the old quarter, past the bombed homes, and still up and up, resting to look over the sea, until you come on San Rocco. All over north Italy you 'come on San Rocco'. You meet him all the way from his church in the Rue Saint Honoré, in Paris across to Venice, where nobody can miss him, because he is buried in the great Church of San Rocco. It is not that I am devoted to San Rocco. I am very sceptical about him: with reason; for he is also buried in several other cities of Europe—his cult was immense—and several places that do not claim his entire body claim to have parts of it. His insignia are a dog, and a wound in the thigh which may be a plague-boil, for his fame was due to his power of curing people of the plague. He was a Frenchman, Saint Roch, from Montelimar, on the Rhône. There he was found, at the end, an unidentifiable, unkempt vagabond who had been thrown into the local jail to die and then to be revealed, amid general dismay, as the Mayor's long-lost son.

His church up these stony steps has no aesthetic interest. It is silent, dim, candle-lit, gaudy. Each time I went there one or two old women were praying in the quiet dusk. Having said that little I have no more to say about it. It is so affecting a memory that it ties my tongue. All I know is that it had, for me, an extraordinary appeal. Is it that it is so unexpected in that cobbled lane? So secluded? So intimate? So unadvertised? Such a contrast to the roar of Genoa below and yet so very evidently a veritable place of the people?

It may be that I was fascinated by its ex-voto offerings: that ancient by-product of religious art in which Italy abounds. You see examples of them in every church, especially the little metal simulacra of hands, hearts or arms. It is a practice whose origins go back to the age of paganism, indeed the age of savagery, when men modelled their afflicted members so that the numen in wreaking his vengenace on them might release the actual body from sickness or pain. Christianity gave to this savage custom a sweeter sense. The little models now give thanks for favours received in answer to prayer. Sometimes those models are not in metal, but in wax, or even plaster, being actual impressions taken from the afflicted members. More rarely they have been found in gold, or richly jewelled, as when a pair of eyes glitter from the centre of a piece of goldsmith's art. But the offerings stray far from models. A soldier back from the wars may hang his bayonet in the sanctuary; a sailor fix a piece of hempen rope to a statue's hand; one may see a pair of fading epaulettes. In Saint Mark's I remember being distracted all through mass by a little silver revolver hanging on the wall of the left-hand side-altar. I kept wondering what its story might be. In some churches they are there by the hundred. Look up at the walls behind the high altar of Santa Maria della Salute in Venice. They are like the fingers of the doomed clambering out of their misery, clutching at the hem of hope. Every single one means some secret human sorrow hung about the neck of a patron saint.

Here in San Rocco there are other ex-voto offerings which are even more touching—pictures of incidents, felt as miraculous, which the worshipper wishes to commemorate. These canvases by local *maîtres populaires* are crude, candid, and melodramatic, but they are also as sincere and spontaneous as only non-professional painting can be. You will see in each a signature of thanks; the letters V.F.G.A., which means in Italian *Voto fato, grazia avuta,* and in Latin *Votum fecit gratiam accepit;* 'the vow made, the grace received'; or, sometimes, P.G.R.—*Per grazia ricevuta*: for grace received; or P.M.O.—*Per miracolo ottenuto*. In this little church I stood long before an elaborate painting of a subject common enough to provoke some slight curiosity as to the reason for its frequency. It shows a child falling from a window into a hay-wagon put there miraculously as the parents felt, or 'opportunely' as journalists would say, to receive it. I have seen similar pictures in which an angel is waiting below to catch the child. The essential feature of each picture is the cloud of glory, the *nuvole di gloria* framing the saint through whose benevolence the grace has been granted. Often three or even four figures are thanked.

I do not think anybody is in a position to look coldly, or merely inquisitively, or even quite objectively at these naïve pictures. To me they come from an age when the world was still an acknowledged mystery: which is to say an age when even to accept life was to make an act of faith, to acknowledge an open mystery where nothing lay between man and the other world but, as Valéry has said, a pane of glass through which we look, but which we cannot penetrate.

In the end I think that, perhaps, the reason I came back to San Rocco again, and yet again, up the winding steps, into the empty dusk, was not to be away from the roaring city below, but to be one with it, to share with it some experience we two held in common. Their poverty is their own poverty, their wealth is their own wealth, but their 'superstition' is my 'superstition'. I did not come there to think. That would be to share nothing. I came there just to be there. The seaman like Carl who comes ashore and has his booze and his women and, when tired, returns to his ship, cutting it all off with a slice of gangway, has no thought but a thought as remote as home, or Stamboul, or the Egyptian shore, or the next day's job. Yet he owns Genoa. I could not do that. The shipowner who works in his office on the port, or the banker on the Garibaldi, lunching at the Grattacielo, lying on his verandah to scan the French or Italian papers, possesses this vast port without an effort of a thought. I could not do that. But whenever, while I sat here, a poor woman dropped in for a few moments I raped her soul. I felt that for that moment I possessed a scrap of intimate Genovese life. I felt that even her poverty was, for that moment, no longer hers; its consolations too well known, its sublimation too old and worn. Back in Ireland there are dim churches like this, rubbed well by appealing knees and fingers; and by the holy wells, in lonely places, there are thorn-trees decorated with bits of rags and string and holy medals and safety-pins rusting in the rain, foreign coins and tin brooches, any old scrap from the detritus of a peasant's pocket, tutelary trees that are fragments of the same myth and the same depth of savagery and the same peak of civilisation, squeaking and moaning to heaven when there is nobody by but the wind.

There is nobody here. The candles gutter before the statue of the thaumaturgist. Genoa rumbles far below. I sit and wait. An old woman shuffles in. Our souls mingle. At once I feel at home. These are not only Genoa's poor. They are God's and the World's.

And that, I think, is where Italy betrays herself. If she has found some way of reconciling Venus and the Virgin she has found no way of reconciling Genoa and Godliness.

Mazzini

THIS brings me to my last pilgrimage in Genoa, out to its great cemetery, the largest in Italy, famous for its realistic monuments of mothers and fathers of families as large as life, copied from some old daguerrotype or family portrait in full detail—watch-chains, dresses in folds, creases in trousers, hats in armbends, the tassels of a sofa, a lady's glove or a gentleman's pince-nez—all minutely carved, a wilderness of Carrara ghosts. Oddly, it was my friend Carl who suggested the expedition, and not to see these curiosities, but to pay a visit to the grave of a man about whom his first captain, an Italian, had often spoken to him in the night-watches—Giuseppe Mazzini. He lies in a great granite vault on one of the highest terraces of all.

Poor Mazzini! He was one of the noblest of the many backroom boys of nineteenth-century Europe. One sees him in his lodgings on the Fulham Road, or Brompton, or Eastbourne, passionately covering pages upon pages to proclaim the religion of the future and to outline the blue-print of a brave new world. For though to Catholics his name is anathema, or was, for I suppose later devils have long sent him to oblivion or made him seem a mild poor devil by comparison, he was essentially a religious man. Disheartened by pointless *émeutes,* he wanted to generate a revolution of the spirit; to elicit the spiritual formula of the epoch. It was to have been a synthesis of all the best in the past plus one new element, for which he sought as devotedly as a mediaeval alchemist looking for the touchstone. Was it the principle of Duty? Was it the religion of humanity? It could not be the Individual; of that he was certain, for he saw in individualism the slough of materialistic egotism and ultimate anarchy. Was the great enlightening principle to be Unity? If it were, it could only be established by the revelation of moral principles without which the world would fall into 'scepticism, materialism, and indifference to everything superior to the individual'. The philosopher's stone was certainly not the Rights of Man, for rights are merely secondary to duty. All he knew was that it must be a religious ideal. 'Religion and politics are inseparable. Life is one. . . . You cannot say to the people, *Thou art half free and half enslaved; social life is thine but religious life belongs to others.* You cannot dismember the soul. Liberty is the gift of God, who rules over, blesses, and renders fruitful all the faculties of man, His creature.' 'To desire to abolish religion . . . is to create a void.' He says it over and over again. 'It is as a religious party that we must rise again.' 'The religious idea is the very breath of humanity.'

Were he alive to-day such a man could certainly not be a Communist, and it is a fair guess that he might even still be a Catholic. For his revolt against the Church was a revolt against a temporal power which has now, except in the title and the symbol of that garden in Rome, no bigger than St. James's Park in London, passed completely away. Even the modern adoration of 'the people' could hardly please the man who said the 'people' is too often a caste in rebellion against other castes. His weakness, as I see it, was that he did not recognise that order and unity imply hierarchy; as Garibaldi, the man of action, instinctively did. He did not see that if there is not the hier-

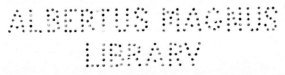

archy of one aristocracy there will be the hierarchy of another, for whether we call it 'aristocracy' or 'the dictatorship of the proletariat' the thing is the same: the 'rule of the best citizens'. The reason we quarrel with Communism or Capitalism is not because either is inherently a wicked idea, but because their 'best citizens' are generally far from being the best, and because both have got bogged in a sordid materialism. If it were not for that one might philosophically commend the world to wait until the robber-barons of twentieth-century Communism, having arrived at the end of the same avenue as their predecessors of a thousand years ago, become the civilised 'best citizens' of a thousand years hence. But their hideous dialectical materialism closes all such avenues forward. Goethe said that Luther put back civilisation by five hundred years. These abolish it.

Mazzini is to be respected for hanging on so insistently to the idea of religion against so many legitimate local and contemporary temptations to think it hopeless. But it was a formless thing to which he clung—religion as a ghostly spirit not as a physical vessel. My good Carl and his old Italian captain thought of him, however, only as a nationalist leader, not as a philosopher; and they were right.

I think one of the most happy moments in his sad and strenuous life was the reconciliation with Garibaldi described by Trevelyan in *Garibaldi's Defence of the Roman Republic*:

'When in 1864 Garibaldi came to our island to receive as the redeemer of Italy and the chosen hero of England an ovation so tremendous that it frightened Europe and even Palmerston himself, on one of those festal occasions he "looked through all the roaring and the wreaths" where sat a certain patient, neglected figure, come among the rest to honour him, and his heart went back thirty years to the days when, as a young merchant captain, he had first met Mazzini at Marseilles. Since then bitter quarrels had divided them; but the sight of his old friend overwhelmed all meaner thoughts of him. "I rise," said Garibaldi, to the assembled company, "to make a declaration which I ought to have made long since. There is a man amongst us here who has rendered the greatest service to our country and to the cause of freedom. When I was a youth and had only aspirations towards good I sought for one able to act as the guide and counsellor of my youthful years. I sought for such a guide as one who is athirst seeks for the water-spring. I found this man. He alone watched when all around slept, he alone kept and fed the sacred flame. This man is Joseph Mazzini. He is my friend and teacher." '

Cooks' tourists do not 'do' Genoa. It has no Charm. They miss the most vital city in Italy. For it is Milan and Turin and Genoa and Rome that are, to-day, the hubs of Italian life, and I, when I say this, am not forgetting that three-fourths of Italy is peasant, conservative, traditional and Catholic. After all, so is, or was (certainly as for religion), three-fourths, and more, of Russia. They are the hubs because it is from these places that ideas radiate and I believe in the force of ideas, when they are born of actuality and are not brain-spun like so many of Mazzini's ideas; though not all of his ideas were that, and one must never forget that it was among the slums and lagoons of Genoa that Mazzini and Garibaldi hammered out that great dream of an Italian Republic, which, in the end, Garibaldi, Cavour and Vittorio Emanuele sold to the men of wealth and position. There is no point in thinking of Italy in terms of old masters. Who are its new masters? Where will the next Garibaldi spring from? Who will . . .

But there I go! Questions, questions, questions. And from there I went, as I had from Turin, and my old Devil looked after me sadly, fondling his apple in his hand, for I was making for the Riviera, which is no place for clever people.

Quarto Dei Mille

During his lunch-hour a Genovese worker can, for a penny or two, swim, eat and bask in the sun on the beaches of the Italian Riviera. It runs from the French frontier to Spezia. All that the word means is a coastline, or a stretch of coastal country. If the word raises other expectations, few would consider them fulfilled by the noisy, cheerful, shouting *bagni,* or bathing establishments with dance-halls attached, often beflagged and belanterned, which line the seaside suburbs of Genoa. The rattling trams and the endless thump of traffic beat louder on the Golden Road than the soft fall of wavelets. The road passes for long stretches through narrow streets and under tall houses, indeed all the way to Nervi, which is itself one long and narrow street. Up in the hills there are some pleasant homes among the grey-green olive-groves. Closer to the shore one sees a few rather moth-eaten palms and lemon-trees struggling to exist. Dust rises. Houses peel. The age of Italy peeps through the wrinkles and the rouge. Yet in a picture it could all still look wonderful. The colouring would be delightful if we could separate it from the neglect, the noise and the smells. The sun and sea are unsoilable.

The pious traveller must, however, make at least one pause on his way out of Genoa; at Quarto dei Mille, five miles to the east. He should visit it for history's sake, and if possible at night, when the shouting mobs of sea-worshippers and sun-worshippers have gone—I doubt if the trams ever stop—and preferably when the moon enlarges the ocean as it did that night of the fifth of May 1860, when Garibaldi embarked there with his thousand men for Tuscany and Sicily and the battles of Marsala and Calatafimi.

'O night of the fifth of May! Lit by the fire of a thousand

lamps with which the Omnipotent had adorned the Infinite. Beautiful, tranquil, solemn with that solemnity which swells the hearts of generous men when they go forth to free the slave. Such were the Thousand, my young veterans of the war of Italian liberty, and I, proud of their trust in me, felt myself capable of attempting anything . . .'

He descended by a rough path to the foot of the cliff, and there—Carducci describes the rock,

> *Breve ne l'onda avanzasi*
> *striscia di sassi . . .*

—he stood by one of those little inlets into which only a single boat could glide at a time, the helmsmen whispering, phosphorescence dripping from the oars. Boat by boat, in dignified silence, his men rowed off to meet the ships that had been commandeered in Genoa.

Trevelyan's description of that scene clings to the memory: the silence, the respectful crowds, the tension, the men sitting here and there under the palm-trees, waiting for their leader to emerge, and then Garibaldi's appearance, in the moonlight, dressed in his red shirt, South American cloak, and slouch hat, a costume and a man that has since become one of the inspiring figures of history; as familiar and recognisable as Napoleon or Lincoln. As they embarked the dawn was coming up over the headland of Portofino, and as the two ships smoked away down the sleeping coast to Bogliasco and Camogli, and thence across the Ligurian sea to the coast of Tuscany, the sun rose before them in symbolic splendour.

> *Cheti venivano*
> *a cinque a dieci, poi dileguavano,*
> *drappelli oscuri, ne l'ombra*
> *i mille vindici del destino.*

> *And silent came by fives and tens*
> *His shadowy companies; vanished in the dim light,*
> *A thousand avengers of destiny.*

Something almost mythical here; and all along this coast; his vestiges and his glory; a fame little understood, but deeply felt by every worker and peasant, as if a god had passed in the breeze and touched men's lives with his wings. He seems to personify the Italian ideal—the dramatic gesture, the guerrilla's dash, intense and swift, the insane risks, the capacity for endurance, the warmth of comradeship, and the conscious, sensuous awareness of the wonder of the hour.

Nervi

NERVI is the first place where the traveller can possess the Mediterranean. It has a long quiet seashore promenade where he can sit at ease, under a coloured sunshade, at a café high over the sea, away from the noise of the road, forgetting it completely, happy to hear the whisperings of the waves hundreds of feet below, watching yachts pass gently, a speed-boat with its white wake, bathers brown as Africans on the rocks below, and a few miles to the east the great headland of Portofino, whose nearer slopes are speckled with the white and pink mushrooms of remote villas. Genoa is now well distant to the west. He will be, at first, aware only of the baking sun and the spread of sea and the vault of light, and the eye keeps on roving eastward to that greater beauty and to the peaked mountains which strenuously suggest a climb whose reward may be that he will see on the horizon the dim whale's back of Corsica. Here for an hour the setting will seem evocative enough to satisfy all expectations. But it will be only for an hour. Nervi's promenade, its narrow strip of seclusion, its few seaside hotels and cafés hold at bay a seediness that is almost squalid enough to be exciting; though I can well believe that if I were an Italian, accustomed to the cheerful down-at-heelness of everything and content so long as I had sun and wine, I might not notice this squalor at all.

To how much does not the sun and wine of Italy reconcile us! Or has all strangeness a power to please, and all travel a power to suspend fastidiousness? If I can be fascinated, for a while, by this lower-middle-class dustiness and mustiness of Nervi, it is probably in large part merely because it is both a sunshot and an unusual sort of mustiness and dustiness, and if Southend could be transmogrified into Capo del Sud, and if the sun blazed on it, and if the wine were flowing, I should probably be indulgent to it, too.

From the start Nervi was a sell. The kind and friendly clerk of the tourist agency who had pressed me to try Nervi had said: 'Take a tram; it's only ten minutes out of Genoa.' This had seemed ideal. I could, from so near as that, continue to explore Genoa on any day I cared to do so. The tram actually takes an hour, and is a bore, for it is crowded, and even the constant jovial chant of the conductor, 'Avanti signore per favore' (so much more amusing and pleasant than 'Move along, please'), cannot make it any less uncomfortable to be jolted, standing, in oppressive heat. *Dieci minuti,* like *pronto* and *subito,* mean, of course, nothing to an Italian. Ten minutes or an hour, what's the difference? This kind and friendly tourist expert had also pressed into my hand an attractive, illustrated folder advertising a good *pension.*

'*La casa, completà di ogni comodità moderna, al centro di un parco ricco di piante di aranci, limoni, olivi e rose offre ai suoi ospiti un soggiorno confortevole, riposante ed ameno.*'

How green I was! It was so impressive I feared it would be a luxury beyond my means. In German it was even more impressive.

'*Das interessante Patrizierschloss der Grafen B——, aus dem 17. Jahrhundert stammend, bietet seine Gästen durch seine charakteristichen künstlerischen Innenraume, ausgestattet mit allem modernen Comfort ein behagliches vornehmes Heim . . .*'

I should not have let myself be so easily deluded. True, the *pension* is comfortable enough. But I also find that when a once-fine villa has declined to a boarding-house its latter end and its memories of former luxury mock one another to an effect that is almost macabre. I awaken each morning in a colossal bedroom, ruthlessly cut in two by a papered partition, to gaze at naked pink nymphs gambolling on the ceiling (the partition cleaves them like a sword); at relict bits of mottled marble statuary in the corners of the room; at chipped modern furniture from some Genovese department store; and I feel I am in a house fit for a seedy Conrad novel, its air midway between sauerkraut and suicide. Why, I ask myself, over and over, as I survey those heaving pink rumps, have Russians and Germans always favoured Nervi as, I am told, they always have done? To have a Riviera address? Or was it Slav nostalgia? Or are Black Sea resorts [1] at all like this? If so, why want to see any more of them? But, I recall that Mazzini, in his old age, sighed for the pier at Eastbourne!

I could imagine Dostoievsky's gambler taking refuge in this *Künstlerisch* villa, broke to the world, pining for the casinos of Venice or Monte Carlo; rising to walk moodily along the promenade before lunch; carrying himself like a grandee—hiding the holes in his socks—despising it all as too domestic, too bourgeois, too reach-me-down. He would sit at the café, and sip *cinzano,* and look across at Portofino, and wonder if Rapallo had a good casino? He would scan faces eagerly, smell an adventure and discover a commercial traveller; strike up a flirtation with a countess and unmask a Genovese waitress. In the end he would lose his last lire dicing with sailors in the port, and go beserk in a brothel.

I was fascinated daily by the ceiling of the dining-room. Those spattered holes could only be bullet-marks. Were German troops quartered here? Was it just a night of drinking? But why did 'he' get so very drunk? What storm of the heart, or brain-storm, sent the blood rushing up behind the cropped neck? Such houses are like novels with all but Chapter One

---

[1] Now, I believe, all raucous with 'rest-camps' for workers, far removed from the sleepy Yalta of Chekhov's day.

torn out. Black and yellow marble staircases lead by the light of dim twenty-five watt bulbs to great central landings, lofty halls —as my folder had said *signorilmente arredato*. But led once where else? To whom? To what dreadful or luscious nights? No, not a novel; a curtain rising on an interior where no character will ever appear; only the stage hands, the management, infinitely kind, willing to do everything possible for the guest —except to evoke the play.

'Ah!' says the attentive German manageress, 'but you must imagine the play; we provide only the wine and the food.'

And the play of the living guests? Some Italian mothers with children; two old grandmothers on whose table come daily three bottles of wine, a bottle of *acqua minerale* and a mighty bottle of digestive medicine. Two lovers, French. Three Swedes. A fat Dutch boy who can only say 'Goot! Goot!' Two girls, surely typists? No Russians, alas! But the inevitable Père Goriot complains daily of his food, which is always inferior to everybody else's food, except on the one day when two daughters and a son-in-law come and he is treated by the staff like royalty—falling back the next day, with a sad, unheeded growl, on his mountain of *tagliatelle* and his marked bottle of mineral water that he sips with a grimace.

Orange-trees? Yes. Lemon-trees? Yes. Roses, oleanders, palms, blue sea? Yes. All that. Villas, seaside hotels, gardens? Yes. All those, though built about, crowded in with barbed wire. The palms are dusty. The paths are dusty. The barefooted porters are dusty, and the grocer's boys invade dustily, and shouts float up from the public beaches over the occasional rattle of the trains; and one steps out of each enclave into narrow dusty streets where two people dare not walk abreast on the tiny pavement, and even one pedestrian must draw in to the wall when the trams swoop past, brushing his shoulder.

'But,' the spirit of my good and kind Italian tourist agent might protest, 'the bands played at night? The moon sent its ladder across the sea to the shore? Girls and boys went promenading arm in arm singing?' (Yes. They even sang *O Sole*

Mio.) 'And you bathed,' he persists, 'and lay about in the sun on the rocks, and rested well in the afternoons, and bathed again, and dined well?' (Moderately well, I interpolate. He ignores this. . . .) 'You strolled, had a good brandy for a nightcap, watching the crowds come and go, in exquisite weather, and felt,' he cries, mounting to a climax of astonishment at me, 'felt utterly content in body and mind!' His hands are spread wide. His face is a vast question-mark. 'What more?'

In the very early mornings, sometimes, about six o'clock, I used to bathe when the beaches and rocks were quite bare, when the sea did not stir so much as to breathe, was not yet even tepid, when the silence and the boundless spread of light enveloped the shipless sea and kissed the peaked mountains with their lofty shrines. I would slip then, alone, into twenty feet of clear-blue virgin water and know 'what more'. It is not just that this place is shabby-genteel in the outward or physical sense. All holiday resorts are shabby-genteel in their souls. They pretend to be what they are not. They do not belong to the place where they are. The seaside village which has its own natural life, winter and summer, belongs; but these, which go dead in the off-season, have just painted fake life on top of whatever real life there was before they became 'resorts'. Lives have been immured, not under new life, but under a 'lick of life'. You get a creepy feeling as if a corpse were hidden somewhere and that everybody is in the conspiracy to conceal this corpse; shopkeepers, porters, touts, cadgers, fishermen, maids, proprietors. It is as true of Blankenberghe as of Brighton. It is as true of Rapallo as it is of Nervi. The only places that are immune are places that have existed and would exist if never a tourist came there. Geneva is a pleasant place to idle. It belongs to where it is. If you come they are very glad to have you and you will be well served. If you do not come they will make watches.

Sori

WHERE is this romantic Riviera? For by this I am sufficiently seduced—even by Nervi!—to want to enjoy sea and sun at their best. In the bus I move anxiously down the coast to Sori. Streets fade out and do not reappear.

Villas and gardens thicken and these gardens are freshly tended. They look cool and soothing. We are beyond all sight or sound of tram tracks now. We are out of reach of the paws of Genoa. The coast road drops and crosses a deep river valley which debouches on a shingle shore beneath a long viaduct blown by the R.A.F.—but just rebuilt. The peaked hills nod over each other's shoulders. The village in the valley is strewn (strewn in every sense, for it has been bombed) down to the edge of the water. One senses an unabused life, a veritable countryside, a traditional rhythm. These may have to be searched out. Miles may have to be walked back up the valleys to find them. But that is not abnormal. Egdon Heath was a long step from Weymouth.

There is only one serious blemish to this exquisite little paradise of Sori—residents are sensitive about it and could hardly be otherwise—the load of motor traffic that keeps rumbling day and night with scarcely a pause along this corniche road. It has ended those happy days when one would have seen only the carriages, under their white awnings, lifting cloudlets behind them as they clop-clopped in the thick dust. It was a narrow road in those days—the Roman roads were not wide roads—but now they are widening it everywhere, sheering off corners, shoring up wider sweeps, improving the camber for these great lorries and streaming cars.

Sori is a lovely place to dawdle, and I wish now I had stayed there longer: for unless you are one of those intense notebook reporters who write a travel-book once a year you will let Italy seep into you, and seeping is a slow absorption. The trouble about your idle wanderer is that he refuses to wander once he has found a happy corner. He will never know more than the minutest scrap of this Riviera, perhaps no more than his *pension* and its garden where he will contentedly lounge weeks away; and the rocks below it where he will bathe and sun-bathe; and take in random images, such as that great pine overhanging the cove, that crooked path to the sea through the olives, that wide view of the blue ocean, seen again and again and again, morning, noon and night; heavenly sensations of sun and heat and languor and content.

I do not think I should have adverted to any other kind of Riviera if there had not been at my *pension* an accursed Scotsman—a very nice fellow whom I much liked; which does not prevent him from being accursed—who represents the natural, though unforeseen, outcome of Mazzini's secular 'Religion of Humanity'. He was a Socialist who believed in nothing but disbelief. He didna believe in God, and he didna believe in Churchill, and he didna believe in President Truman, and he didna believe in Stalin, and since he was an agnostic—which means a fellow who goes around proving the might of reason by demonstrating that it can tell us next to nothing—he didna even believe in himself. He was the agin'-the-government type. Only long afterwards did it occur to me that he was my Devil in disguise. One day he brought to me as I lay in the sun of the garden the following extract from some old book he had found in the *pension* library. It must refer to about seventy years ago, but it is probably still largely true. He read it out, his voice harsh with anger:

'"Compared with the state of the English poor, there is very little real poverty on the Riviera. In the coast villages the men gain a good subsistence as fishermen or boat-builders, the women making lace or plaiting straw. In the country almost everyone has a little olive-ground or orange-garden which they can call their own. A young couple seldom marry until they have hoarded up 400 or 500 francs (about £25), for which sum a house may be bought in one of the seaboard towns or villages, and then they save till they can purchase a piece of rock, which by perseverance and hard labour . . ." '

Jock repeated these words with an accusing glare, as if it was I who had written them.

' " . . . *a piece of rock, which by perseverance and hard labour* may, in this climate, soon be transformed into a fruitful garden. Here they often labour all night long, and lights are to be seen glimmering and songs heard from the orange-gardens of the poor all through the dark hours. The first year they carry up earth, prepare the ground, and plant wild orange and lemon-trees; the second year they graft them; and the third year they begin to reap the fruits. The oranges and lemons require watering all through the summer, but the olives require more than this. They have to be constantly trenched round to give air to the roots, without which they do not flourish, and once a year (March and April) they require to be manured with rags, which are very expensive. During the rag season the smell from the olive groves is most unpleasant and the effluvia from the ships which convey the rags to the ports is so offensive that unloading them becomes a service of the greatest danger." '

Jock looked at me.

'Imagine that! I expect the bit about the rags is out of date. But the calm way the mon writes! Without one tittle of an iota of indignation!'

I looked at him unhappily from the hammock.

'Jock, I'm on holiday. And anyway, I'm an escapist.'

He was as shocked as if I had said I was a sodomite.

'But you can't ignore facts like that.'

'You'd be surprised! Matthew Arnold says that the Celt is always revolting against the despotism of fact. The truth is that the Celt always refuses to see any facts he doesn't like to see. Anyway, Italy isn't our responsibility. Isn't that why we came here?'

People like Jock ought really not come to the Riviera. He

had no trouble in proving to me logically and inescapably that in 'the moderrrn wurrld every country's affairs are inextrrricably parrt and parrcel . . .' and so on, while I envied his Victorian traveller his benignant assurance, happy detachment and placid conscience. I could only get rid of Jock by pointing out to him (it is the only argument which silences reformers, by choking them with fury) that the people are as cheerful as sandboys, which is true; and that reformers (like Jock) take away from the peasants the only three sources of wealth they have, their content, their religion and their traditional mode of life, which is also true; and that, having done this, the reformers drive the peasants into the hell of the cities from which there is no escape, which is only too miserably true.

'*I* didna make the cities!' Jock roared. 'The capitalists——'

'Don't make them any bigger. Hands off the land.'

'But the people canna *live* on the land.'

'They have been doing it since the days of the Antonines!'

'Do you call *that* Life?'

Behind the Riviera

IT is a hard-working life. Back behind the fashionable strip of coastline the important trees are not the myrtle, tamarisk, oleander, pine, yucca, peach, palm or ilex, decorative trees. What counts here are figs, olives, sweet chestnuts, almonds and vines. When flour is scarce, as it almost always is, the people up in the hills will subsist on dried figs and on flour made from the sweet chestnuts. When I ask Jock why this is so he explains to me that Italy does not produce enough of that large and long-eared wheat called *grano duro* from which the best paste is made—the pastes or doughs which we call macaroni, tagliatelli, spaghetti and so forth—so that extra grain has to be imported and added to the poorer native kind. Even then there is not enough flour to make enough of any kind of *pasta* or of bread; and, as anybody can see for himself, Italians eat mountains of both. Jock had a theory that the excessive amount of iodine in the surrounding sea is so stimulating that they have to have some such sedative food. They certainly eat little meat; the peasants of the south eat practically none. Growling at Jock I began to ask questions. This is what I gathered.

Italy's food problem is all too obvious. The land is so mountainous and poor that although the people plough 42 per cent of the total surface (the highest proportion in Europe), further supplies of every vegetarian food stuff, bar one, have to be imported: barley, maize, oats, rye, wheat, even olive-oil. Rice is the only arable export. With all that, the peasant still must tighten his belt. That summer the bread ration was minute, about the size of three rolls per man per day. The most casual traveller will see at once why life is good for people with money all along this ribbon of villa-covered coastline. Labour and its products are cheap for exactly the same reason that they were cheap in Ireland when its people used to depend on the potato, the *pasta* of Ireland, and when a few pence could often stand between the peasants and starvation.

On the Riviera a maid will wash, cook, housekeep, launder, dust and scrub all day long, merrily, for the equivalent of £1 per month. All local food products are cheap in proportion. In any one of these Riviera villas a household of, say, five people could live for about five guineas a week, all in. (When I mentioned those two facts to a friend in the Foreign Office in Rome he shrugged, pointed out that a First Secretary probably gets the equivalent of about £7 a month, out of which he has to pay for everything while living at a high standard, in a capital; whereas this maid was fed, housed, and doubtless got many presents.) Many of these village craftsmen do fine work, such as shoemaking and tailoring, at prices which they may consider high, but which the villas consider cheap. In Sori one could get a first-class pair of ladies' handmade shoes for £2, or of gentlemen's fine kid for £3 10s. One day Jock wanted his watch mended. The local man went specially into Genoa, had to search it all over to get a missing piece, travel back, and mend the watch; he then charged a fraction of what Jock would have paid at home in a big city.

Much of this labour is evidently not measured. The Italian gives his heart to his work. He is inexhaustibly kind and interested. One evening I had promised to dine with a friend near Sori. The cook's brother, a fisherman, heard that there had been some hitch in the food arrangements, got up at dawn and went fishing for polpi, those small octopuses which are so succulent in a *fritto misto*. I am sure he felt sufficiently paid by the thought that he had saved the situation.

None of this is meant to suggest that the people are exploited. Coming here from Ireland I felt all this was very familiar; the personal touch of the response to a crisis, the cheerful interest, the feudal-friendly relationship. All it means is that when two different standards of living exist side by side the richer is richer because of the poverty of the poorer. The rich do not produce that poverty. They alleviate it. They can do nothing else about it. If the poor demanded higher wages and higher prices, the villas would be empty; and nowadays, when incomes are taxed heavily at source, they would empty all the sooner.

What the traveller, casual or otherwise, will further observe is that there is little spirit of revolt and much patient endurance. The Communist witch-hunter may quote statistics, in terror or in anger, pointing out how many local elections were won by the Communists, in 1946, after the Liberation, or in 1948. But to read statistics is never as informative as to visit a pub. This little village of Sori was one of the places run after the Liberation by the Communists. A few nights in the Sori taverns makes one realise that these 'Communists' are *sui generis;* what one might call 'nice' Communists, more interested in playing cards, drinking wine and letting off a lot of gab than in red revolution. (They won their position here simply because the Christian Democrats were completely inactive during the occupation; anything done was done by the Left.) I should be surprised, for example, if the local parish priest bothered his head very much about his Reds. Their easy-going philosophy, their old traditions, their atavism, their womenfolk all combine to keep them to the wine, the cards, and the gab.

The first minute I stepped off the bus at Sori I saw a perfect image of the easy-going Italian. A worker, dressed in canvas shorts and a paper cap, otherwise as nature made him, was tending a petrol engine. He sat beside it, in the broiling heat of the sun, indifferent to the roar and rattle, while a ganger higher up screamed some order to him, unheard or unheeded. He was holding between his fingers a pink flower at which he gazed with pleasure, twirling it this way and that between oily fingers, whistling softly and, apparently, happily to himself. As I passed I pointed upward to the ganger. He glanced up, kissed the flower and waved it. The ganger grinned, and then shouted something. The workman shouted 'Subito!' When I looked back he was still twirling the pretty petals.

Not that they do not work hard; those half-naked workers slaved as they padded barefooted along that dried-up bed of the river, endlessly wheeling trucks of dump before them. I have enquired what their wages were. A road worker earns 1,000 lire per day.[1] *Pasta* this summer was about L400 per kilo, and flour L340 per kilo: roughly 2 lb. A hard-working labourer will eat, I take it, about 2 lb. a day of bread and/or pasta, which will cost him L370 or one-third of his day's wages. Compare with British costs. Suppose 2-lb. loaves cost 9d. If that were one-third of a British labourer's wages per day, his total wages would be 2s. 3d.; or 15s. 9d. per seven-day week. (A later note: bread in July 1948 was 7d. per lb., far too dear for the poorly-paid worker.) This is a saner way than to compare money 'values'. That summer the average exchange-rate was around L2,000 to

---

[1] These figures were given to me in 1948. In addition the employer has to pay in to the roadmen's *libretti* (a species of bank-book) L600 per day, which is for old age pension, insurance against accidents and tuberculosis. He must further pay 26 per cent on the L1,000 per day for holidays and *festas* which are not paid for, and to provide for thirty days' holiday per annum.

the £1, so that counting by the exchange an Italian roadman might appear to be earning 10s. per day, or £3 10s. per week. The cost of living makes his money worth far less in practice.

Jock alternately drove me mad and entertained me vastly by his scientific probings into the lives of the peasants. Not that I believe that no foreigner can pierce into the lives of another people, though it takes genius and time, and he must have some bridge across the gap of racial difference. I do not think that Jock had any bridge. He relied on cold reason. It was both a pleasure and an embarrassment to watch this perfect machine clog up one night when a resident who has known Sori this fifteen years was telling us, with a nice mixture of amusement and sympathy, about the 'miracle' which happened one summer when the valley was suffering from a serious drouth. It was August 15th, the big local Feast Day when the statue of the Virgin of the Annunciation is carried on the men's shoulders up and down the roads of the parish. The night before the procession a few of the local lads had come upon an unsuspected spring and partly for mischief, partly from a sense of drama, partly from a sense of piety, they planned to release the stream of water just when the procession and the statue passed that way. So they did. *Ecco! Un miracolo gradito!* But it is one thing to plot a miracle and another thing to deny it; and presently our young men not only found that their 'miracle' was accepted on all sides, but began themselves by degrees to wonder if perhaps in the end there had been something miraculous about it. Jock chuckled and chuckled until I said:

'Well, maybe there was something miraculous about it.'

'But,' Jock explained politely to me, 'he's just told us that the local lads let out the water.'

'They might have been merely human agents of a superhuman giver?'

He looked at me as if I had two heads. Yet, after all, that was how the participants felt about it, and was it not their minds that we were discussing?

Our host told us several other stories to illustrate this romantic, religious, imaginative, or sublimatory element, as one chooses to call it, in the Italian nature.

'Isn't it all just superstition?' Jock cried in the end.

But does this element not affect *all* their lives? Such as politics? The whole Fascist adventure was in large part a bit of romantic d'Annunzian make-believe; it was also an escape of the imagination from the plodding routine of life, a vulgar escape admittedly, into the violent emotionalism of Italian Grand Opera. This imaginative quality of the Italian nature has its great faults and dangers; it has its rewards and qualities also; and its reactions. They will believe their own fantasies and the courteous foreigner will do well to pretend to believe them, too, if only in kindness; for they must suffer a bitter disillusion, poor devils, as all romantics do, whereas the foreigner can contentedly go back to drink in the sun, basking like a lizard on his favourite rock, or dreaming the day away on some verandah like a prow, too happily mesmerised to bother his head any more. They will eventually do that, too, a little sadder and no wiser and ready to flare out at any instant just as before. I cannot but sympathise, being one of a race that has always suffered from the same slavery of the imagination, whose journey towards intellectual and imaginative freedom has been as prolonged and painful.

I got so bored in the end with Jock's applications of the salve of pure reason to these wounds and fissures of the heart that I had to say to him that one can probe men and nations *too* far. To keep on excoriating the mind in order to explain it is often as pointless as to keep on peeling the globes of an onion to show how it is made; reasons lie behind reasons; you do not simplify man that way, you make him smaller. Once we have exposed the one main motivation of a man or a people there is little to be gained by going any further.

The English have a gift for ruling. The Italians have a gift for enjoying life. The Irish have a ruling passion for revolt. They are three different sorts of human adventure. In our time the English have been driven from the search for conquest to

the search for security. The Irish have sold their natural re-
belliousness for an unnatural obedience. The Italians were
never empire-makers and in their Fascism were false to their
natural bent. They are a brave people, but they are not a war-
like people, and they cannot 'keep it up'—their rages die in
them, their passions flood out and are gone, and these blazes of
passion die the more readily because they have that long, long,
long traditional memory which seems to say to them: 'We've
been through all this before, you know!' So have the English;
but England has not been overrun a dozen times, been the
cradle or the grave of three civilisations. That is why every
Italian family has, as a matter of verifiable history, always
aimed at giving one son to the Church, one to war, and a couple
to politics, one on each side. No wonder the oldest noble names
exist to this day, surviving every revolution: Doria, Chigi,
Orsini, Colonna, Barberini, Ruspoli, Massimo, Borghese. That
was how the great republics lived. The Florentines were poor
soldiers; but they knew how to manoeuvre. It may not seem a
noble technique, but it is based on endless unrest, and it gives
opportunities to all sorts of men to rise to great station; most
of the popes were men of the middle-class, or of the poor.

They had, to be sure, their bold adventurers, too, in plenty,
their *condottièri;* they were signalised as adventurers, lone
wolves employed by governments to do their fighting for them.
One of the first of them was an Englishman, John Hawkwood,
who was buried in the duomo of Florence. It was a doubly dangerous profession. A failure might be killed by his employers.
One was too successful; his employers, feeling inadequate to re-
pay him sufficiently, decided to kill him and worship him as a
saint; which they did. Perhaps Mussolini partook of the type,
and paid the price of ingratitude as well as of tyranny.

Camogli

FROM Sori I moved on down the Riviera to a little fishing village which is the gem of the whole coast from Savona to Spezia. Camogli is well off the main road, and this has preserved it from modernisation. It is a functional fishing village, not a tourist resort. It is so crushed down to the seashore by the hills that its houses have had to be built to an unusual height to contain all its inhabitants. As they rise up, one behind another, on the steep hill, the whole village looks from the sea like a cluster of skyscrapers that glow in the sun like palaces carved from coral. In these tenements families are piled on top of families in crowded warrens which are entered under dim arches that lead to steep stone stairs. The lanes are almost as narrow, as steep and as stepped. Down along the shingled beach, and between the beach and the tiny cluttered harbour, there are more crooked houses on every square foot of crooked space, all this way and that way, with taverns built over the water, a ruined castle to top the rocks, and a gaudy, glittering, golden church approached by a flight of noble steps. Being so crowded, Camogli has a beautiful restless vivacity. The sails, the boats and the yachts and the sparkling water are never for a moment still; sailors and their womenfolk go up and down all day long. Your eye wanders, delighted, from the harbour to the tiers of houses, from the houses out over the Mediterranean, is recalled by the tawny children plunging into the harbour, caught by the endless come-and-go of the fishing folk, or by their arguments over the wine-flasks, the cards, or the political papers from Genoa, on trestled tables under trellised vines. The whole place is brilliant with allure for the painter. Its war of colour is not to be described. The gaudiest blue-and-rose of a picture post card cannot do it violence.

I have never seen a place with so vibrant a personality. I loved it because it is a place where there is an intense local life. The very name of the village throbs with emotion: Camogli, that is *Ca'* (popular for *casa*) *mogli,* the Wives' House, or Home, in reference to all the wives who have been widowed by the sea. You feel this bond immediately you climb the steps from the quays, which gleam with fish-scales and smell of petrol, into the church which gleams with gold and smells of incense and wax. You notice, first, on the wall outside, the plaques recording the years when the Mission came to Camogli for weeks of high-pressure salvation. They evoke pictures of a packed church at night, intense religious emotion, daily morning masses, the final renewal of baptismal vows on the last night when every brown wrist in the church would hold a tawny lighted wax candle and every throat would roar defiance at the Devil. They would have been precious weeks and sad weeks. As the plaques tell us, Plenary Indulgences were granted at the end of each Mission, to be offered in passionate pity for those dead bones that sway under every swell of the sea outside.

As I knelt there in the half-light and silence I became aware that the silence was not absolute. There was a soft weeping sound, a gentle groaning sound, falling rhythmically to a whisper as of wings in the air. I looked at the altar, shaped gracefully like a boat, and gradually I realised that this gentle and regular throb came from behind the apse. It was the sea pulsing eternally on the shingle below. That muttering of water pervades Camogli. Children are born to its rocking, sleep to it, live on it, age on it, and too often sink into it. Around the walls of the church are several lovely *ex voto* models of sailing ships—lost and saved—and black obituary photographs. I see again, with special vividness, the face of the jovial, fat, moustached sea-captain in the jaunty straw hat smiling down at me; while that old siren outside, beyond this shadow that is a light, the blue, placid and seemingly innocent sea, sighs like a dreaming tiger.

The sense of the sea's power is everywhere. Here, in the sun of the quay, is a woman in black, cross-legged on the ground, sewing a feather mattress into a snowy case; a pleasant and public way for a widow to work. One of the tall houses behind her is the *Casa di Riposo per la Gente di Mare,* the inevitable 'Sailors' Home'. Old Ligurian seamen sit all day long in these windows, watching the ships go by. It is held that the best captains of the Italian mercantile marine come from Camogli, and always did. Once Santa Margherita also served the sea rather than the tourists; its little dockyard famous. Rapallo never had the same reputation. They called it *Il Golfo dei Nesci,* i.e. *dei gonzi,* the Gulf of Ninnys. Here in a niche in a wall is a Madonna di Buon Viaggio. A prayer invokes her as the Sailor's Hope—Spes Nautarum. Here is a long crocodile of small children coming from the beach to the Orphans' Home. Later you may see them seated at supper, row on row, each child with its small tin mug, tin plate, spoon and knife, and hope to God they will not go to bed hungry. The very names of the boats appeal: the *Padreterno,* or the *Speranza.* They trust in God and in themselves. The *Due Fratelli.*

Black Magic

Deeper underneath that trust what might greater intimacy uncover? I had a curious experience one day. It was disturbing, too, because I could not be quite sure that it really happened. That afternoon as I strolled around the narrow lanes with Jock my eye caught a scrawl on the sunbaked, peeling stucco of a jut of wall under an arch, a scrawl that had been cut there crudely with a knife. It was in the shape of a starfish.

I passed on, hardly noticing it, listening to some new indignation from Jock. Then suddenly I remembered, at the back of my mind, that I had seen that mark before, in some book, and that it is called Solomon's Seal. My doubt did not concern the actual seeing of the hieroglyph. I did see it. I strolled back and looked at it again. My doubt was as to whether it had any intent. It may have been, and probably was, scraped there by some doodler unaware of what he was doing. I should not have thought twice about it if I did not also remember that my friend whom I have already mentioned as an old resident in

Sori had said a couple of days before, with a laugh, that one would probably find every known superstition in Camogli, down to the Black Mass. This last I do not believe to be a fact, and neither, I am sure, does he. Nevertheless, the sight of that scrawled hieroglyph stuck in my mind with such a torment-ing and somewhat uncomfortable insistence that when I came home to Ireland I spent several days in the National Library in Dublin and in the Irish Folk-Lore Institute searching for in-formation about it. Under the heading of Black Mass I could find nothing. Then, by the merest chance, in an old Italian folk-lore journal in the Institute I found out something.

It is undoubtedly a form of the sign called Solomon's Seal. (That much anybody can find straightway in a good diction-ary.) It is sometimes also called the Seal of Mercury—why, I do not know. One meets various references also to Solomon's Ring, which told him everything he wished to know. One guesses that the idea was widespread that all occult wisdom came from the East; and that the Saracens might have brought this piece of it across the Mediterranean. Similar mystic symbols and talismans have come from much farther away than the Levant; such as the swastika, which it is said is, to this day, used as an emblem among the Buddhists and Jains of India. Probably people have always been fingering these signs, changing a swastika into a circle by curving the arms, imposing a circle or a square of triangles on the cross—which was a mystical emblem long before Christianity gave it new life—as in the Celtic cross or the so-called Saint Bridget's cross which is still woven from straw in Ireland on her feast day. Wherever the idea came from, Italian seamen have been known to invoke heavenly or diabolical aid by means of Solomon's Seal. Their tradition is that when the angels were driven out of heaven some made their homes on the sea bottom and there now stir up storms. If a boat is surprised by a storm, and if there is a first-born in the boat, he may undo his belt, expose to the evil spirits *le parti che tacere è bello,* while the others cry for mercy to God, calling on Saint Francis or Saint Barbara with some such half-illiterate jingle as:

> *Santa Barbare affacet' affacete*
> *Ca mo passe du colonne*
> *Hine d'acque, hine da vende,*
> *Santa Barbare fa bon tempe.*

Though why Saint Barbara should be called on is itself a puzzle, since she is, I believe, the patron saint of locksmiths and gunners! If there is no youngest child aboard the boat the Solomon's Seal might then be scrawled on the prow, and transfixed with a knife, which thus killed the adversary. Another form of the seal has, it is said, been used to call up winds. This one is an elaboration of the swastika.

Affixed with a nail to the prow—so the legend goes—it is whirled about, presumably like a toy windmill, while some incantation called the *paternoster verde* is recited. One contribution to the folk-lore journal which I have mentioned suggests that this 'green paternoster' may be a parody of the true paternoster and so be part of the whole parody of the Black Mass; but another derides this and says that the prayer, whose jumble he gives, is a country joke. But only trained folk-lorists could sieve these traditions, and at the end of my researches I felt that I had only been led astray in a dark wood by that

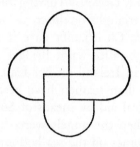

scrawl on the sunny wall, and I relapsed into my first opinion that it had been made there by an idler recalling he knew not what.

San Fruttuoos

AND yet, it may have been more. . . . No outsider can be sure of such things. Pious and impious legends have always flourished along this rocky riviera. Just around the headland of Portofino, across the bay, out of sight of Camogli, is a tiny cove called San Fruttuoso. As you pull into this cove the weathered tiles of the old abbey's hexagonal cupola built on arches over the shingle rise against the wooded cliffs. Mountain paths wander perpendicularly up the travertine hill under storm-twisted trees. It was once a Benedictine hermitage endowed by the Genovese Dorias, some of whom were sailed there for burial. It is now crapulous and dirty from a thousand years of storm and neglect. From here come two very different sorts of tales.

The first is about the Gran Diavolo, a brigand whose amusement it was to ask his victims their opinion of the Devil. If they praised him he let them go; if they reviled him he sent them, as he hoped, to join his master. He was captured, killed and immediately buried on a hill called Monte Oliveto, whereupon an enormous tree at once grew out of his grave. One day a poor woman of the hill, weary of invoking the saints, invoked the tree, saying: 'If you do not help me, who will?' A head appeared out of the tree, took a number from its mouth, another from its nostril, a third from its poll, combined the three numbers and bade her buy that ticket in the lottery. She did and won. The dead know all things.

The other legend invokes a famous Irishman. For all this region northward to the famous monastery at Bobbio is an Irish pilgrim's way. Bobbio was founded by Saint Columbanus. Once, while on his way down through the mountains, he passed through the village of Moranego, which is still dedicated to him; he persisted southward to this San Fruttuoso di Capodimonte—how, it is hard to tell, for even to-day it is the rudest mountain country—and left there a small cross to be preserved in memory of his visit. Formerly the people of Moranego used to make the same hard pilgrimage to San Fruttuoso in his honour. It is no great hazard to guess that as they came there they would as readily have recalled the one story as the other, and, perhaps, believed each as readily.

That remote cove must, in winter, seem like the end of the world. And what a strange contrast it is with everything about it. A few villas nestle along the Portofino headland. At Punta Della Chiappa there is, or was, a famous restaurant. The sophistication of Rapallo, Santa Margharita, Paraggi and Portofino are barely around the corner. But San Fruttuoso is so difficult of access that few people go there. In the summer a few gay motor-boats do pull in, a few holiday-makers stay there, and under the auburn fishing-nets swung high in the air over the water, veiling the white walls of the old abbey, a few oiled sunbathers recline on the beach or dive into the clear water. They merely underline its solitariness.

No cenobite, no castaway, can have looked more detached from the world's way than the ancient limpet who comes back to my mind as I saw him one day, perched fishing from a ledge under two hundred feet of sheer cliff, smoking at his ease, looking at his line—how he got to that rock none of us could see—not even glancing at our boatload as we passed by on our way into the cove in the morning. He was still there, like a barnacle grown into the rock, as we passed out in the afternoon, a symbol of San Fruttuoso's retirement.

But when autumn comes, and those few oiled sunbathers have gone, and the pretty motor-launches have chugged away under cover, what a dark and desolate corner it must be; seeing little of the outer world but the steamers passing along the brief horizon by day; and then, at night, only the more adventurous lights of the fishing-fleet floating out around Punta del Buco. When they tire, then, of discussing boats, food, the lira, tourists, politics or fish, how do they pass the long wild nights when the the Dorias snore below? Have the old men more stories like wind howls up from Corsica and the trees creak overhead and that one of the Gran Diavolo? Or of wrecks like that one which is pictured so wildly and dramatically in the *ex voto* painting in the church? Do they relapse week by week deeper into the past, as in Irish glens the people do who, in the summer, emerge for a spell into the twentieth century out of the Middle Ages? I suppose nobody but themselves knows what dreams rule their minds, and not even they themselves fully know. I have been a visitor, off and on for thirty years to one of the most mountainy parts of Gaelic Ireland, more or less accepted by the people, able to talk the language fluently, and I am sure that I do not know more than a tiny fraction of their minds, and I am as sure that much of what they 'think' is dark even to themselves. This wild corner of Liguria and any wild Kerry cove are probably much alike, being both relics of an ancient civilisation buried now under the detritus of centuries, to be excavated only by scholars who have the training, or the genius, to think, with them, like children of time.

Around the headland of Portofino comes elegance and sophistication. They are charming bays and in the season full of liveliness and brilliance, but places like Paraggi and Rapallo are alike beyond my purse and outside my interests and I far preferred the cove at Sestri Levante, with its little boats and yachts, its woods of oak and strawberry trees, its hilly paths, its open view back to Rapallo and its natural Italian atmosphere; for few foreigners stay here. It is, however, best in summer. In the winter the northern winds would steal down the slopes of Sestri, but would break against the hills behind Rapallo and only be felt four miles out to sea in the gulf.

At Sestri I left the Riviera, lured by the mountain roads.

To Spezia

As we climbed out of Sestri Levante, winding up and up among the barren mountains, with the driver hooting at every turn, as well he might, his muscles straining on the wheel, sweat beading his neck, never a moment's rest, I kept wishing that another mode of travel had not passed away—the two-horse carriage. How much more restful the quiet clop-clop of hoofs, to alight and walk while it is still cool; to pause at the inn at Bracco for a glass of wine, still within view of the heat-dimmed sea; to spend the livelong day on that incomparable thirty-five miles of mountain road, swung high over the valleys; or to break it for the night at the Albergo at Borghetto di Vara. That is twenty-two miles from Sestri, enough for one day, even with two horses, on such a hard-pulling road. Unless you travel slowly, it is hard to get the full impact of the wildness, stoniness and barrenness of the Appenines, to have leisure to consider how, at home, one would be seeing—as one hardly ever sees here—pleasant green fields and spreading trees, not this scattered scrub like a veil or a shadow, herds of grazing cows. In Italy the cow lives for the most part in the shadow of its stall, fed like a rabbit or a pig; the cow in the Christmas manger of Nativity pictures is there in the summer, too. But to come close to the detail of daily life one must leave the motor roads and climb back into the hills. Perhaps it would be of all forms of travel the best not to travel much at all, to sink a deep well in one mountain village and to come there again and again. Few could practise such self-denial.

Horizons rise behind horizons. The rivers in the valleys dwindle to streams. Those dramatic churches perched on mountain crags that, from below, seem abandoned or silent hermitages are half fort, half village, houses and church and rock all stuck together like a cluster of barnacles, lively as hen-runs, dusty and cobbled; life crumpled together in the most familiar way. You soar above them. You possess the sky. And, then, you think, this is only one of ten thousand such exciting roads down to the toe of the peninsula! The morning wears on. You become merged with what you look at. The scene mesmerises. Unexpectedly, in the midday haze the 'soft, Blue Spezian bay' glimmers far ahead and far below. Such vastness of space! Such a palpitant undulation of land, sea, waves of air, sparkle of veiled light! The Apuan Alps lift, beyond the great bay, their jagged peaks, crystalline with the limestone from which comes the marble of Carrara. The rocky shore is softened by its umbrella pines. On this nearer side of the harbour's sweep the hills circle splendidly southward to Porto Venere—below which is that cave which is said to have inspired 'The Corsair'.

The descent is an exchange of elements, like coming down to earth in a plane. It is a descent to earth in every sense, for you may wish you had remained on the heights when you find yourself down at last in a bombed and battered Spezia, dust on its yuccas and orange-trees, its hotels gapped, its monuments splintered, its docks empty. That day we stopped dead in the Via Domenico Chiodo, held up by a mob of angry strikers. The women of Spezia had made their men draw lorries across the street and halt everything on four wheels while they crowded in a black mass about the Prefettura howling for food. They were led by a tremendous hay-mow of a woman, their La Passionaria, bare-armed, bareheaded, all but bare-bosomed, a scarlet kerchief swept about her head, a jolly, furious woman pouring floods of good-humoured abuse on anybody who dared to try to manoeuvre a way past her pickets. For two hours we sat in the grilling sun. Across the Piazza there were occasional bursts of cheering and booing. To them it was life or death; bread or starvation. To us it was a bore. As I turned from the vacant waters of this one-time great naval base, once a speckle of cruisers and battleships, to the ruins of the front, and watched the cheering mobs of hungry women, I knew that I was attending a tiny but pathetic epilogue to history.

Rebecca

By the time the cars and trams at last began to move, the long, dusty coast road down to Viareggio seemed even more uninviting than it is. The scattered detritus from Carrara's quarries paints the hills a graveyard white, blinding in the sun. Factories line the way. Dust clogs the air. Little wharves nose out to sea for the shipment of the marble. From such wharves they would have sent out the marble blocks when they were building the churches of Lucca and Pisa. Nevertheless, I was looking forward to Viareggio itself. A handsome young Jewess at my side was telling me how she used to spend her holidays there as a girl, and she spoke lyrically of the pine-forest that stretches its cool and sighing silence, its dim Turgenevian boskiness, for six miles along the beach. She was half-English, half-Spanish, green as an olive, dark as a sloe. Apparently, for reasons that we shall never know, just as Nervi had once been a haunt of Russians and Germans, the Americans and English of two or three generations ago made Viareggio the most popular bathing resort in Italy, after the Lido. All I knew of it was that Shelley had been burned somewhere on this shore. Later I was to go on a pilgrimage to the pyramid of Cestius outside Rome, where his ashes were scattered, and to his rooms below the Spanish steps, where Keats died.

Alas, small girls with long curls grow into young women with short curls; and intimate beaches become big resorts. The Viareggio of to-day is just one long row of hotels on the landward side, and on the sea side one long row of restaurants, ballrooms, skating rinks, *bagni,* cafés, cinemas, shops. Rebecca looked at it, and looked at it with eyes that slowly changed from longing into accusation. At last the grave Moorish eyes surrendered. 'It is too big.' Change, that enemy of all pleasure, yet without which there is so little pleasure, spoils every return. Even in her childhood Viareggio was still romantically aloof. In Shelley's day this great beach would have been desolate and soothing. The smoke from his pyre rising under the eyes of Byron, Hunt and Trelawney would have been a lone pillar of smoke on a vacant shore. There would have been no sound but the wind in the pines and the falling waves. The forest is now grubby and dusty and gapped. 'In the mornings,' Rebecca sighed, 'we used to ride there and not see a soul.'

A great marshland extends behind this flat shore; in time it may become a lagoon. Ruins here; wreckage of war. The canal leads past the enormous lake which sucks the valley dry. More factories; an impression of slavery, desolation and breathless heat. We were glad to climb out of it towards the 'free town of Lucca'—free until Napoleon, that 'pagod' of liberty-loving Byron and Shelley, ended its four hundred years of independence and gave it as a little present to his sister Elisa. After her it tumbled into the hands of Stendhal's ineffable Dukes of Parma. It is a town to pause in; but hardly to stay in; the plain is hot, and treeless, and the river is distant. But it is a compact walled town with impressive tree-shaded ramparts and a colourful tree-shaded piazza and a splendid cathedral; a busy, effective little town; old enough to have its Roman amphitheatre, and a church founded by one of our wandering Irish monks, one Frigidanus. But friends who knew Lucca in its best days tell me that people never cared to stay much in the town itself. They preferred to go to Bagni di Lucca, about fifteen miles back into the hills, a favourite place with Florentines for *villeggiatura* (the country season), high, cool, green and old. The Brownings came there, and the Shelleys; Hugo, Liszt, Lamartine, hosts of the famous. Then the habit fell away. It must be one of the best places from which to explore up to the very backbone of Italy.

There is one other and supreme reason why travellers do not often pause at Lucca. They say: 'We will come back here from Florence.' They press on to that city whose 'name is like a spell.' It had need to be. The approach to modern Florence from this seaward side is dismaying. One is not greeted by the famous campanile, or the tower of the Palazzo Vecchio, but by the chimneys of far-flung industrial suburbs, the inevitable battered airport, and the casual concrete military road. As with Venice, where one simply refuses to see Mestre, where one cranes beyond it for the first lagoon, and palpitates at the first glimpse of some filthy *sandalo,* as like a gondola as a barge is like a skiff, here one must crane for the first glimpse of the Duomo and see nothing else until the familiar outline cuts the limpid sky. Then, a sigh of joy. It really *is* so.

Florence

As to what is so, we receive from that unmistakable skyline, as unmistakable as New York or Paris, both a confirmation and a prediction—a promise that our little fund of reverence and knowledge will be further and fully fulfilled; and all the more surely, says campanile and dome, if to reverence we add patience and modesty. Whistler, often impatient and always immodest, said of Rome, in irreverence and ignorance: 'This is a stucco city. Ruins don't count. I'm quitting,' and left after three days. If that sort of disappointment and disgruntlement has been an almost universal first experience in Florence and Rome, and I could quote a dozen examples offhand from Hawthorne to Zola, it is largely because we expect Florence and Rome to give up their stories at a glance, as if the age of each were not a hundred times overlaid by a lava through whose cracks it slowly steals, one might say is lured. Nobody can read Rome without footnotes. Florence is not an open book. Its otherness or strangeness and its human appeal are neither superficial nor immediate.

So, in spite of the promise of that skyline, I have to admit that the face of Florence was at first sight far from attractive. It is a heavy, dusky masculine face. It has what the Spaniards call bullishness. Why it was so popular all through the nineteenth century I do not understand even yet. The last thing anybody could call it is pretty. It has immense human interest. It contains countless beautiful things. It has many picturesque corners and views. It has many natural charms. These could not have sufficed to give it its fame. It was certainly not its climate which attracted so many foreign residents and visitors. Some physician has said that he could not understand how anybody dies there in the summer or lives there in the winter; though, in practice, it is in summer that the residents leave it for the sea or the hills. Why ailing Elizabeth Barrett Browning chose to live in Florence and, unlike Landor, not on the heights, but down on the flat of the city, is something that I cannot explain; for the heights are lovely. Probably the popularity of Florence developed accidentally. One traveller came and loved it; then another, and another in his tracks until the habit grew. Why is it that most Italians in Dublin have come from one small region outside Rome? Why do Venetians gravitate to the north of France and Tuscans to the south?

One of the first things that struck me here—it seems a rather childish remark—was that there is a great deal of stone. The windows are set far apart and seem, thereby, smaller than they are. My second impression was that the streets are oppressively narrow. So, it is true, are the streets of Genoa; but Genoa has the sea. True also that many of the Roman streets are dark; but Rome has those seven hills which lift us above the tiles, and more open spaces. The streets of Venice can be stifling; but Venice has her vast lagoons. And in those dusky, narrow Florentine streets the buildings are of a cyclopean ponderousness which, for a while, overshadows their grace of form and the detail of their decoration. They are as forbidding as an attractive but over-sized woman. Everybody's first impression of the famous palaces, with their rough-hewn ground-floor façades and thick-barred windows, the Palazzo Riccardi, or the Pitti Palace, has been one of awe. Not until we have lounged often and idly about the Boboli Gardens and mentally placed the immense palace in its magnificent setting of walks and avenues, its thickets of sweet bay, of cypress, laurel, privet, quince, poplars, oleanders and stone-pines; become familiar with its fountain, pool and lofty belvedere, its statues of gods and goddesses, heroes and hermaphrodites set in shadowy niches; not until one has come to long for its several views, such as that from the belvedere north to San Miniato, or from the corner by the balustrade back between the smoking cypresses at the rose-stalk of the Palazzo Vecchio, which is one of the deservedly best-known 'little views' in Florence, or down the terraces at the gleam in the Vasca dell' Isotta, all of it a vital contrast of dark foliage and blue sky; not until familiarity and association have made us accustomed to the forceful character of all Florentine architecture, in its setting, do we come to enjoy its fascinating mixture of Roman order, mediaeval strength and Renaissance ambition whose final satisfaction is a sense of magnificence and muscularity like the *David* of Michelangelo.

This weighty duskiness was always in the character of this

city, but in its hey-day there would have been more variety and higgledy-piggledy, less anatomy, less classic line and far more colour. The citizens then carried brilliance on their backs, even as they lavished the green-veined marbles of Genoa on their churches as if in thirst for some relief from the ubiquitous brown stone. One may at first be almost shocked by the gaudiness of the Duomo and the Campanile. How oppressive the two would be if they were masses of northern Gothic devouring the sun! And is not much of the joy of San Miniato, set against dark foliage, the satisfaction of this same unconscious thirst for colour. Ruskin wisely warns travellers in Italy, approaching Venice for the first time, to expect coloured architecture, so novel to us in the North; he might have warned us, too, to expect the delight and force of this Florentine contrast. Besides, the *pietra d'Istria* of Venice is much more kind to the eye than this grey stone of Monte Ceneri, flatteringly called *pietra serena,* which is the dominant tone of Florence. It may once have been *sereno,* clear or bluish; it has aged forbiddingly.

Our century does not counter duskiness with colour. It lets in light. A good comparison of the results of our method greets the traveller to Florence immediately he arrives, if he comes by train, in the spaciousness and clean openness of the modern railway station, opposite the brilliance of Santa Maria Novella. Each building is admirable in its way; both are products of Renaissance man; the emphasis being now on science rather than on poetry; though Ruskin would have gasped to hear anybody say a good word for a railway station.

The Quattrocento Sun

THIS duskiness of Florence puzzles me. Did the Renaissance Florentine not feel our thirst for light? To see the Baptistery ceiling properly one has to have the electric light switched on. The interior of Or San Michele is cavernous. Gozzoli must have painted the frescoes of the Palazzo Riccardi chapel by lamplight, for it originally had no window at all. Over and over again one is well advised to accept the guide-book's ominous advice—'morning (or evening) light best'.

Quattrocento man could certainly not be called 'light-conscious'. He never paints direct sunlight. He virtually ignores shadow. His paintings glow; but with colour. Faces and bodies are moulded; but not by the effects of sun. Never—I think it is safe to be so positive—does one come before Tintoretto on a picture in which light recognisably streams from its source, from any source, as in, say, Vermeer's 'The Artist in the Studio', in which the light pours from the left through a window hidden behind a dark curtain in the foreground. Never do we come on a landscape like Corot's 'The Road from Sèvres', with its translucent shadows thrown across the road and its sunlight pouring from behind a screen of trees. Botticelli's 'Pallas and the Centaur' is an exquisite example of this fifteenth-century Florentine treatment of light. A few frail shadows, cast by the near-zenith, point the artificial rocks, and the hairy part of the Centaur's body seems to darken the ground beneath his hoofs. Everything else, the face of Pallas, her hands, breasts and thighs, and even her toes are visible, thanks to an all-enveloping calm diffusion as of early dawn, and ambient, universal lucidity sieved from nowhere and distributed everywhere like the air itself, so that every detail is seen as by the magical luminosity of its own colour, independently of the sun. Light in our strong modern sense does not exist in these pictures.

Tintoretto threw the bridge across from sun to shadow. He liked often to occlude the sun so that his figures and his foliage, as I recall them—I am thinking of 'The Flight into Egypt' in the Scuola di San Rocco in Venice—seem to be radiant as with a nimbus, and their shadows are presented to us. But I wish now I had looked more carefully at them for I seem to remember a darkness rather than a direct shadow. You may remember that Alice Meynell paid tribute to this daring innovation in her poem 'To Tintoretto in Venice'—she is speaking of the earlier, more modest art when she says:

> *Long had she sat content*
> *Her young unlessoned back to a morning gay,*
> *To a solemn noon, to a cloudy firmament,*
> *And looked upon the world in gentle day.*
>
> *But thy imperial call*
> *Bade her to stand with thee and breast the light*
> *And therefore face the shadows, mystical,*
> *Sombre, translucent vestiges of light,*
>
> *Yet glories of the day . . .*

Caravaggio, who was contemporaneous with the elderly Tintoretto, took this naturalism of light and shade to the limit.

'How sad!' Ruskin might have said, expounding the triumphant 'infinity', as he called it, or the 'idealism' which the old unnaturalism managed to achieve. But, then, Ruskin does not explain why it was that those homes are sometimes so poorly lighted, those churches often so obscure that we cannot properly see their triumphs. He must have frequently seen, as every traveller still may see, an obliging sacristan ingeniously lighting a picture in a dim church by means of mirrors; standing one mirror against a bench in the church and running out into the bright campo with another to direct the sun inwards on the first mirror, and so on to the face of a picture otherwise lost in the dusk. Colour the quattrocento loved; light, as such, it did not see. Ruskin loathed and reviled classical architecture, and suspected everything painted after 1508, but it was, ultimately, classical architecture not Gothic architecture which let the sun into the study. I can only remember one modern building which Ruskin praises wholeheartedly: the little church of Saint Margaret's, a stone's throw from Broadcasting House in London, and it is as dark as a coal-hole.

The precision of that date 1508 is amusingly characteristic of Ruskin. In Raphael's twenty-fifth year, he records, he began to decorate the Vatican for Julius II. 'In the first chamber he decorated he placed a picture of the kingdom of Theology presided over by Christ. On the sidewall of that same chamber he placed a picture of the kingdom of poetry presided over by Apollo. And from that spot and from that hour the intellect and the art of Italy date their degradation.'

He was inordinately fond of these years of doom. Speaking of the rebuilding of the Ducal Palace in Venice, begun in 1423, he says: 'The first hammer-stroke upon the old palace of Ziani was the first act of the period properly called the Renaissance. It was the knell of the architecture of Venice—and of Venice herself' (*Stones of Venice,* Vol. II). Earlier he was more precise. Unless he gave the hour he could not have been more so. 'I date the commencement of the Fall of Venice from the death of Carlo Zeno, 8th May, 1418.' But he does add that the *visible* commencement began five years later with the death of Doge Mocenigo (*Stones of Venice,* Vol. I). One does not have to be a Marxist to think it more likely that the 'Fall of Venice' began in 1497, when Vasco da Gama rounded the Cape of Good Hope and Venice ceased to control the overland trade route to India. In fairness to him we must remember that he excepted certain achievements from this general Fall. He had to. Tintoretto and Veronese take us to the brink of the seventeenth century, and he pronounced Tintoretto's 'Paradise', in Venice, 'the most wonderful piece of pure, manly, and masterly oil-painting in the world'.

Cities are not Museums

THERE is one other all too obvious reason why Florence does not immediately please. One may expect to see an old city: one finds a modern one. When Ruskin was writing *Modern Painters* in the 1840's modernity was already overlaying much of the old Florence. In his second volume, which appeared in 1846, he was already listing the ravages which he characteristically attributed to the moral decay of the century. 'There is not a monument throughout the cities of Europe that speaks of old years and mighty people but is being swept away to build cafés and gaming-houses.' One can hardly accept so patent an exaggeration; we may in sympathy let it pass, for he had and we have much to regret. Here in Florence he saw a whole street being wiped out, the Via dei Calzaioli ('The Street of the Stocking-Makers'), once a cobbled street of towers and casements, where Bronzino lived, and Donatello and Michelozzo worked, and where stands the lovely church of Or San Michele (if one could only see it), a church once so revered that anybody who made too much noise in the street could be fined sharply, and if he did not pay he was ducked in the Arno. The street was destroyed and rebuilt in the French style at public cost. "It consists now," he remarked, and it is still true, 'almost exclusively of shops of bijouterie and parfumerie.' And he goes on to record, in legitimate wrath, that the old refectory of Santa Croce had been turned into a carpet factory, so that he had to stand on a loom to see the frescoes; even as he speaks in horror of seeing Gentile da Fabriano's 'Adoration of the Magi' lying supine under the rain in a cart, until he protested, whereupon somebody threw an old piece of matting over it and wheeled it away *per essere pulito,* a cleaning process he interprets bitterly, having seen the 'divine distant landscape' of a Perugino painted over in French ultramarine with a common house-brush.

Yet did not the golden age itself carry Cimabue's Madonna in procession through the streets in every weather, with immense respect, but scarcely with immense prudence? And how much of Renaissance Florence, and indeed of all Italy, grew on the bones of the Middle Ages? God knows what the seventeenth century did to the sixteenth! When we find that decrees had to be passed in Florence in the seventeenth century to prevent works of art from being taken out of it we can form an opinion on what made them necessary. Botticelli was neglected completely for four hundred years after his death. His 'Pallas and the Centaur' was first discovered under the dust in an attic of the Uffizzi in the late nineteenth century by Walter Spence, and it was Rossetti who mainly restored to his name its rightful fame.

Every age has changed and meddled with its inheritance, sometimes impairing it, sometimes enriching it. The architectural history of the Piazza San Marco is a wholly successful mosaic of the endeavours of many generations. Santa Maria del Fiore, begun in 1296, was not finished, in its present form, until 1887. When we stand on the Capitol to-day, silenced by its countless memories, we are excited rather than depressed by the knowledge that it has undergone change after change from the days of Romulus to the seventeenth century. The Venetians were working on the mosaics of San Marco in Ruskin's day; destroying them in his opinion—though he was probably right in that, even though, if he had lived in the sixteenth century, and had his way, he would have likewise damned almost everything 'new'.

It is right that people should argue about changes and innovations; but are not many changes disliked rather because all change is felt as a betrayal than because every change is for the worse? People are never done complaining about what has been done to Rome. 'No other city', Mr. Raymond Mortimer wrote in 1946, 'has been so deliberately spoiled by its rulers.' Is this true? I agree that the approach to Saint Peter's is at present monstrous. We can only hope that some day it will be enlarged further and laid out in gardens, with tall poplars or cypresses spearing up against the great façade. But the main question is, Was it ever a good approach; and what is the meaning of the word 'spoiled' if it was not? I disagree with him about the Via del Impero, which I find spacious and noble. I regret with him, but think it a futile regret, the withdrawal of country greenness from what were once the city's outskirts; for this, surely, was not deliberate and it has been going on for hundreds of years. Seventy years ago Mr. Augustus Hare felt that Rome was already ruined. 'Fifty years of United Italy', he wrote (it was one of his milder outbursts), 'have done more for the destruction of the artistic beauty of Rome than all the invasions of the Goths and Vandals.' Ruskin was cursing change sixty years before that and, if Keats had lived on into Ruskin's day he would probably have sighed for the perfection of the Rome of 1820; so small, a country town, with goats lying in the streets and cows being milked below the Spanish steps. Ruskin adored Saint Mark's. Countless buildings were ravished to create it. He adored the Middle Ages, which, for a thousand years, used ancient Rome as a quarry, or a foundation, or a rubbish-heap, and forgot the very name of the Forum. And so back and back to the days of Juvenal's savage regrets for a still older and better Rome.

Cities are not museums. Bruges is like a lovely stuffed bird. Carcassonne, so carefully 'restored' by Viollet le Duc, is literally stone dead; whereas Aigues Mortes, despite its name, vibrates still. Pompeii is a museum, dug up, though awesome. Ravenna still palpitates, though sinking into the earth inch by inch. Abandoned Torcello pulsates with the memory of its infancy. Cities must not only be seen to be believed, but felt as growing, living things. The only people who can demur at this will be those who see buildings pictorially. To know buildings we must get their physical impact, their movement under light and shadow, the livingness of their surroundings, the to-and-fro of people, their noise, dust, heat, smells, grime, all the fingermarks of time and use. Purely visual Rome or visual Florence is a disparate collection of post cards. Florence in stone is what you touch, you living and the stone living and the people living behind the stone; and for all this we have to take the rough with the smooth, permanence enlivened, even when insulted, by mutability. Architecture is dead. Buildings have blood in them. It is as impossible to study cities out of books as it is to study men, and neither can be ordered to stop growing. If Florence and Rome are the Herculaneum and Pompeii of the centuries, the modern dust we blow away to reveal their beauty is also part of their age. Modernity is part and parcel of their continuum, for Florence and Rome were always modern. I agree that the act of imagination which reaches backward, to pause at some part of the perpetual flux, can be incited by a perfectly preserved ruin, but I think it is helped far more by a perfectly managed café—provided it has been created in an unbroken tradition with the living past. It is only when the continuum is arrested that the past dies. Then we really do get the most horrible sort of modernity, that is another age, another race cut off from its roots. If we really want modernity in that horrible sense let us preserve the past. If we want to avoid it we must accept endless growth and endless alteration.

Past and Present

THIS may be the secret of Florence. It may have always been the most popular Italian city with foreigners not because of its past, but because it opens its doors, its somewhat austere doors, slowly at first, but in the end wide and welcoming, both to the past and to the present. Venice, by contrast, is more generous with its treasures of the past—being so little changed in outward appearance, so outwardly like what it always was—but, as for its continuing or present life it is, like the Venetians themselves, secretive, aloof and remote. It is the one drawback of Venice that it is so exactly what you expect it to be—lagoons, gondoliers in ribboned hats, deserted islands, winding lanes, songs under the moon on the Adriatic, lost ramos, all the trappings of romance—that you find yourself living not in a mortal city, but in a fairyland. In the end I found myself looking there madly for a dentist's brass plate.

Guide-books do us a certain disservice by romancing about the mere paraphernalia of strangeness. Writers on Florence often begin on such a top note of lyricism that you wonder where on earth they will end. They start with talk of the City of Flowers and would be pained if one reproached them afterwards that the characteristic smell of Florence is horse-dung, its characteristic noise motor-cycles and its characteristic sight money-changers. Browning is a better guide than any guidebook. After all when he lived in No. 9, off the Piazza San Felice, and entered

> *Under the doorway where the black begins*
> *With the first stone slab of the staircase cold,*

stumbling on the step as he still read his square old yellow book, he had not only stepped across several centuries to the Past but found the way thither in the Piazza San Lorenzo market, all tumbled and jumbled with its realism of

> *. . . fire-irons, tribes of tongs, shovels in sheaves*
> *Skeleton bedsteads, wardrobe drawers agape,*
> *Rows of tall, slim brass lamps with dangling gear*
> *And worse, cast clothes a-sweetening in the sun . . .*

Trappings seem romantic only when they are gone or when somebody (like Browning) has made them seem so. We could so easily become sentimental about Carabinière in red facings and cocked hats, horse buses, Austrian bands, bottled springwater from the Mugello, warming-pans, gentlemen carrying shoulder-shawls in the Pitti, Spagnolette Avana, Vienna bread, Miss Penrose's school for young ladies in the Villa Lalletta, the English Club, soldi, scudi, 'The Florence Herald'—a list I compile out of an old Baedeker—if we did not remember that to the man who bought that Baedeker when it was new these things were as normal as motor-cycles and money-changers to-day.

For all that, the Past has to be excavated; doubtless by a mixture of imagination and historical knowledge. But, what kind of knowledge? On this Rebecca and I soon began to argue passionately. For I had by now discovered that she is an art expert, and I was eager to learn from her. Her father had been a collector who travelled a good deal in Spain, often in remote places, so that he often travelled the hard way, on mule-back and on foot. He married a Spanish girl, whence Rebecca's lovely Moorish-looking features and olive skin; a mind I begin to discover as ceremonious as the Talmud; and a temperament, as Péguy said of all Jews, so accustomed to sadness as to be happy in it alone. I liked her reverence for the past. She is not ardent about it, which I attribute to her austere English training, but she is as devoted to Art as if it were a religion.

I remember how those arguments began. One wonderful starry night we went up over Florence to dine at Fiesole, and after dining we climbed into the oncoming dark up the steep, cobbled lane that winds to the old monastery of San Francesco. Half-way up there is a small terrace, an old wall, some crinkled *quèrci,* and an exciting night-view across the Arno valley. The silence was absolute and dominating. A chattering group came down the lane and ran gaily against the little parapet. In two minutes the far-off lights of Florence and the lofty stars and the dark valley and the darker mountains had laid a finger on their lips. I felt how easily any Florentine of the great days, standing here, under these eternal stars could see in these lights of Florence the Beginning and the End, his complete, self-sufficing world replete with every human activity that man has ever compassed, every mortal question posed in the round, every possible act of the imagination—war, religion, art, politics, commerce, philosophy—explored to the limit of genius. In such a place as these lofty steps of Fiesole, darkness and silence enclosing our bodies, expanding the imagination, I could understand the old impenetrable Florentine arrogance, that satisfaction of the compass-leg which knows that all human gyrations swing on its fixity as the stars on the Pole, so that a humanist like Pico della Mirandola, a mystic like Savonarola, a man of affairs like Cosimo de' Medici, would have as little wondered there what Rome, London or Constantinople were thinking as a Parisian intellectual, leaning on the parapet of Sacré Coeur, might wonder to-day about the thoughts of some least provincial town of France.

'What are you thinking?' I whisper to Rebecca.

'It is so lovely,' she whispers back.

'Only that?'

We walked back in silence to the little Square below, with its coloured lights and babbling strollers. I said something about Savonarola, in whom I have a special interest. I had once thought of writing his life—the prophet in the lions' den, the mystical realist-tamer devoured in the middle of his act—until I found that he was really not intelligent enough to bear probing. To my surprise Rebecca was interested. For I am always surprised when anybody is interested in Savonarola, apart from the usual vulgar interest in the savage Puritan who burned valuable works of art in a Pyramid of Vanities; and I could not help being especially pleased that a Jewess should be sympathetic to a Dominican mystic. It opened up for me the whole question of how far a non-Catholic can understand the mind and art of a purely Catholic century in a purely Catholic country. As we sat under the lanterns she said that she had spent the afternoon in the Monastery of San Marco and talked of the Fra Angelicos whose loveliness is like music transformed into colour. I felt that it was a comment on us both. For although one of the first places I had visited—and with what emotion!— was the spot in the Piazza della Signoria where Savonarola died I had not yet seen the cell where he lived, mainly, I think, because they have reduced the monastery to the ignoble condition of a public museum: 'preserved' it, or in other words killed it stone dead.

It may be imagined that our discussion was futile. And yet, I could never drop it completely. After all, it seems to me that just as Fiesole, lovely as it is, is something more, much more than a lovely place, these Fra Angelicos are also much more than lovely pictures; that Fra Angelico was also the result and the receptacle of a great many spiritual combinations not only in the life of his period, but in the traditions that fed his period, that he is part of an immense spiritual ferment which cannot be reduced to the level of a purely secular criticism. Can the smell, flavour and interior glow of a wine ever be realised by a teetotaller?

Rebecca's argument was that emotional sympathy and technical knowledge are enough; and they are, indeed, essential and they are a great deal. My argument was that we also have to have that other kind of knowledge which becomes, by long and intimate experience of his way of seeing life, an instinctive understanding of his inmost faith. I was there holding on to my own position that we 'feel' Italian painting as we 'feel' Italian architecture—as part of a living civilisation endlessly fluxive yet basically unchanged since the Middle Ages. Rebecca shrugged.

It is probably this belief in the continuum of things that once attracted me so powerfully to Savonarola. He stands in the swaying flux of the mid-Renaissance like a traffic policeman, a stern one, and I am afraid not a very intelligent one, for he was not satisfied as a good traffic policeman should be to direct the traffic on its way, but wanted it all to go one way, which was rather a nuisance for everybody. He was too devoted a mystic; he asked too much of human nature. As Shaw has said, he thought that because *he* could live on top of Mont Blanc for an hour everybody could live there for ever. He relied far too much on divine wisdom and not enough on his own human wisdom. Nevertheless, he did try to accommodate tradition and change, and I like that in him. He was certainly far more than a rabid burner of 'indecent' pictures. His Pyramid of Vanities was, it is certain, not comprised of 'priceless works of art'. There is no knowing what he sent up in smoke.[1] Besides, he was also the man who preserved the Medici Library, and who was admired by the Della Robbia, Lorenzo di Credi, Fra Bartolomeo, Michelangelo, and others whose opinion we

[1] The main evidence is Burlamacchi's *Life*, which Ranke rejected as a forgery, and which Villari only accepted as a document written by several hands, first published about three hundred years after the event, and by no means reliable.

must respect. I was drawn to him, in brief, because he was a traditionalist who tried to mate the Present and the Past.

How that theme recurs! Rogers once wrote of life in Florence:

> 'Tis the Past
> Contending with the present; and in turn
> Each has mastery. . . .

I wonder if either ever has or ever had the mastery, or for long enough to matter. Few experiences here are static. I think of nights on the Piazza Michelangelo, one of the most charming places to dine in midsummer, in the open, perched high over twilit Florence, with the wide Piazza spread before you, and a bronze cast of Michelangelo's *David* in the middle of its vacancy. Below, the city lies spread to the Cascine gardens in the west; in front the heights of Fiesole are already twinkling; the crumpled range of hills behind Vallambrosa are slowly fading into the dusk. It is one of life's unforgettable experiences to sit here of evenings with a pleasant friend, over excellent wine and food, watching the lights come up, the statue slowly becoming silhouetted against the green of the northern sky, and charm yielding place to awe. The Duomo and the campanile grow dim. A bat squeaks. The pines breathe. All the treasure-houses where you have been drinking beauty and energy through the days fall dark, and sleep. It is an immortal sleep and your heart so flows and fills again that the stars might be the eyes of the dead and the silence becomes a prayer. It is nights like these that make life worth living. A jeep tears suddenly into the Piazza; two young American soldiers leap from it, look over Florence; up-river, down-river; get in again, whirl on two wheels about the *David,* peek out, and are off. Done it!

Two old ladies, who might have eluded E. M. Forster, with two young girls, who might have escaped from Elizabeth Bowen, now approach; they sit and begin to chatter at the table next to ours. One old lady actually wears a blue veil in the time and fashion of *A Room with a View.*

'Have you seen San Miniato, Angela?'

'Yes, auntie. I think I'd like an orange squash.'

'Are you sure you saw the Della Robbia *Virtues?* Aren't they sweet?'

'Yes, auntie, Gloria, won't you have an orange squash?'

'The bronze doors are remarkable. I wouldn't have an orange squash if I were you, not before dinner.'

'Oh, hang it, yes! I must have a squash. Have you got all my post cards, Gloria. Oh, you are a pig! I'll pay for it with my own money if you like. Gloria! You've torn my scarf! Pig, and double-pig!'

Two young lovers hold hands. His arm is about her neck. He nuzzles her ear. A quiet party of four dine in a corner of the verandah by themselves. The restaurant walls are pitted by bullet-marks. The ceiling in one place is torn by something heavier, perhaps a bomb, perhaps by shrapnel. Did not General Mark Clark survey Florence from these hills behind? As Charles VIII did in the days of the Borgian Pope. Time merges. Every scene has another scene behind it like a film exposed many times.

'That Horrible Tower of Giotto'

I RECALL one evening when, as we sat there, after visiting San Miniato, with five words Rebecca got her revenge for all my teasings about her infidel disabilities in the presence of Christian art. (I must have bored her intensely with my endless arguments.) As we looked down at the bulb of the Duomo and its slim tower I ventured to say that the campanile had failed to impress me as much as I had expected.

'After all,' I said, 'you could describe it as just a rectangular tower covered with white, pink, green and black slabs of marble.'

She was at first too hurt, or too exquisitely civilised, to do more than look at me as reproachfully as if I were a G.I. on tour. Then she said, with a shrug,

'One must compare many examples.'

Naturally. (I switched quickly to something else.) Without that sort of practical, as against theoretical knowledge, even the most intelligent person may look at any work of art and no more see it than a blind man. I was amused, a few months later, when I had educated myself a little, to read Somerset Maugham's reference to this campanile in his account of his first visit to Florence, aged twenty. '. . . I spent laborious days, Ruskin in hand, visiting the sights. I admired everything that Ruskin told me to admire, even that horrible tower of Giotto, and turned away in disgust from what he condemned. . . . I returned to England very much pleased with myself and actively contemptuous of anyone who did not share my views (and Ruskin's) of Botticelli and Bellini.' If Mr. Maugham, writing in his sixties, can thus beat his breast, not because he once found the campanile 'horrible' and now knows better, but because he once trusted Ruskin that it is beautiful and now thinks he knows better, it is plain that Rebecca's advice is sound.

It is, indeed, as I have said, not enough to read books. Before I came to Florence I had observed that Ruskin warns us that the first sight of the campanile is generally unpleasing; it did not sink in until I saw the campanile for myself:

'In its first appeal to the stranger's eye there is something unpleasing; a mingling, as it seems to him, of over severity with over minuteness. But let him give it time, as he should to all consummate art. I well remember how, when a boy, I used to despise that campanile, and think it meanly smooth and finished. But I have since lived beside it many a day, and looked out upon it from my windows by sunlight and moonlight. . . .' It is in *The Seven Lamps of Architecture;* a fine passage, well worth reading again, and noble and sensible as Ruskin always is when he is not chasing some brainspun theory.

The tower has to be looked at, and looked at, and, as Rebecca

said, compared with many other towers, before one can understand the nature and fullness of Giotto's achievement. Besides,
most books use such meaningless words about architecture! I
have just taken down from my shelves the first Italian travel-
book to hand to see what it says about the campanile. 'Fair and
slim as a lily, as light as that, as airy and as full of grace . . . so
fair, so undreamed-of a flower . . .'

Giotto did not invent anything new. For four hundred years
before he came out of his eggshell men had been building campaniles; the belfry of that lovely little Santa Maria in Cosmedin
in Rome (every tourist knows its Bocca della Verita) has been
ascribed to the ninth century. The Florentines would have
seen several belfries all in the surrounding countryside. Travelled Florentines had seen them by the hundred all keeping to
the same aim and all keeping within the same broad limits.
True, there were relaxations of those limits. There were varia-
tions as between regions. Some might be round; Pisa's leaning
tower the most famous. Some regions, such as Lombardy and
Venetia, liked to have the sides unpierced by windows, or by
only very small slits, to achieve an uninterrupted soaring flight.
Recall the great bell-tower of the Piazza San Marco, whose lofty
faces are divided into four blind arcades by slim, soaring pilas-
ter strips; or the faces of that most impressive tower of
Torcello, which is divided into two tall blind arcades that carry
the eyes upward in one long swoop to the belfry. Compare
these with the campaniles of Rome, whose divisions are
marked horizontally, storey by storey, and agree or differ as
you please with those who think the Roman style the more
beautiful. Some campaniles rise clear from the ground, like
Giotto's; some are welded into the building; some are of plain
brick; some are adorned; some use marble, some porphyry,
some majolica; some have octagonal roofs; some have spires—
Giotto intended his to carry a spire. I do not think we should
include military towers in the convention like that of the
Palazzo Vecchio, or the town hall of Siena, whose projecting
eaves and machicolations make them so interesting in point of

outline. One must, indeed, see many examples, and make many misjudgments, before, at last, daring to look critically at Santa Maria del Fiore.

For a while I thought I preferred, from among those near at hand, the campanile of the cathedral of Siena. It is both appealing and dramatic, with its alternate vivid courses of black and white marble, and its traditional window-plan whose clarity and simplicity—simple when you are familiar with it—could alone impose form on that dazzling striped front. The effect of this plan is that as you look upward into the diminishing perspective of the outline you enjoy the contrast of an expanding series of windows; that is, a single-arch below, then a double, then a triple, then four arches, then five, and lastly six arches open for the bells. At Florence, I found, the plan is more subtle; first two delicate single arches, one on top of the other; then two, side by side, mullioned; then two more imperceptibly taller; then a soaring triple with fine tracery, twice the height of the two below it; a harmony more felt than seen. I next noted the novel angles or octagonal projections all down the four corners, delicately panelled, and saw how this combined the soaring effect of pilasters with the horizontal divisions as at Rome. I absorbed the rich corbels; the proportions of the panels of marble throughout; their cunning varieties of colour; the balanced distances between the string-courses; the inset statues, some masterpieces in themselves; then the reliefs, some by the sculptor of the Bapistery gates, some by Andrea, some by Luca della Robbia. . . . But, once I thus began to examine it after even a slight experience of other competitors the thing proved to be a mass of riches.

Nobody but a practised and sensitive architect could weigh all the problems it must have presented to Giotto. Should it really have had that missing spire? Is the present termination too blunt? One certainly thinks so at first. And, yet, does this squareness not go well with the façade of the church beside it, which is insistently rectangular; for it has eschewed volutes— those flying sweeps that sometimes fill the abrupt angle of the façade between nave and aisle, as in Santa Maria Novella and San Miniato. And yet, again, there is a pleasing hexagonal tower on top of the campanile at Verona which was intended also to be flat-topped. How long Giotto must have worried over such problems; and over the problem of the relation between the string-courses of the campanile and the horizontal lines of the church. And what a subtle harmony of Italianate and Gothic he achieved; and how much thought and imagination must have gone into that blending! One can imagine how furiously contemporary Florentines would have argued over it all; one back from Rome comparing it with the belfry of SS. Giovanni e Paolo—one of the finest in Rome—which is inlaid with coloured tiles; or with the dainty Santa Maria in Cosmedin and the modest S. Giorgio in Velabro; or another back from Verona contrasting it point for point with San Zeno Maggiore; but why keep to contemporaries—Giotto would be mentioned in every century after him whenever a new campanile was being raised in any corner of Italy. It may be imagined that I did not mention campaniles to Rebecca for a long time!

The Northern traveller, whose eye is trained to appreciate more ascetic material, to concentrate on cold agglomerate clusters of limestone carvings and statues, whose mind is tuned more to the symbolism and idealism of the mediaeval spirit than to the sensuousness and ambition of later centuries, may easily turn away blindly from this coloured stalk. He may well leave Italy declaring that he prefers the tower of some remote country church, reminding him, perhaps, of some familiar Saxon church at home. He may go so far as to use the word 'horrible' to describe this dazzling, or he may even say gaudy, pillar rising independently from the earth like some brilliant, strange, tropical bamboo. Strange; which is to say, once again, not immediately, and perhaps never, obvious.

Florentine Humour

THE old sage was right, too, to
send us back from—what good English he wrote!—'that serene
height of mountain alabaster, coloured like a morning cloud
and chased like a sea-shell'—to the life of the man who made
it; to the passions and intrigues behind its construction; the
contrasts of its pure inspiration with what one might dare call
the carnal conflicts of the pride and ambition it evoked. Unless
we are to treat the whole of Florence as a dead museum of culture we will instinctively do this all the time; with the
Fornarina, the Botticellis, San Marco, the Medici tombs, everything. We will not look at the skill and power of the *Perseus* of
Cellini in the Loggia dei Lanzi as a statue only; we will see him
again madly throwing his spoons into the mould, falling into a
fever of misery, taking to his bed, rising from it to feast in delight with his friends at his statue's triumph. How *can* anybody go through the Pitti or the Bargello as through a museum; or through San Marco, even though it *is* now no more,
and as sepulchral, without peopling either with the men who
made it? And so on with every house, church, street, statue and
picture. And why do we do this? Surely, in an effort to feel the
continuity of the Florentine tradition? Not that we can have
much hope of sure success; whereas to a Florentine this continuity which we laboriously, and in an external way, induce or
infer would be instantaneously palpable. He would see the very
face of Renaissance man in the faces of to-day, and where a
stranger can only guess and grope wink down the centuries at
the original of each modern echo.

Consider any Florentine tradition, say, its humour. For the
uomo piacevole of tradition, specifically a Florentine, had the
reputation of being the chief jester of Italy even before the time

of Aretino, than whom only the papal court produced satirists as bitter. 'Sharp eyes and bad tongues' was the traditional phrase for Florentines, and one still hears other Italians describe them as the greatest cynics in Italy, a compliment of some force in a country cynical to its toes. A native would trot out examples by the score. One drew my attention one day to a sentence in the newspaper describing how a lady overtaken by a *crisi di nervi,* due no doubt to the great heat, had tried to throw herself into the Arno from the Ponte alle Grazie the previous afternoon.

'Somebody observed her, held her and persuaded her from the insane intention,' said the reporter, using the word *trattenuta,* which has a nice nuance of entertaining a person while detaining him. 'Then at S. Maria Nuova a good dose of sedative restored her, *we trust permanently,* to a more cheerful state of mind.' That little grin would not appear in an English, nor even in an Irish newspaper. I liked, too, the self-mocking spirit of the man who had painted across the back of his ramshackle cart: *È brutto ma mi serve.* "It's crude, but it suits me!" It was a kind of apologetic, good-humoured grinning gesture to the Giottos and the Bronzinos. The notices that one finds painted on restaurant walls are of a common Italian humour. *Il padrone di casa sono io; chi comanda è mia moglie.* 'I am the proprietor of this house. My wife is the boss.' A gay picture of a cock bears this inscription *Quando questo gallo canterà, Di credito si farà.* 'When this cock sings you'll get credit.' And so on. But one, which stumped me for a long time, had an original touch. *Non mi far di cacio barca, ni di pan, Bartolomeo.* Literally, 'Do not make me a boat of cheese nor of bread either, Bartholomew.' I can only take it to mean that this is what patrons should say to the proprietor, i.e. 'I want a good meal, Bart. Don't try to make me a boat of bread and cheese.' In other words it is a roundabout, impish, and delicately polite way of saying, 'No cheap meals served here.'

Those were in a little cellar of a place big enough to hold about four tables, where the padrone cooked like a wizard or an alchemist in a cubby under the stairs as dim and big as a coalhole. It was the first, but not the last, place where I drank *Zuppa alla Pavese,* whose very name is, I suggest, a joke, for *pavese* means a shield (I do not think it has anything to do with Pavia), and the specialty of this excellent soup is the fried egg *gules* on the slice of fried bread *sable* floating in it. I think it was there I was told that all Florentines eat a piece of cheese with their pears, preferably *pecorino,* or failing that *pastorella* (Rebecca insisted that they were joking the innocent tourist. I insist that it makes a delectable combination, provided the *pecorino* is not too dry.) But they surely jested in the names of their streets? *Hell Street,* and *Purgatory Street,* and *The Street of the Beautiful Ladies.* One never knows if there is a jest in the air. While bargaining one morning for a fourteenth-century-style triptych in the Via delle Fosse I said the price was high. The maker replied with a sad smile: 'I took four whole days to make it!'

The Piazza della Republica

I FOUND this quality of dry humour nowhere else in my wanderings. If it were not for it Florence would not have been half as pleasant. Of all the tourist cities in Italy, it has the fewest amenities. There is no swimming-pool, and the Cascine gardens have been reduced to a shambles by the liberating armies. The only place to sit at night for a drink is in the Piazza della Republica, a smug 1880 reconstruction with an elephantine triumphal arch on the west side. (I need hardly say that it was originally called the Piazza Vittorio Emanuele.) Here one meets friends night after night, before dinner and after it again. It is the most popular and the ugliest rendezvous in Florence. And, yet, even this vulgar *piazza* has an air. It belongs. And all its clients and supernumeraries belong, down to its guttersnipes and its beggars, its poor women, its cripples, its shabby nuns with their little tin cans into which the drinkers throw a coin worth about a farthing, or the jovial white-bearded friar passing among the tables, with his friendly 'Pace e bene'. (How different, I thought, to Ireland where the poor laity beg from the priests!) I remember the ragamuffins with particular pleasure. There were a couple of these minute pirates, selling black-market cigarettes, whom I used to look forward to meeting every night, they had such vivacity, they were so brimful of roguery. Even the adult pirates in rolled-up shirt-sleeves, wandering up and down, pulling bundles of notes from their bosoms or their hip-pockets, nudging, whispering, disappearing conspiratorially into the recesses of restaurants and reappearing with knowing looks, even these were infinitely more engaging than their colleagues of Venice, Rome or Genoa. Those others are vulpine or servile; Florentines never. They give out a good-humoured, ironical, roguish sting and tingle as of people whose enjoyment of life is not lessened by their amusement at it. Three musicians who came around night after night playing on their guitars to the drinkers and diners, the same old tunes, every day, every hour, had an engagingly sardonic air of being entertained even while they were entertaining. Their captain was dressed in a blue and white striped pullover, short-sleeved, round-necked, as if he owned a yacht at Rapallo. He would murmur the names of the tunes to his two stooges, play with an idly mechanical skill, his dark eyes roving quizzically over the faces before him; finish just when they had played enough to entitle him to his ransom; stuff it into the upturned guitar case; and then he would lead his companions away on a brisk half-trot that had a faintly contemptuous air of dismissal. All day from lunch-time to midnight he did this, resting always in the Loggia dei Lanzi under Benevenuto Cellini's *Perseus,* as indifferent to the sixteenth century as to the nineteenth. There only did the three overtly unbend, joke and laugh. I had a

strong feeling that they rumbled internally all the time. I liked
the ingenious poet who sang his own verses in French, Italian
and English; all about love . . .

> . . . *Ma il piu bel ricordo che mi resta*
> *è quella goccia di luna*
> *sulle tue labbra*
> *come una stilla di rugiada*
> *che cade sulla rosa*
> *Allo spuntar del dì.*
>
> *Mais le plus beau souvenir*
> *Que j'ai conservé de toi*
> *C'est cette goutte de lune*
> *Sur tes lèvres,*
> *Comme une goutte de rosée*
> *Qui tombe sur la fleur*
> *Lorsque paraît le jour.*

Which he signed; Umberto Girlanda. I even liked the cursed
tifoso who seemed to be always demonstrating his brute of a
motor-bicycle *con brio* around the Post Office.

I have felt lonely in that Piazza, sitting alone, the Americanos
gone to my head, but never once bored; never depressed. It is
easy to talk of the 'magic' of the lagoons, or of the Pincio, or of
dawn and night on the Mediterranean, or of the 'enchantment'
of the Adige when a thunderstorm is hammering like a thousand Thors in the Alps, of the Arno swirling under a new
moon, of campaniles pale as ghosts or olive-groves faint as
clouds in the great heat, of a hundred hours and places in Italy.
As it happens, it is easiest of all to talk of 'magic' in the Piazza
della Republica. What else but magic could so transmute its
squalor as to make it a happy memory? It is a human magic.
The subcutaneous tingle that comes up through the austere
stones of Florence, the mysterious resonance of its swarthy and
narrow streets is clearly and unmistakably its latent human en-

ergy still vibrating across seven centuries. The past of Venice lives as a remembered dream. Rome is a dark perspective flitted with shades and whispers. Florence has altered, but has it changed?

Dante and Joyce

I WOULD often ask myself, while walking in the Pitti or looking at the pictures or frescoes of some church: What work of art here best sums up, and will crystallise in the memory, this persistent aura? And I always felt that I should select something that was vigorous, human, and unmistakably local. The Fra Angelicos are tempting; but they do not compass the Florentine vigour that, drowning all cynicism, all humour, all tolerance, so often bursts its bounds in a flood of destructive passion. Rebecca proposed Botticelli's 'Nativity', now in London, and although this pleases me trebly, by its own grave and solemn beauty; by its summary of all that the Florentines believed in; and by its personal association with Savonarola, whose influence on the painter and the picture cannot be denied, still I thought it too lyrical for my purpose. In a similar way the church that I think the loveliest—San Miniato —is ruled out because it is too beautifully Byzantine, and Florence is essentially a Renaissance city. I wanted something monumental and fiery and severe, and if there were more fiery mobility in Masaccio, or if the *Lorenzo* in the Medici chapel were not so much a single, personal portrait, or if there were not an almost excessive grace in Donatello's *David,* any of these perfect things would have been the chosen symbol. One morning, still at a loss, I said to Rebecca: 'If we were asking this question not about Florence, but about Paris or London or Dublin . . .' and before the question was ended the answer was evident. For just as one would inevitably choose Balzac for Paris, Dickens for London and Joyce for Dublin, there is only one possible name for Florence.

Thinking of Joyce, I became excited by the many parallels between the two men; not only for the mere interest of these accidental similarities, but because to think of the story behind the *Vita Nuova* in terms of *A Portrait of the Artist* helps to dispel the cocoon of awe which we have been resolutely spinning about Dante's passionate flesh ever since the doorstep gossips of Ravenna muttered as he went by: 'There goes the man who has been in hell.' The story of Beatrice has become too much of a romantic myth, a hazy legend, not without a great deal of help from Dante's 'taste for enigmatic roles', as Joyce says mockingly of himself; and this romantic approach will not do, because, although we may accept the basic truth in Dante's highly literary reconstruction of a passionate love-affair, to accept it wholly is to erode and polish away all its human accidents until we are left without an intelligible, human, natural boy and girl in whom we can believe. Curiously, at an opposite pole, Joyce tried to do much the same with his fleshly, naturalistic Beatrice. She is quite palpable, as if hot and warm from the bed, in *Stephen Hero,* a spur alike to love and hate, obviously some girl who once stirred him so much that he could have surrendered a great deal for her; but she appears in 'A Portrait' as a dim shadow without a name. There he gives only her initials, E—— C——, having given her name in the earlier version; even as he now refers with a fastidious vagueness to incidents which he will no longer describe. Dante also suppressed the torments of the flesh. His whole life, his vast arrogance, his relentless pursuit of revenge on Florence for banishing him show him as a full-blooded, passionate, angry, bloody-minded Italian; and it is pertinent to remember that even while he was idealising Beatrice Portinari he was married to Gemma Donati, and had a round flock of children by her. But that he did idealise her, or, as we say nowadays, sublimate what she evoked in him, does not mean that he did not bite the sheets at night and grow pale from dreams of her body's touch.

They were two grim figures; self-dramatising, passionate, down-looking, undershot of jaw, stalking moodily through the lanes and streets of their little cities, observing the men and women that each was to put into his masterpiece, neighbours and fellow citizens who were not in themselves, for the most part, of the least interest, but who were to be given an intense interest by the obsession of their recreators. Each loved and hated his native city. Each found it noble enough to admire and base enough to disdain. The Florence of Dante's day did not, of course, possess a tithe of its later riches, neither the duomo nor the campanile, nor its great palaces, nor a hundredth of its statues, its paintings or even its memories. It was far from being the seventh city of Christendom. Each could say, as Dante said, in individual assertion, that

> *. . . of thyself to make*
> *Thy only party is the better way,*

Each was steeped in mediaeval Catholicism. In each there was a struggle between lyricism and brutality. Each was a lover of words and of learning. Each was disdainful, secretive, inturned, lonely, poor and patronised. Each was exiled and died in exile. Each was unhonoured by his native city even in death. Not that the chasm between them is other than immense. They are, in every sense, an age apart. Florence, though small, was virile and creative. Dublin was a servile eunuch. And since each is a measure of his country's civilisation, there is no least question which is the greater man.

As I pursued the parallel, still mainly in order to dispel the romantic fog from about the Florentine, I was amused to note further that neither of them discovered any new subject once the gates of his native city closed behind him. A single obsession filled their lives: one small handful of common life observed in youth. One result is that although these two big books differ in a dozen ways they are identical in one thing; that each is so local and personal that we have to read them with footnotes. Neither man could construct a self-contained work of art, which is the great appeal of all classic art; whereas the con-

centration of one man on his own emotions and his own experiences is the antithesis of the classical and postulates a book
which cannot be fully understood without study—the *Inferno,
Ulysses, Gargantua and Pantagruel, The Faerie Queene,* a great
part of every contemporary satirist, such as Pope or Voltaire;
and of every personal book such as the 'Confessions' of
Rousseau or of Saint Augustine. Such books will always be
more praised than read, sometimes dismissed by the impatient
or uncultivated as unreadable, but when we do master such
books they have an intimacy which the classical can never
achieve, being not only works of art, but human testaments.

Dante, if we could come to see him as naturally as we can see
Joyce, would come down from his pedestal in Verona or Florence and breathe beside us. He makes those swarthy streets
teem again. One name, one passage from his pen can evoke all
the passions of an era. I am thinking of one scene where two
heads lift out of their tombs in hell to stare at him. One of them
looks eagerly behind Dante and then back at him with: 'Where
is my son?' It is old Cavalcanti asking for his son Guido, Dante's
lost friend, a name powerfully evocative for anyone even
slightly acquainted with the history of Florence. The other
skull, Farinata,

> *Proudly his brow and breast swayed upward
> As if he held all Hell in scorn . . .*

pours out in his angry talk of exile and exiles the whole boiling
cauldron of that rage and pride of Guelph and Ghibelline,
Bianchi and Neri, Albizzi and Medici, which put stone on
stone and tore stone from stone in the making and unmaking of
this great city.

'And if your faction never found its way home,' taunts Ali-
ghieri, 'that was because it never learned how!'

'A lesson,' taunts the protruding head, 'that you, before long,
will find it as hard to learn . . .

But I stood alone when all the rest would
Have swept Florence from the earth. Alone,
And openly, in her defence I stood. . . .'

They are the sort of words that, like the words of Shakespeare's
Henry before Agincourt, turn past history into present life and
put us at the sideline of the game. . . .

The traveller in Florence will fall back often into summer
idlings and vacant dawdlings; but not for long. He will take
his pleasures wandering thoughtlessly along the quays, watching the sun on the weirs, strolling along old streets, in and out
of old shops, passing in and out of churches, of whose riches he
is daily sated and for which his hunger is daily renewed; and
then when he is most idle, most thoughtless, a head rises slowly
out of the tomb, all his senses leap alert, and he is grappling
once again with present immortality.

Neverness is the word for Venice; everness for Florence. The
clocks of other cities are synchronised; the clocks of Florence
have two faces, then and now; and both are right, since time
here is never immobilised, the past never dead, the present
never supreme. When one looks back at Florence from Rome,
where one is so utterly overwhelmed by the past, one feels the
difference at once. Here, one feels, things do not so much occur,
or happen, or arise, or begin, or end, as prevail, endure, come to
pass, cut and come again.

I say 'one feels', for I can only record an impression. Doubtless everness has enemies. The clocks of Moscow and New
York also tick loudly. More folders than Umberto's love-songs
pass about the Piazza della Republica. Perhaps what I read as
everness is just a stopped clock? Perhaps one day a machine-
gun will scatter its works in a vicious burst of hate and bore-
dom, or a natural, healthy, boyish longing to own a brand-new
Ingersoll. If that ever happens my impression is a heard echo, a
hail and farewell, a memory of the good old days before the
(usual) revolution. If it comes to that, where should a revolu-

tion more suitably occur than in a city whose chief exports for centuries were cut-throats and condottiere? And if that is not the Florence of Baedeker it is the Florence of Browning. But I find myself on dangerous ground and begin to get cold feet. I should like to be taken seriously about some things, but these are matters on which no passing traveller has any right to speak. What could an Italian know about Irish or British politics unless he lived among us for several years? For all I know that group conversing eagerly, head to head, in that corner of that restaurant, those two leaning over the quay-wall of the Arno, that late light in that lofty window, betoken plotters or mystics propounding heaven or hell. I know that the Communist party is active in Florence. I know that there is an intensely mystical Brotherhood of poets in Florence, called the *Ultimi*. I never pierced them. I am merely a man travelling for pleasure. Pay no heed to me whenever I seem to forget it.

Siena

SOUTH of the Italian lakes Maggiore, Como and Garda, the main attractions of northern Italy are the Riviera and the cities. Between Florence and Rome one is bewildered by the variety of appealing towns, villages and mountain hamlets. I wanted, naturally, to go to La Verna, to Siena, to Montepulciano, to Perugia, to Gubbio, to Assisi, to Orvieto. . . . But I am a lazy traveller who idles the days away; and the joys of Italy cannot be clutched in handfuls.

Of all those places I most profoundly regret La Verna. Friends who had been there—two of them had escaped from the Germans and hidden here, high on the wooded col between the Tiber and the Arno—and everything I had read about it made this remote Franciscan hermitage profoundly appealing. Day after day I said: 'To-morrow I will go to La Verna.' When at last I felt like moving on somebody said: 'You must see the Palio in Siena. We are driving there to-morrow.' The coin fell in favour of Siena. And once you are in Siena there is the road calling you through Orvieto to Rome. How often in those hours I envied people, many of them my contemporaries, who had travelled in leisure through Italy, and some on down to Greece and into Asia, in the good old days when you could do it often and freely on a few pounds—young men and women like Robert Byron, the Sitwells, Elizabeth Bowen, Morgan Forster, Christopher Sykes, Harold Acton, all in their gilded youth while I was wasting my years on Irish politics, or talking Gaelic with old men under West Cork hedges, in the rain, instead of lying with my gob open to the sun in Calabria. I suppose we get something out of every experience. We had better! If a man could only have six lives. Or even two. Or even one and a half?

The road to Siena is a winding vaulting road of little valleys and wide horizons where towers and towns appeal from afar across volcanic hills. In winter it might all be grey and bleak. To-day it glowed and sang. On the way I passed another long-dreamed-of name, San Gimignano. All I could do was close my eyes, and sigh, and swear to come back again and yet again.

The approaches to Siena were jammed. From all over this part of Tuscany people were pouring into the town in cars and buses. As we crawled into the winding crowded streets the whole place vibrated with the noise and tingle of a fiesta in an effect at once delicate and dramatic, with its universal contrast of thrusting mobs, pink walls and blue sky. There is another constant contrast; black and white like a leit-motif of sun and shadow. You find both on the Piazza del Duomo in the striped white and basalt of the cathedral; and where the bricks of the old walls merge into pale stone with black outlines to each saracenic window-arch; and in the campanile that climbs up, course by course, in silver and jet; and on the terrace of the church, itself a draught-board dazzle, there were nuns in black and white and Dominicans in black and white; and over many doorways the final frequent assertion of the arms of the Bianchi and Neri—and all, remember, made doubly dazzling by the blazing sun and the flawless sky and the crowds surging along in high excitement. On any normal day one is almost surprised to come on any other colours than rose and black and white, or if not white a whitish yellow, soft as worn sea-shells, but on a special day like this day of the Palio when flags and banners in red and cerise and gold flare in every street Siena simply laughs with colour.

If you think of Siena when wandering around Renaissance Florence the secret of Siena's particular charm will at once occur to you; or if you think back to it from Rome whose perspective of history is so strikingly gapped from the eighth century on to the beginning of the Renaissance. For while Siena has seen three civilisations, the Etruscan, the Roman and the Mediæval, the first is for archaeologists, the second is for historians and it is the Mediæval which remains before the eye. The Cathedral epitomises it, far more suggestive of Gothic—in spite of its horizontal lines—than S. Maria del Fiore. The old walls; the great town hall with its soaring campanile; the soft brick floors of the winding lanes; the church of S. Domenico; the political and religious traditions of the town, such as the Palio, all evoke the fourteenth century. This Gothic insistence, midway in time, as in geography, between Pagan and Byzantine Rome and Renaissance Florence, brings us into immediate intimacy with Siena. Its streets, walls and houses are part of a tradition we have always known. We accept at once the dazzling exuberance of the Cathedral which might otherwise overwhelm us, because its spirit, though expressed in a manner totally different to our Gothic, is so evidently that old mediaeval spirit we know so well; and as we come to recognise this we must be enchanted, too, to discover that in architecture the heart can expand in other ways than one, that the language of a perpendicular symbolism is but one of its idioms.

For in encrusted ornament, and above all in the dome, religious emotion also took wings, burgeoned and expanded visibly, and with as many, or even more, practical results as to light and space below and above, and, if with a less evident sense of emotion rarefied and subtilised with an even greater impression of dignity, solidity and strength. But the dome can also express the fullest subtilisation of the spirit. It is the most abstract of forms, and when it passes the limits of the half-circle and seems drawn upward by some attraction of the heavens, as if it were about to break out of its arched round into an ogee, and fly a pennant like a wild oriental lance, it is as much an expression of spiritual desire as any soaring spire.

Italian Gothic does not express its emotion by this northern attempt to soar, though its campaniles are ladders to the sky, any more than it melts towards deliquescence by whittling its stonework to lacework. It is much more controlled and articulate, with a clear all-over design, so that even when it breaks into flower, coruscating and clustering on every side rather like a foxglove, if one could imagine a foxglove of a hundred tints, all the parts which tend to confound and bewilder us in Northern Gothic are here subdued to the plan of the whole. The dome is a sign of this. This final floating bubble over all, though itself a last crown and cluster, also gives weight and balance to the interior ornament; much as the heavy striped horizontals control the exuberance of the façades. (They may also be, as Ruskin suggests, images of the desert's wide horizons.) The Cathedral of Siena is thus a masterpiece of the triple native Italian genius for brilliance, expansiveness and constructive science.

To me, brought up by the insistent habit of our Gothic of the North to think of the spirit of the Middle Ages as grey and ghostly, wild and grotesque, Siena was a revelation, although the painting of the Sienese school alone should have long ago broken through my obtuseness with evident demonstration of the opposite. I saw, in delight and astonishment, what, I suppose, everybody else has taken for granted since boyhood, that the Middle Ages were just as gay and glittering as the Renaissance, and in architecture at least just as scientific. Standing that day before the brilliance of this firmly balanced beauty of the Cathedral I began to feel for the first time in a position to strike a just balance between the loss and gain of the Renaissance; to understand and sympathise with Ruskin's extravagant, if often madly unjust detestation of it; and to realise that not until one goes well south of the Alps, to see the wedding of Gothic and Byzantine, the meeting of the tides from the Aegean and the Mediterranean, is one really able to realise the immense loss to Europe when the centre of its civilisation moved from the south to the north, from Spain and Italy and Byzantium to Britain, Germany, and even, for all its glory, to France. I began to see that the domination of these great flesh-eating Northern giants has given us an unbalanced picture of European civilisation, and as if in counter-balance, I could feel soft winds calling me from the Bosphorus and I sighed with them to think that I shall probably never see one speck of that other procreative and spiritualising southern half of Europe which we have relegated and banished and excluded from our consciousness so stupidly and schismatically under the title of the East. Culturally and historically Europe, I began to see, extends to 30° long. and 50° lat., to Cairo and Bagdad, to all Palestine and Syria, to whatever Rome touched or the Crusaders saw. Without the deserts of Arabia and Persia there could have been no Saint Mark's, no Venice, no Ravenna, and Siena would be something less interesting than it is.

All this I might just as well have seen in Santa Maria del Fiore. The surrounding weight of Renaissance art had prevented me from realising that Brunelleschi did not invent his dome but borrowed it from the East. Here I am about to force a point a little early and might better wait until Venice to develop it. I must record it as it occurred to me. I saw that wherever we see a dome we must think of the desert, and think how strange it is that it took so long to strike the imagination of Europe. One might say that it is a simple idea and that without the Orient it might have risen in Europe. It is, indeed, simple enough; it is merely the barrel-vault rotated on an axis, and the barrel-vault is merely the arch extended longitudinally. But what seems to have inhibited the north from developing arch and barrel-vault, and thence the ribs and thence the whole Gothic complex sooner than it did was a simple thing—the North had timber and the desert had not.

With timber you can easily build a flat roof, and so avoid stresses, and so never come to the problems of construction that budded and flowered out of the use of the arch and vault. The basilica is one of the simplest of buildings in point of construction: a row of pillars with arches supporting a wall, and a flat wooden roof across it, and then two aisles with sloping wooden roofs; the rounded apse being the only and not very difficult constructional problem involved. For seven hundred years men went on building like that when the East was raising the lofty, floating dome and the cross-in-square pattern of Santa Sophia. Some did not even have arches springing from their columns, but, as in Santa Maria Maggiore in Rome, still used horizontal lintels in the old Roman style. Such is the conservatism of builders when there is no functional urge to invite originality. If it had not been for the example of Syria and Persia and Egypt flat roofs might have gone on being built far later than the budding of the Gothic style—out of the arch and vault —in the tenth and eleventh centuries. There would have been no soaring spirit at all, apart from the campanile, neither arch nor dome nor spire. It was the desert, now forgotten and perhaps still decried by some, that lifted thought and building heavenward.

The eye thus functions readily with the imagination in Siena. Its age is unabused. Its secret is patent. It speaks its own traditions. As you wander around the old narrow streets, under the tall houses, down the steep lanes, softly treading time as on a carpet, it needs little effort to invoke the fourteenth century; to see Catherine toddling at night with her swaying lantern along these scarcely altered alleys, on her endless work of mercy; or Bernadine with the little circular tablet that he always carried, bearing the monogram I.H.S. in a halo of golden rays. But if one could be in Siena either on Catherine's Feast Day in May, when her embalmed head is shown in her home to

swarms of devout pilgrims; or on either of the two Palio days
in July and August, one could hardly need to invoke the imagination at all. Their pageantry re-creates the past under our
eyes. Then *Magis cor tibi Sena pandit* 'Siena opens more than
her gates to you—her very heart.'

The Palio

THE Palio is a horse-race,
which lasts about two minutes, thrice around the wide piazza. In
those two mad minutes if your heart does not swell until it fills
every cranny of your body, out to your eyes and your ears and
your teeth, strangling all your guts in an orgasm of delight in
the glory of man, sport, horses, colour, sun, the spilling, bub-
bling drunken wine of being alive in Italy, among a race that of
all races of the world best knows what it is to devour life not
only to the last crumb and drop, but to the eating of the cups
and plates as well—if this does not happen to you at the Palio,
then you cannot know even the meaning of 'man', 'horse' or
'sun', let alone know how to enjoy them.

Only two minutes? But to those two minutes the build-up
has been enormously elaborate. It has been going on, for the
Sienese, for weeks beforehand, and on the day of the Palio the
race itself is merely the climax to a scene of prolonged pageantry which, even without the race, is unique, delightful and
exciting.

You must imagine you are sitting at the edge of a piazza of
great extent, shaped like a mollusc-shell both as to its outline
and its delicately hollowed centre, based on the town hall, surrounded by tall houses, rosy and serrated, with wooden stands
beneath them, and every inch of space, except the track, black
with a swaying mob of fifty thousand people. They stand
jammed shoulder to shoulder on the square. They sit on the

roofs. They bulge through the windows. They clamber up
poles. They crowd Jacopo della Quercia's lovely fountain. That
dark sea is never at rest. Every so often there is a flurry: somebody has fainted, or someone is fighting. To-day, too, there is a
faint, and unusual, threat of rain, and the black sea keeps making little white blossoms of waves as faces lift to the sky. Otherwise we are all impatiently watching the clock tower and the
far corner of the square. When, at last, the beginning of the
procession appears and the great Sunta bell on top of the Man-
gia tower and all the bells of Siena begin to clang, and the multitude begins to roar, we know what the noise was like in the
Roman amphitheatre when the first lions bounded in.

Group by group every parish appears, dressed in brilliant mediaeval costumes, carried so unselfconsciously that grace and
realism are one. Each parish has its drummer, its captain, its
men-at-arms, its horsemen, its recognisable standard, and its
two flag-wavers who perform traditional and flawless agilities
with their great coloured flags. They flap and wave them, fluttering and crackling this way and that way, passing them under their elbows, behind their backs, in and out between their
legs, ending up with the splendid trick called *sbandierata* when
they throw them high in the air, like flaming torches, one to
the other, while the audience roars frantic approval. I do not
know how long this procession lasts; parish after parish; display
after display; always the silver trumpets braying, the bells
wildly clanging, the rising and falling cheers. Excitement never
palls for a moment. By the time it has come to an end the mob
is already worked up to a pitch of delirium.

The race itself lives for me in the memory of the frenzy of a
woman beside me when the horses leaped from the tape. The
jockeys were riding bareback, still wearing their mediaeval
costume, somewhat simplified for these two minutes, but including still their steel casques, since it is within the rules that
they may not only lash their horses, but lash one another if they
want to. Two of the turns are most dangerous, one a right
angle and the other a sharp bend at the end of a slope. From

the second of the start to the second of the finish that mob went mad, flogged by the thyrsus of an invisible god; but I cannot believe that any of those fifty thousand *tifosi* was madder than the little dark bulbous woman beside me. She screamed continuously and hysterically at the top of her voice; she clasped her hands; she went white as the marble floor of the Duomo; she danced up and down; her eyes dilated; her entire soul and body was in the horse and the man for whom she screamed.

And, praise be to the Great God of Glory, he won! Whereupon she stopped dead, both as to her shouting and dancing, and as the winner, a handsome devil, mahogany brown, came around the course, triumphantly flashing his snowy teeth and waving his whip to the crowds, she gazed at him in adoration. As an Irishman I would have said five minutes before that I knew what the excitement of watching a horse-race can feel like. Compared to this one the end of the Thousand Guineas at Punchestown is like the Dead March from Saul.

The Palio answered a wonder that has often come to me in Italian towns, like Siena, rich in natural beauty, art and tradition. I have wondered, simply, in pauses of delight, if the people themselves ever feel about it all as intensely as we strangers do. Or do they take it all for granted, scarcely aware of the wealth of their surroundings, imbibing from them but as rarely as they advert to them? Oh, I know—Italians are proud of Italy—at least of her art if not of her politics; and they say so clearly in both cases. Italy made the Italians. The Italians created Italy. And this created and re-created Italy goes on making Italians in every century. Country and countryman have become indissolubly one. The appetite grows by what it feeds on; and no doubt, the soul, too, is an appetite.

But, though this is all plausible and persuasive, I could not help doubting it occasionally. For is it always so? Go from the great mediaeval Piazza of Siena to the modern railway station of Siena, and build me the bridge between the two of them if you can. It is, or was, a splendid railway station. So is the railway terminus at Florence. But they are not Sienese; or Florentine; or even Italian; or even European. And I do not think any-body would deny that modern Italian taste is not of the surest? Is the bridge down, then? After Palio day I decided that the answer for Italy, and Siena, is the same answer for every country. There is a runic language that men do not speak with their mouths, a language that may be forgotten for long periods, but never dies. If it is spoken too often it becomes vulgarised, and there are even times when one thinks it should not be spoken at all. I remember a gallant, blazing day in Venice. As I crossed Canalazzo in a ferry an English girl beside me said: 'What heavenly weather! I wonder do they appreciate it.' The gondolier, who must have understood English, at once cried out, *'Oh, che bel giorno di sole!'*, and began to sing, of all songs, *'O Sole Mio!'* I felt I was in Blarney or at Niagara Falls. But when the Barcajuolo, at night, without seeming to notice what he was doing, instinctively guides one's gondola along the track of the moon, one knows.

The Palio is one of the rare occasions when Italy says that she knows. For there is far more at work here than the excitable temperament of Italy. The Palio is a synthesis of patriotic feeling, love of sport and religious emotion. When that race ended and the followers of the winner crowded him about, with a few *carabinieri* to protect him from the rage of the losers, the bells of the Oratory rang out a peal of triumph as they streamed through the packed and narrow streets to the church of Provenzano for a final benediction, a solemn Te Deum in thanksgiving to God. The trophy is a banner resplendent with the image of the Virgin, reminding us that this city is dedicated to her. The festival commemorates the fighting days of the Sienese republic, at Monteaperti and Montalcino; and no doubt evokes other martial memories, from Calatafimi to the Piave, as such events can always do without a definite reference. More than once I have spoken of the Italian 'jumble', of the many seeming contradictions of their lives. I begin to wonder if their greatest art is not an art of reconciling life's complexities and varieties, an art, when all is said and done, more practical and less theo-

rectical than the French art of living, less intellectual and fine
drawn also; and so, less adaptable to adversity, because much
less self-aware, but far warmer, and more capacious, much
more elastic; a great bursting bag of life, though by that I do
not mean to suggest any lack of grace. The cornucopia, for all
its abundance, perfectly combines the idea of lavishness and
beauty.

I have a friend, a writer, who has travelled all over the world.
He is a very fine writer, indeed a man of genius. He stoutly
maintains that culture does not mean doing, but being. To him
a fine-bred horse is culture. A waiter bringing food to the table
with a flourish is culture. He records in illustration a good story
of a Brazilian sent by his Government among the farmers to
make them develop their farms. He came to a farm where the
owner sat on the verandah, strumming a guitar, and he addressed him eloquently, pointing out the splendid things he
could do with his farm. 'Yes,' said the farmer, still strumming.
'That, señor, is all true. But, you see, I have no time.' Perhaps
the Italian has arrived at this mystical state of being instead of
doing, and, perhaps, who knows, it is culture. No Italian man
or woman can as much as stand without adopting a posture of
absolute grace. To see them talk is to watch something as graceful as a ballet. In their natures there is grace—I had almost
given it a capital letter and called it, as if it were a gift of the divine, Grace . . . Well, if they were content with that, with just
being, and stopped from doing, would that not be enough?
How horrible Fascism was, in such a people, making them suddenly begin to *do,* and do so hideously. But that is the apple of
Eden again, and there are, are there not, many eager and ambitious and clever Communists in Italy to-day? Of course, there
is one great weakness in my friend's argument. Even to breed a
fine horse, to make a good wine, you have to 'do'.

A Wine-fair

WHILE I was in Siena they held the Wine-fair. There was livingness enough there, and doing enough, for it was good wine. Where they held the fair I have forgotten; on some rampart from which one looks across a glen at the impressive bulk of San Domenico and the rose-bouquet of the city behind and about it. It was a wine fair and an agricultural fair in one, so that country-folk could savour the wines and see, if they still could see, the latest agricultural implements: tractors and ploughs and so forth.

Our passage from booth to booth here was a pilgrimage through the vineyards of Italy, for each booth was a little coloured café surrounded by tables and chairs where for a few pence we imbibed in comfort, sun on the poll, Siena in the eye, and wine on the palate. I recall clearly only a part of that blissful voyage. The Moscato I did not much care for. It was too sweet, a sherry-coloured, syrupy wine. The Orvieto was very good; mild, white, gentle and dry; a pleasant wine. That booth was hard to leave. The Mileto was not quite so good, though it is a gentle wine. The Frecciarossa was excellent. 'Oh, but excellent!' I recall the Bigi less acutely, and the wines of Emilia hazily. The Soave-Bertani must, I know, have been heavenly, for Siena seemed by then like the gates of Paradise, and Rebecca, who had come down from Florence for the day, was a Mahommedan peri. Surely the next wine was Barbera? All I remember of it is a red northern roughness like a sturdy Beaujolais. Or was that Broglio, which is a wine from the Chianti hills? But it cannot have been. Broglio, though a Chianti, is the best Chianti, a mild red wine. I feel it *was* Barbera, for its red roughness still tingles my palate, and I can still see San Domenico through that rough redness, and still recall how I wondered what San Domenico, good soldierly man, drank before soldier became saint. The best wine of all was the Lachrimae Christi from the slopes of Vesuvius.

O wines of Italy, not honoured enough, not known enough, not *drunk* enough; from Spoleto above the Sabine hills, where Barbarossa hacked, where Lucretia Borgia lived, and which one mad Major O'Reilly once chose, I have forgotten why, to hold against the Piedmontese, up to these shimmering hills of Chianti behind this beloved Siena. O grapes of joy, from Umbrian Orvieto, where a Borgian pope took refuge from a French king while a Ferrarese Dominican cheered from the pulpit of San Marco (and was duly burned for it), up to the sparkling Asti of the plains of Piedmont, and down again, line on line, to Frascati and Genzano, those two great wines of the Roman Castles which one should drink in Frascati and Genzano themselves as one eats a salmon fresh from the stream or a peach from the tree. If these are culture, lead me to it.

The wines of Italy are, taken all in all, much more sleepy than the French and never quite so slow and gentle in their diffusion through the soul; though I shall never forget a cool, insidious, straw-coloured Soave-Bertani at Torcello—even there on a sunny day, on a Venetian island, for Venice is not a good city for wines, having, perforce, no cellars. I wish I knew more of them and knew them better. I wish I had gone south to Naples and Sicily to drink the old Falernian (*old* the essential word); and I have never, alas, drunk the Moscadello from Montepulciano, *il vino nobile* of which it is said that *Montepulciano d'ogni vino è il re;* nor 'Est-est; nor the Aleatico of Elba, which, I am told, is dark and sweet and aromatic. Of all these, and there are many, many more, how strange that the only ones well known to us are the vines of the Chianti hills, and these never differentiated, so that people just ask for a Chianti without saying, for example, 'A Broglio.'

That is all I remember of the Wine-fair; except the roaring jollity of the *contadini* and that the queues at the public convenience were nearly a quarter of a mile long. Indeed, that is the last I remember of Siena, for I left it in a haze of wine that night for Rome.

Rome

THE night-train to Rome becomes a day-train early in the morning, and by that hour everybody is physically and mentally in shirt-sleeves because of the gathering heat. An Italian *wagon-lit* in summer is as hot and friendly as an Italian tenement. When in a *wagon-lit* to Rome *magis tibi cor Romanus pandit.* All you have to do is to stand in the corridor and pick up life-stories for the listening. There is no metropolitan chilliness about Romans. Rome is the home-town, the village, the ancient mother: and Italians, like Americans, have a tremendous mother-cult. The only obstacle to heart-to-heart talks that morning was the wearying heat, and my head. Even to look out at the exhausted land whose yellow drouth must be what the desert looks like in high summer, seared the eyeballs. The river-beds were dry as old bones. The barren land was fissured like a volcanic lake that has ebbed bare. The olives were pale as exhausted ladies. The white dust under the hoofs of the white oxen was too weary to do more than puff with husky tongues. When, at last, the Tiber came it was a tawny trickle and the Campagna was a crackle of sere reeds and arid grass. There is no 'Ecco Roma!' on this route, no distant, heart-lifting outline, no rising excitement and gradual satisfaction, and when you are at last spilled out into the rau-cous street you might, if it were not for the great Baths of Dio-cletian mounting before you in the square, be in London or Birmingham. What is more, you hardly care. You do not cry out 'Ave Roma Immortalis!' You cry out loudly for a taxi, a bath and breakfast. Rome, you say, can wait; and so it can. It has, after all, been waiting a long time already; longer far than Paris, Byzantium or Bagdad; none longer except the fabulous cities of the East, Benares or Pekin; and none at all in which one may at a single glance look down so long and varied a perspective of human endeavour.

One afternoon, when I had been about two weeks in Rome, I found myself reading *The Marble Faun* in the farther corner of the Pincio garden—the reading of books about Rome in Rome is a pleasant sentimental occupation—looking from time to time over the edge of the Viale del Muro Torto northward along the valley of the Tiber into a shimmering haze of heat. Hawthorne, I found, had once stood here and looked also at Mount Soratte, some twenty miles away. Afterwards he had written this penetrating remark: 'In the blue distance rose Soratte, and other heights, which have gleamed afar, to our imagination, but look scarcely real to our bodily eyes, because, being dreamed about so much, they have taken the aerial tints which belong only to a dream.' The sentence reminds us that Hawthorne deliberately chose Italy for the setting of his story as affording a sort of poetic or fairy precinct where actualities would not be so terribly insisted upon as they are, and must needs be, in America. His novel is a dread warning against letting Rome overwhelm the imagination. It had already overwhelmed mine. Not until I read that sentence of Hawthorne's did I understand the process. I put my finger into the book to ponder on it.

We come to Rome less to see a real city than to verify an ideal one. We have all been here before, many times since childhood. Mount Soratte? We look at it and we are straightway back at school and our old headmaster is chanting, *Vides ut alta stet nive candidum Soracte* . . . pausing to comment: 'Ah, you see, that is a mountain outside Rome and Horace is telling his friend to look out of the window and to notice that the snow is still shining on the top of it.' When we look at Soratte we verify not only one blue hill, but all the blue hills of youth. The verification is inevitably troubling as well as delightful. One or two have failed to bring it off and have left Rome dissatisfied with reality, as Whistler did with a scornful jest, and as Luther did with an ominous growl.

I forget the name of the villa in the Pincio, now turned restaurant, on whose terrace one can sit and have tea or a *spremuta,* or ices (at Pincio prices) and survey Rome like a king. That afternoon I sat there and, still without finishing Hawthorne's passage, began to consider whether Rome has not a highly deleterious effect on whatever little sense of reality Italy will have left to the traveller by the time he has arrived here; as well as on whatever small conceit he may have had of himself as a cultivated man. 'Overwhelms', is, I think, the word for this city. Of the three great thoughts that have passed through it, the Greek, the Latin and the Christian, the vicissitudes of any one would have alone sufficed to evoke Shelley's pregnant summary:

> *Go thou to Rome,—at once the Paradise,*
> *The grave, the city and the wilderness.*

But when all three civilisations have mingled and persisted, with countless mutations and resurrections, and when every generation has recorded the prolonged battle visibly and magnificently, and when these metamorphoses lie under and over one another, what we look at is less a city than the long and complex story of mankind; one so miserable when we think of all the suffering it has brought to men and women like ourselves, and so chastening when we consider the price of its greatness that it may well subdue us with thoughts of eternity rather than of time, and become under our eyes less a monument than a tomb.

Rome lies spread beneath me in the setting sun. The Angelus is ringing in many tones, deep and piping, from the sea of roofs, domes, cupolas, campaniles and ruins below these still-flowering oleanders, cypresses and evergreen oaks. The city, dusted by its own evening depths and oncoming shadows, is

gradually growing more transparent and less likely. The sil-
houette of Saint Peter's is soft as a bubble to the west, and three
lesser domes decline in perspective to the south-west, one behind the other like images in receding mirrors. As the hour
fades the solid mass appears to sink into the earth. Indeed, it
might, at this hour, seem not so much to have risen from this
mortal earth, century after century, as to have ascended from
another world beneath it, and I begin gradually to think of her
as another Persephone who has come to us again and again
from the arms of Pluto, blossomed with splendour and beauty
and vice, these fading monuments her granaries, these motes in
the sunset a living dust from her flail, until as roofs and domes
become at last a mere veil of light, and Hesper gleams in the
flawless sky above the Campagna, I could imagine that Rome
would at any moment fold into herself and vanish as a star.

Most deleterious, I decide, shaking myself awake and calling
for a cinzano, the price of which at least may restore some sense
of common earth and of a more familiar Rome. I begin to imagine a counterpart to Thomas Mann's *Death in Venice* which
Henry James or Edith Wharton might have written as a modern *Love Among the Ruins*: the story of a man of intelligence,
gifted also with some imaginative sympathy, who comes to
Rome for a brief holiday and is lost in it. He should be a
scholar, familiar with Jerome and Clement, Eusebius, Zosimus
and Tertullian, Justin Martyr and the Apologists and the Acta
Martyrorum. He would have married a beautiful but obtuse
woman; and he might even have a grown son and daughter
who would come to Rome to search for him and have interesting encounters with very modern Romans, such as high Government officials or, it might also be, sceptical detectives. When
his wife has found him she will no longer want him and when
he sees her he will no longer know her, or desire her, or any
woman, for he has been living too long with this ageless Pro-
serpine, sleeping with her in garrets, eating with her in cheap
restaurants, dreaming his life away in a blissful fantasy of the
past that her wonders have hourly fed. It could happen. Paris

has done it. Even London has done it. Rome probably has done it, even to the most hard-headed Americans.

'When we have once known Rome,' it is Hawthorne again who said it, 'and left her where she lies—left her in utter weariness, no doubt, of her crooked, narrow streets, so cold, so alley-like, into which the sun never falls . . .' and he goes on with a long list of her disillusions and discomforts, 'tired', 'worn out', 'sick at heart', 'half lifeless', 'disgusted with the pretence of holiness and the reality of nastiness . . . crushed-down in spirit by the desolation of her ruin and the hopelessness of her future—left her, in short, hating her with all our might . . . when we have left Rome in such a mood as this, we are astonished by the discovery, by and by, that our heart-strings have mysteriously attached themselves to the Eternal City and are drawing us thitherwards again, as if it were more familiar, more intimately our home, than even the spot where we were born.' The disgust apart, which I have not yet experienced, but which many others have, the rest is doubtless true. Yesterday I performed, at my cabby's suggestion, the ritual of throwing a coin into the basin of the great Fontana Trevi, because, if one does so, he said, *'On aura la nostalgie de revenir.'* It already seems unnecessary to have purchased the inevitable.

My Map of Rome

THERE must be some hope of conquering this centaur, half god, half beast. Let us begin by anatomising him, very simply, as if we were looking over his prostrate body for the first time.

Imagine that you are sitting beside me under the sunshade of this terraced restaurant in the Pincio, looking westward over the roofs, toward the sea. The Tiber flows through Rome from north to south, beneath us, that is from our right to our left.

Across the river the Vatican slope rises gently and the Janiculum hill stretches off to its left. The river here sweeps away from us towards Saint Peter's, hits the shoulder of the Janiculum and sweeps back again to our side, directly under the hill of the Capitol. In that sweep lies modern Rome. There the force of the river's current has cut its broadest course and scooped out an island, the Isola Tiberina. Below the island it made a swampy backwater in ancient Rome, between the Capitol and the next hill you see, which is the Palatine. The great public sewer or Cloaca Maxima was cut there, under the Forum, to drain the swamp. It came out in the river below the ruins of the Pontus Aemilius and the Pontus Sublicius. Any day when you go into the Carcer Mamertinus, into the cold underground cellar beneath the small church of San Giuseppe dei Falegnami beside the Forum, they will show you a small, rusty iron door, which, they tell you, leads to this Cloaca Maxima. The dead—many of them the great dead—executed in this cellar, the guide will tell you, were chucked through that door into the sewer. Perhaps. They were, more likely, dragged at a horse's heels and tumbled into the river. So the Tiber flows yellow to the sea whose blue line you may sometimes detect from loftier heights of the city than this Pincio.

Look now again at all those roofs below us, inside that big sweep of river, the armpit of the tawny Tiber. This is the 'plain' as distinct from the hills—the Campus Martius. As well as being the chief modern part of Rome, it is also the oldest living part of Rome, for although its origins are not so ancient as the ruins of the fora—it only spread out gradually from these, a vast suburb with fine gardens and noble houses—it was never, unlike the hills, deserted in the days of Rome's contraction, days when only the Campus remained alive, when the Capitol was a waste called Monte Caprino, the 'Hill of the Goats', and the Palatine a network of ruins and tilled gardens. The result is that this city of the plain is now a typical Italian jungle. It is impressive when softened by twilight, the echoes of the Ave Maria dying away, like Paris from Sacré Coeur; but, when we descend into it, it is all a Marais quarter. It has not a single avenue, boulevard, or impressive street. Its so-called streets are often mere lanes, narrow, dark, grubby and odorous, sunless in summer, damp in winter, always busy and crowded, a terrible jumble of poverty and wealth, of palaces and garrets, of sophistication and simple virtue, of antiquity and modernism, so that all that most visitors, and I imagine most residents, too, know of it will be a few shopping streets, or their favourite churches which they dig out of the surrounding warrens, or a few favourite restaurants islanded in them. It is a babel of noise. Trams and buses rattle through it, packed to suppuration. Once I saw a car so full that a late arrival hung on to the man hanging on before him, and then yet another jumped and hung on to the second, and a third ran after them and still found room for a toe-hold and hung on to the fourth, and so they trundled away at thirty miles an hour like a galloping caterpillar. It is impossible to pretend that this Rome is elegant, though it has elegance; or that it forms a graceful city though it has enclaves of nobility. There is something almost American about it, or is it that there is something Italian about America; it is so raucous, so friendly, so frank, with its jammed pavements, its pedlars and pimps and shoeshine kids, its lamp-post advertisements about virility, piles and varicose veins.

Rome is not a beautiful city. It is affecting and interesting. It contains more impressive buildings, monuments, ruins and memories than any other city in the world, and we are so dazzled by these jewels that we may, in retrospect, forget their setting; forget how quickly one passes from the splendid viewpoint of the Janiculum to the slummery of Trastevere or from the grace and quiet of the Pincio to the dull rattle of the Campus Martius. Rome, from end to end, hardly contains an impressive street. One cannot even use that word about the mile-long Via del Corso, cutting this plain as straight as a ruler along the line of the old Via Flaminia and Via Lata, for all its baroque façades, its magnificent beginning in the Piazza del Popolo and its fine conclusion in the Piazza Venezia. (Let

us not speak of the 'Wedding Cake'.) Old lovers of Rome complain (I have quoted one or two when writing about Florence)
of Mussolini's efforts to create wide and airy thoroughfares in
Rome, yet had Napoleon the Third not torn Paris asunder it
would be, like this Rome of the plain, a maze of insignificant
streets and all its splendid things be, as these are, gems set in
pig-iron: the Pantheon, the column of Marcus Aurelius, the
exquisite baroque Piazza Sant' Ignazio, the temple of Neptune,
its many churches and palaces. Since our first experience of
Rome is inevitably in a taxi or carozza or on foot about this
central quarter it is well to defeat disappointment by expecting
it. We should quickly drive to the Janiculum or to the Pincio
and survey the city as we are now doing.

This pleasant Pincian hill is not one of the more famous
seven hills of Rome, nor is the Vatican nor that Janiculum
across the river. Their centre, the original citadel or *arx,* was
the Capitol, the Romulan cradle, and the Palatine beside it, the
focus of the empire. Around these two in a crescent starting
from this Pincio, lie the other five; the Quirinal, up to our
day the site of the royal palace; then the Viminal and the
Esquiline, either of which you may climb to visit Santa Maria
Maggiore; beyond it, across the hollow of the Colosseum, the
Caelius on the green edge of the city (though, alas, much less
green now than even ten years ago) where you will go to see
Santi Giovanni e Paolo and that strange, disused church of
Santo Stefano Rotondo, specially interesting to an Irishman,
since on its walls there is a plaque commemorating the death of
Donough the son of Brian Boru, King of Ireland. Last comes
the Aventine between the river and the towering ruins of the
Baths of Caracalla, under whose pink bricks you may, in the
summer, hear Italian grand opera by moonlight.

Three other chief quarters remain and then we have at least
the layout of Rome clear in mind: first, directly across the
river, below this Pincio, the Prati di Castello, once level and
pleasant river-meadows, now laid out in modern rectangular
lines of houses and apartments; secondly, in front of us, the

quarter called the Borgo, around the Vatican; and then, down-river, underneath the slopes of the Janiculum, one of the old-est quarters in Rome, called Trastevere, or 'Across the Tiber', for the most part an indescribable swarm of filth and poverty, for centuries a ghetto in fact and still one in appearance. Through it you will probe upward for Santa Maria in Trastevere and San Pietro in Montorio, again an Irish pilgrim-age, since the last chiefs of Gaelic Ireland, the exiled princes O'Neill and O'Donnell, lie there, near the body of the un-happy Beatrice Cenci, underneath a dark slab on the sweaty floor. From its terrace, or from the open space in front of the monument to Garibaldi a little farther on toward Saint Peter's, you get the best view of Rome and the hills to the east. It is a view that reminds me of the wonderful panorama over Flor-ence from the Piazzale Michelangelo, with the Alban Hills in place of the heights of Fiesole and the foothills of the Sabine mountains stretching along the horizons towards Soratte in the north. It is the place from which to watch the sun rise over Rome, to hear its sleeping swarm of life begin to throb and babble again. . . .

Having thus, for the benefit of an imaginary companion, scribbled order on a blank page of *The Marble Faun,* a sweep-ing double-line for the river below me, a bold straight line cutting it, for the Via Lata, now the Corso; indicated the Forum of the Republic under the Capitol, airily sketched in the Fora of the Caesars behind it; and, 'There,' I say, moving my pencil swiftly, 'is the forum of Trajan, and then of Augustus, and Caesar's is here, and that squiggly thing is the great Basilica of Constantine, and next to it comes the Temple of Venus, and everybody knows where the Colosseum is'; I stab in the chief churches that I know, where I think they are, close my book, shove my expert map in my pocket, and paying my (large) bill, stroll away down the terraced road that passes Santa Trinità dei Monti. There I lean over the balustrade above the steps and survey the view again. And I am in five minutes as lost, drowned and happily overwhelmed as ever before.

Ghosts

ROME is too rich. Everywhere
is a grain of history, and every grain a mustard-tree, and every
name a lifetime's study. This Pincian hill, alone, never a memorable part of the oldest Rome, halts one at every step. I look
about me and consider the happy confusion of this one spot
alone. Just behind me, and behind the convent of Santa Trinità,
by the corner of the Aurelian wall, stood the villa and gardens
of Lucullus, patron-saint of gluttons who, like so many Italian
generals of our time, became wealthy in war and obese in
peace. To recall him is to evoke Pompey and Cicero and to
wish I had a Plutarch to hand to be amused by further memories—until I recall suddenly that Messalina also lived here,
plotted murder here, wantoned here with her paramours, shivered here when her husband's final fury threatened her life,
and at last died here by her own hand. At this hour the French
nuns of Sacré Coeur are singing Benediction hymns where
those sanguine ghosts for ever shiver at the fatal dusk, above
those convent steps where I am promised to climb some afternoon next week with messages from their sisters in Dublin
and Chambéry; and I wonder whether they ever sing the piece
that Mendelssohn wrote for them in admiration of their sweet
voices and disgust at their bad music. But why should they
worry about ghosts? There are too many for them to segregate,
or to discriminate. Under the terraced road lies one of Rome's
eighty Christian catacombs; their church was built by Charles
VIII, plundered during the revolution and restored by Louis
XVIII; the obelisk before the church door came from the gardens of Sallust; Nicholas Poussin lived next door; across the
street Claude Lorraine; a few doors farther down, Rossini; from
their back windows they look at the Villa Malta, where
Cagliostro flourished; many a time Keats must have climbed

these 'Spanish steps' in front of this church, with heavy heart and panting breath, before at last he heard this world's last faintest murmur in that room in the corner house on the left which no lover of youth or poetry can visit unmoved. . . . So, I could go on for pages, peeling off stratum after stratum of passionate life without ever once leaving this balustrade, or letting eye or mind wander more than a hundred yards away. It is the same in every corner of Rome. It is all depth and no surface, like a great bay at night, when each dim light is a downward finger.

The full story of the life of any one such corner of Rome would need to be printed in columns, like geological zones, century under century. But even that image is inadequate for a city whose age has so often been exhumed to enrich its youth. There is no image in nature for the growth of Rome, a mingled process of intertexture like weaving, reversal like the tides, of inversion like ploughed soil; a fugue of music; a cycle of death and resurrection. No wonder the favourite motifs of its tombs are the peacock whose flesh was thought incorruptible, deathless Proserpina among the flowers, Christ as a nimbate and radiant charioteer, the Sol Salutis, the tireless sun. We need never hope or wish to hold by any faculty less agile than the imagination a city at once so perishable and so permanent. That Lucullan garden and house is an image of it all. Where are the marbles and mosaics now that Lucullus and Messalina trod? Some are away across Italy in Ravenna, rifled by a Visigoth. Some of the mosaic floors are underneath the floors of a near-by house in the Via Sistina. Everywhere in Rome something has gone somewhere else, become something else. The thought is bewildering, delightful and unsettling. It induces a certain sense of insecurity amounting at times to a sense of irreality as if the ground beneath one's feet were a shifting sand.

The 'Real' Rome

You remember that amusing book of Percy Lubbock's called *Roman Pictures*. It opens with a meeting between Lubbock and an old school-friend named Deering, a lily-frail creature, powdered as to the nose, corpulent as to the rump, dressed in undertaker's black and in a large black Roman hat, who insists on telling Lubbock in Italian (naturally; a six-month baby) that the search for the 'real' Rome is not conducted out of books—one imagines Deering's faintly curving lips and faintly lifted, condescending eyebrows as he says so—and not to be directed towards antiquity. Oh, no! It should be directed at red, raw, and I am not sure if Deering permitted himself so vehement a term as bleeding life; and it should be conducted among the cafés of the Via Nazionale. It is a highly entertaining encounter the veracity of whose characterisation is doubled by its quiet self-satire. We must all have nourished an unadmitted wish to know 'the real Rome'. We must all, if I can coin the word, have unadmitted, in this unadmitted wish, that we feel the constant oppression of a more evident and less real Rome; though, indeed, this feeling of irreality troubles us all over Italy, and reaches its climax in Venice whose beauty must sometimes strike even the most cycloid amongst us as having been arranged for our brief joy —an 'exhalation from the deep' which will vanish as soon as we leave it. Most veracious of all, this Lubbock-Deering encounter carries with it the sly intimation that there is, in fact, no way past the mirages of romantic Rome towards the refreshing oasis of the 'real'. So, at any rate, we gather from the last page; and most of us must echo it with sighs of agreement:

'Where would Deering's line have brought me if I had clung to him throughout? In the end, it would seem, to the palace of the Marchesa, which I had reached on my own account. What

I may have missed on the way to it I shall never know. I could declare to him, none the less, that I had seen many things of singular mark, things that I should never have discovered in the state of romantic innocence which he had been the first to corrupt; and for this I thanked him, though on the matter of Rome's reality I was even now in confusion as deep as ever. On the whole I maintained to Deering that my own romance, when now and then I had caught a glimpse of it between the heads of the crowd, had to my eye a more substantial look than most of the realities that had been offered to me in place of it. What had he to say to that? Well, then, he had to say to it regretfully but distinctly, that I was incurable; and one of the Botticelli hands was laid upon my arm in a gesture that resigned me, with tenderness, with compassion, with finality, to the sad ravages of my illusion. "Go back to your books," he sighed; "I have done my best—good-bye!" '

There is no bridge. Not now, at any rate, when the old traditional social life has broken down. There are only bizarre and irreconcilable juxtapositions, divided by the narrowest but deepest chasms. Or if there is a bridge it is a sort of pocket-pontoon we bring with us, as the old tenth-century Irish verse explains:

> *To go to Rome may little profit.*
> *The King you seek you will not find,*
> *Unless you bring him with you.*

It was, doubtless, very foolish of me not to realise at once that I possessed this pocket-pontoon. I was otherwise engaged; gripped by the vast spectacle before me, with all its historical complexities, and all its specious allurements to 'bottle' Rome, some indefinable but apparently essential and intelligible Rome, by going back and back, always farther and still farther back into its winding perspectives flitted with shades that were to elude every effort to grasp them; much as if a man—and there have been many such—hoped to solve the mystery of

Christianity by tracing it from its bayou-mouths back to its
primitive source; or as if a man, as so many of my countrymen
constantly do, hoped by digging deeper and deeper into the
primitive origins and habits of his people to become thereby
more deeply rooted in his nationality. However, I also did, at
least, in that bewildering and ultimately fruitless journey, meet
many 'things of singular mark' that I might not otherwise have
met, and if the reader cares to follow me, and perhaps later
spare himself the same delving, this—in a very truncated version—is the way that I went. . . . .

Death and Resurrection

THE Rome that lies before our
eyes is a tangle and an amalgam because for a thousand years
after Rome's hey-day the Romans quarried into their own past,
carting away thousands and thousands of tons of blocks, pillars,
entablatures, bronze and marble. Constantine was able to protect the ancient temples, but as the 'new' religion spread and
the barbarians invaded the Empire the old buildings naturally
suffered from Christian and pagan alike. Even Nature shook
them down, with an earthquake, and man defiled them. So
Saint Jerome, in the fifth century, found them, with the Capitol
'a mass of filth' and the temples 'covered with dust and cob-
webs'. It is true that the Christian observation was by then
establishing Rome as the centre of a new, religious Empire, and
that the great Saint Leo not only established the Bishop of
Rome as universal 'Pope', in our sense, but, as monarch, turned
back Attila's Huns and saved the ancient Basilica from the
Vandals. It is true that in spite of numerous sackings of Rome
this work of raising a new empire on an old one went on to the
time of Charlemagne, by whose day we may accept the fact of
the Papacy's temporal power. But it was always, for Rome it-

self, a story of one step forward and one step back. The Pantheon may serve as an illustration. One pope consecrated it as a Christian church and buried wagon-loads of martyrs' bones from the catacombs in it to justify its new name of Sancta Maria ad Martyres. Another carried off its bronze-gilt roof-tiles to Constantinople. A third covered the roof with lead. Even so did Charlemagne despoil Rome, in all friendliness, to adorn his Cathedral at Aix-la-Chapelle, and everybody else has ever since likewise despoiled Rome to preserve it or to adorn it. Temples were changed into churches with less and less compunction; or were even built into them; as when Christ was adored on the ruins of Venus in Santa Francesca Romana, or when San Lorenzo in Miranda was built inside the temple of Faustina, the allegedly profligate wife of Marcus Aurelius. In the ruins of the fora we can realise the extent of the destruction, from every cause. As we look at its pathetic stumps and fragments, mere shards of the original potters of Rome, we can only say in consolation for the loss what I have said about the fluid diuturnity of Florence, and of all creative cities, with the addition that here time and change go a thousand years farther back.

The buildings that take our minds back to the first Christian period are, to me, probably because of their Byzantine influences, the most interesting and beautiful of the all monuments of Rome—San Clemente, and Saint Paul Outside the Walls, and the little Greek church of Santa Maria in Cosmedin (so-called from the district in Constantinople from which this Greek colony had fled), with its triple apse of the Greek rite, its delicate campanile and its pavements of *opus Alexandrinum,* which are held by many to be the most beautiful in Rome. And yet some of these early churches are little known and little visited; such as San Stefano Rotondo on the Coelian Hill or Santa Constanza a mile or two outside the Porta Pia. These early churches all date from, or soon after, the recognition of Christianity in the fourth century, though several were rebuilt later, some to their loss, some magnificently. Saint Paul Outside the Walls, which can be considered the finest basilican church in existence, was, though founded by Constantine, and though the old mosaics still remain, rebuilt splendidly in 1870. San Stefano Rotondo, interesting for its circular plan, which is possibly of Byzantine origin—and which never caught on in Rome; they preferred and clung to the basilica—though dedicated in the fifth century, was altered in the fifteenth. It once had three circular aisles, but the outer fell, or was levelled, the inner circle of pillars filled in and an arcade of ponderous size run across the middle, thereby making nonsense of the design. If anybody wants to see Rome in consecutive order he should pass from the ruins of the forum under the Arch of Constantine, up the hill to his left into San Giovanni e Paolo, to see its campanile and crypts; stroll on still upwards to San Stefano Rotondo (ring the bell of the courtyard door beside it); go on to San Clemente and then see the perfection of the basilican style in Santa Maria Maggiore.

After that there is an enormous gap in the architecture of Rome; the Middle Ages. All that we see of them are fragments, an abundance of mosaic and a few twelfth or thirteenth-century campaniles. There is a gap because the mediaeval wars of the nobles, the clergy and the people strangled Rome. When Chartres and Beauvais were climbing with the larks these struggles left the people without money; the nobles without taste; and the clergy, who alone had both taste and money, as well as vast ambitions, were left without originality. The result is that there is not a single spire in Rome and only one Gothic church, Santa Maria sopra Minerva—that characteristic Roman jumble, built on the site of a temple to Minerva; the church of Saint Dominic; the burial-place of Torquemada; the reliquary of Catherine of Siena; the penance-place of Cagliostro; the trial-place of Galileo (or the convent attached to it, now a Government office); the tomb of at least four popes and five cardinals, including one of the English Norfolks. And even this one Gothic church of Rome was built, decorated and endowed not by Romans, but by Florentines. It is not a very beautiful church. It is none the less an extraordinary relief to the eye to look again at the pointed arches, vaulted ceilings, dim clerestory, and broad aisles of the north. But Santa Maria came late, when the great thirteenth century was dying, and after it the Papacy was at Avignon. When they returned the Middle Ages were over and the Renaissance was ready to breathe new life into a now utterly wretched city, reduced by every kind of misery, disease and bloodshed to a mere country town of twenty or thirty thousand souls.

It was then that the main work of destruction and re-creation began. The Colosseum did not merely fall. Its travertine was also gnawed away over three centuries to build churches and palaces; an image that gives vivid meaning to the word Renaissance. Paul II carted away tons of it to build the Palazzo di Venezia. Cardinal Riario nibbled at it for the Palazzo della Cancelleria. Paul III used more of it for the Palazzo Farnese. The piers of the Basilica Julia in the Forum and a great deal of its travertine went across the river to build Bramante's Palazzo Giraud in the Borgo. The *Jonah* of Raphael in Santa Maria del Popolo was sculptured from marble plundered from the temple of Castor and Pollux. Of the eight great Corinthian pillars of white marble that were once part of the Basilica of Constantine we find the only one that remains set up in the Piazza before Santa Maria Maggiore. (That was in the seventeenth century; it was just a thousand years before that the Basilica's gilded bronze tiles had been lifted for the original Saint Peter's.) It was the Barberini pope who took the brass tubes of the Pantheon roof to make cannons for Castel Sant' Angelo and to adorn the high altar of our Saint Peter's, giving occasion for the famous quip that what the barbarians did not do the Barberini did; for though the barbarians did enough they spared the Pantheon so that it is now the most perfectly preserved ancient building in Rome. The process went on into the eighteenth century, when eight lovely grey marble columns were taken from the Villa of Hadrian into the central sacristy of Saint Peter's.

It is chiefly these three centuries from the fifteenth to the seventeenth that affect us to-day as we look over the panorama from the Janiculum or the Pincio; three hundred years of furious and glorious building that impressed on Rome its classic grace, Renaissance stateliness and Baroque magnificence—not unmixed with ostentatious vulgarity and sham grandeur.

Santa Maria del Popolo

ONE can see all three by going into almost any church, even some of the oldest and finest, like Santa Maria Maggiore itself. Thus, if perhaps some day the traveller, loafing in the Pincio, should fall into a pious mood he might naturally descend into the Piazza below him to the Church of Santa Maria del Popolo, hard by the spot where Nero was buried in a haunted grove of poplars—the poplars cut and the ghosts gone a thousand years ago. I doubt if he will pray or meditate for long. The church contains magnificent things: Pinturicchio's lovely 'Nativity', a window by Claude— Rome is generally poor in stained glass—sculpture by Raphael and Sansovino, two exquisite fifteenth-century tombs, and much more besides. But what horrors it contains, largely thanks to Bernini, though we must never forget that Bernini also did splendid things for Rome, such as the colonnades of Saint Peter's. What inspiration can anybody get from the cluttered and gaudy mess of the high altar, and the two altars right and left of it, whose columned foppery suggests nothing at all but a sculptor's delight in his own virtuosity? From the abstractions and banalities of the Crispi monument? Or that weird truant from Madame Tussaud's beside the door, a yellow skeleton looking out through the bars of his vault? Or the haberdashery monument outside the Chigi chapel, composed of yards and yards of trailing red marble, like velvet in a draper's window, with a prowling lion below, looking like Oscar Wilde in a temper, and a snarling eagle above, and two naked cupids hanging the portrait of a long-nosed female in between, and a medley of ropes and tassels and branches and ivied lumps of rock thrown in for good measure? As we look about us at all this gilded, coloured and carven marble, the mosaics and the bronze, the jasper and the alabaster—and these are modest chapels compared with some others, such as that of Paul V in Santa Maria Maggiore, which blinds us with lapis lazuli, tortoiseshell agate, Sicilian marble, bronze gilt and oriental jasper—it may occur to us why Ruskin haunted Florence, Padua, Verona and Venice but hardly paused in Rome: or why William Morris found it all too artificial and superstitious. We understand why this southern exuberance is so often (and so reasonably) antipathetic to the northern mind; we may even feel a sudden passing sympathy for the monk who, in 1510, lodged in the Augustinian convent next-door to Santa Maria, of whom one biographer[1] wrote this passage, not it is true without some exaggerations and inaccuracies:

'He had often in his childhood slept with his head on a cold stone. Here he finds himself walking in a forest of marble, among pillars of alabaster, past gigantic obelisks of granite, dancing fountains, cool villas embellished with gardens, cascades and grottos. If he wishes to pray he will go into a church where diamonds glitter on the altar, gold on the ceilings and mosaics in the chapels, he who, at home, would have knelt in a simple country church whose only ornament might be a few roses laid on the altar on Sunday by some pious hand. He is invited to rest not on a simple wooden bench beside the path but on an antique throne of alabaster recently excavated. If he looks about for some holy image he will see, instead, pagan fantasies of gods returned from Olympus, Apollo, Venus, Mars or Jupiter, caressed and fondled by a thousand chisels. Of all these marvels Luther un-

[1] Audin: *Histoire de Luther.*

derstands nothing. He sees nothing. No ray from the brows of Raphael or Michelangelo dazzles him. He remains cold and silent before all those treasures in all those churches. His ear is closed to the words of Dante murmuring on the lips of the people about him. He had entered Rome as a pilgrim. He would leave it like Coriolanus and say with Bembo, "Farewell, Rome! Any man who wants to live a holy life must fly this city. Farewell, Rome, where a man may be anything he chooses except virtuous." '

One's sympathy will scarcely last the reading of the passage. To make it last longer Luther should have been less dour, more innocent, or less ignorant of the vast panorama of history of which he was seeing but one brief phase, though admittedly he came at an evil time; for the Borgia was only a few years dead and Sixtus, his lifelong enemy, was ruling Italy like a tyrant. But did he really *see* those lovely things in Santa Maria del Popolo, one corner alone of which would make another city a place of pilgrimage? And even if it were all as vulgar and ostentatious, as some of it is, is it wiser to think of this blaze of golden trumpets, this organ-throb of triumph, this fume and drug of incense, as merely wicked and vulgar, as Luther did of all Rome, or to think of it all as part of man's muddled effort to honour Saint Mary of the People? This is not to renounce one's intelligence. One can discriminate in Rome; one must sometimes denounce her; but even if we cannot forgive her a hundred crimes neither can we deny her a thousand glories that cry out against desertion. Doubtless I speak of a blended Rome; the empire, old as Pius Aeneas, the force young as Constantine, Tiberius, or Augustus and those early zealots whom Rome burned and crucified by the thousand, but who ended by absorbing Rome: a microcosm of Western civilisation.

A Mesmeric City

I BEGAN all this with a sentence from a passage by Hawthorne about the hills around Soratte and their tints of dream. The passage concludes thus: 'These nevertheless are the solid framework of hills that shut in Rome and its surrounding *Campagna;* no land of dreams, but the broadest page of history, crowded so full with memorable events that one obliterates another as if Time had crossed and recrossed his own records till they grew illegible.' That sentence also contains a truth, but less impressively. If he must have personifications, and one can hardly avoid them, it would have been better to say that History, not Time, has crossed and recrossed his records; a homely image from the days when people saved postage by writing perpendicularly on a page already covered horizontally. I suppose he did not wish to repeat the word history in the same sentence. The main trouble is that the sentence has a dying fall; and whenever anybody writes of Rome in a monotone, like Walter Pater talking in his sleep, we do well to be on guard. . . . 'And thus it was, and thus, we may think, as dusk falls slowly over the fading scene, that, perhaps, in some such twilit hour, Rienzi communed, alone, among the Caesars, or Paul of Tarsus passed pensively beneath the pyramid of Caius Cestius, or Lorenzo, whom we now call sanctus was at last lightly laid to rest by gentle Hippolytus, a long, long procession, almost a dream, fading into the shadows under the pitiful smile of the Divine.'

It is when we weary of this mesmerism of Rome[1] and the bewilderment of its perspectives, when we begin to feel these waves close over us, that we instinctively look for some small

[1] Is this the weariness that Stendhal felt when he spoke of Rome's *dégoût de l'admiration?*

corner or object to hold on to, firmly. It may be only a restaurant where it is pleasant to be recognised by a waiter. It may
be a corner of a garden that is 'our' corner. We might even—I
did—form a preference for one cabby. For several days in se-
quence I used to sit in the Borghese gardens, under the ilexes,
on a broken column that was too casual and unimportant ever
to invite identification, yet a veritable fragment of Rome on
which to knock out my pipe. But the mesmerism, the lure of the
dim perspectives, never ceases for long. I recall how, one day,
not yet fully chastened to a recognition of the fathomlessness of
Rome, I began to wonder, while sitting in the Forum of the
Republic, whether it might be possible to choose some one spot
here, of an unequivocal history, on which a man could
metaphorically knock out his pipe: a peg on which to hang a
scrap of familiarity.

Oh! Nothing questionable or large. Nothing like the Curia
or the vestal virgins' Convent. A corner of a street would do so
that I might see from it, with some sharpness of outline, First
Citizen—as one might say Leopold Bloom—strolling up Holy
Street (the *Sacra Via*) looking at the jewellers' booths (the
tabernae argentariae) for a cheap gew-gaw for his moll; then,
remembering that his wife had told him to buy a few ounces of
incense, turning to the right up the Tuscus, but suddenly
doubling from a creditor behind the Temple of Castor and
pausing there to drink of the purest spring in the city, the
Aesculapian pool. ('The kidneys are giving me the devil to-
day!') From there, I thought, he might either wander up New
Street (*La Nuova Via*) or pick up the slope of Holy Street
again; and so turn right—as one might say beside The Arch
near Stephen's Green—at the Arch of Titus. . . . I pulled myself up. When was that arch built? How many anachronisms
had I cogitated in three minutes of an imaginary perambulation? What corner's existence coincided incontestably in time
with any other six corners? I remembered that I had read
somewhere that Holy Street had changed its course frequently

when new buildings deflected it. I dropped the fancy like a flea.

Yet Leopoldus Romanus must surely have passed at least some one indubious object? What of the roster in front of Caesar's temple, where Mark Antony made the speech the day they knifed poor Julius? ('A darlin' man,' asserted Mr. Bloom solemnly.) Eagerly I tried to find out all I could about the site and the event. Guides and books assured me that this was, indeed, the very spot where Antony gave the funeral oration. (Guides will assure you of anything.) Then somebody said: 'Didn't Caesar move the *rostra* at one time?' So he did, facing them down the whole length of the forum towards the west and the Capitol Hill. And I began to have more tremors on finding that two other rosters are indicated at that opposite end of the square. At this stage the invaluable Augustus J. C. Hare informed me that 'the changes of position, as well as actual modification, of the rostra at various periods forms a chapter, or volume rather, in itself.'

Besides, it is easy enough to make these imaginary reconstructions in one's hotel, poring over plans of ancient Rome. When we stand on the white rubbled floor of the city, dug out of forty feet of rubbish, looking at its few poor graceful columns, and its pale stumps of pillars like cut trees, and its patches of ancient street-paving, it is not so easy to unroll the years. Many people in Europe must have had this bewildered sensation in recent years when walking among the ruins of the city of London, or in the utter desolation of Stalingrad or Hamburg. 'Here was so-and-so' is a numbing thing to say even when 'so-and-so' had once been of as much consequence as the Forum Romanum. And here nothing softens the impact. No ivy or flowers or trees now grow wildly among the ruins as they once did. The sun beats pitilessly on the fragments of a conglomerate tomb, so that it is well to come here for the first time at night, when the stars are kind and the shadows fight its battles over again. It was on that day, as I passed out of the ruins, with the Arch of Severus on my right, that my final and almost fatal battle with Rome began. I came on a little dark doorway beneath the church of San Giuseppe dei Falegnami. I peered in. I went in.

The Carcer Mamertinus

IT is the dungeon called the Carcer Mamertinus, one of the oldest structures in the city. This city prison contains two cells, one over the other; cold after the great heat, black after the incandescent sun, a frightening maw. The cell below was once reached only by a hole in the floor. Now there are stone stairs. This lower cell must have been as dark as a coalhole, as cold as an ice-box, as wet as a swamp. It is lit now by a single naked electric bulb. It is about six and a half feet high. The roof was originally built in the most ancient style, by projecting each stone a little farther out so that the walls finally met in a cone.

Down into this hole they lowered Jugurtha the Numidian. He was what we would now call a nationalist. He fought Rome for six years, and was betrayed to Sulla and brought from his hot African hills in chains to this ice-box to die. Another nationalist, the Celt Vercingetorix, stumbled after Caesar's triumphal carriage to this spot, and was bundled out of the sunlight down into this hole to die, slowly, week by week, hour by hour, of hunger. Cicero came out of this oubliette to announce the death of Catiline's fellow conspirators with the word, 'Vixerunt!' Sejanus died here. I grew sick of this prison's tales of horror. Some were decapitated, some were strangled, some starved.

But none of all these excited me so much as a low pillar in one corner. 'There,' said the old curator, 'Saint Peter was chained.' In the floor he pointed to a small circular opening, a spring which Peter is said to have caused to gush out at the request of his sceptical jailors. Both are said to have been executed with him, presumably as convert Christians. There is a stone here, now behind bars, where the saint's head and face were said to have been brutally battered against the wall. On this black, worn stone, fingered smooth by countless pilgrims, we now see the profile of a man's bearded face as clearly as if it were sculptured there—as it probably was. I came out of that obdurate subterranean dungeon, blinded by the sun shimmering over the ruins of the forum, deeply stirred by the contrast and image of the triumph of failure. For days I could not forget it. This, I decided, would be my one sacred spot, free of all complications and speculations. I would remember it with feeling and intimacy; a mere hole in the ground; of no least aesthetic interest; impressive beyond words by its associations; a focus from which many thoughts could radiate to the verge of the empire, the old as well as the new. For though I could never hope to trace Saint Peter's journey up from Roman Capernaum, pausing to talk to the Cappadocians, and to those distant Celts, the Galatians, persisting on through Bithynia and across the Bosphorus—or did he come by sea to Rome?—this, at any rate, was the end of the journey, or almost the end; for all that remained for him to do after he left the prison would be to walk across the Tiber to the slope of the Vatican and face the howling mobs in the circus of Nero, which is now buried under Saint Peter's. There beneath the high altar we may look down at the sarcophagus of the second greatest figure in the history of Christendom.

That City Prison bade me dream, if I wanted to, about Rome; it bade me be awed, respectful, impressed; but not to attempt to come too close to its dead. The silence of the past is never silent in Rome, but its whispers are subaudible, its annals are the grapevine and they are as deceptive as the Sybil. The traditions about Saint Peter, I found, are many; all too many. One is shown the chair he sat on; his altar; his chains. But *are* they his? I have already confessed, abjectly, my lust for asking questions. This was of all the questions I have ever asked the most lunatic. Instead of asking it I ought then and there to have turned my back on the City Prison. Somebody should have been good and kind enough to lead me by the hand down one of Mr. Lubbock's less equivocal romantic vistas, or even into one of Deering's chromium cafés. Pigheadedly I persisted. The upshot of it all is that I now know this: that there is not an iota of historical certainty (I do not speak of probability) not merely as to where Saint Peter died, or where Saint Peter is buried, but as to whether Saint Peter ever even set foot in the city of Rome, or indeed what happened to him at all after the year A.D. 50. I might as well have tried to explore the deepest gallery of the catacombs at midnight as to have gone back thus to the primitive source of light.

Not that I entirely regret it. It is an interesting experience to explore the catacombs at midnight.

Where is Saint Peter?

THE question, 'Where is Saint Peter?' is one of the most complex and fascinating of the many unsolved problems of history. For it is heartening, or if, in a jealous regard for historical fact, you choose to regard it so, dismaying, that although there is practically no information available about this man he has become the foremost and most famous human figure in the story of Christianity. His fame rests almost wholly on tradition; the contemporary documents about him are of the fewest and they are most ambiguous, and the archaeological evidences are just as few and just as equivocal. His story, fact or fiction, or both intermingled, has been passed on by word of mouth. And yet, although we have fourteen letters of Saint Paul's and only two from Saint Peter: and although Paul laboured mostly in the West among the Gentiles and Peter in the East among the Jews; and although we know a good deal about the movements of Paul and little about

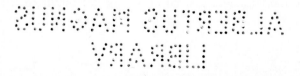

Peter, it is Peter whose name is the more glorified and whose story is the more fully adorned by circumstance.

I will give one illustration of the sort of equivocal knowledge we have about Peter, not in the desire to persuade anybody, but simply to describe the nature of the problem. The only words in the New Testament which would testify to Saint Peter's presence in Rome occur in the first of his two letters, addressed generally to Christians scattered throughout Asia Minor. These letters were never dated or headed by an address, but towards the end of the letter he says: 'She, in Babylon, jointly-elect, saluteth you.' ('She' is generally taken to refer to the Church.) On the face of it the letter thus seems to come from Babylon on the Euphrates. Those who believe that Saint Peter worked in Rome maintain that 'Babylon' is here a metaphor for 'Rome'.

The scholarly historian who insists on unequivocal proof for every historical event is naturally sceptical. He will not even be impressed by the fact that all the early writers accepted that Peter meant Rome when he wrote Babylon. He will say with a shrug: '*Early* is a relative term. It may impress a layman. But when even the layman realises that *early* means about two hundred years after the event he, too, must be sceptical. Otherwise it is as if he were to rely on the authority of a document of our own day for an event that happened during the French Revolution, such as some important detail about the death of Louis XVI. And who would be so credulous as to trust so late a document?' Yet who might not well be justified in relying on so early a document? Consider. Suppose we were to ask the writer of it for his authority, and supposing he answered, 'It is an old tradition in our family', what could that mean? It could only mean something like this: that the writer, James, heard it as a boy from his grandfather, Thomas, who heard it as a boy from his grandfather William, who had actually seen the thing happen. I will put it in the form of a simple genealogy:

WILLIAM (1768–1848), who saw Louis XVI die, in 1793,
    | begot
  JOHN   (1800–1870), who begot
    |
THOMAS (1838–1918), who heard the story from William,
    | and begot
  PHILIP   (1872–1932), who begot
    |
  JAMES   (1908–   ), who heard the story from Thomas
                 and wrote it down in 1948.

Call James by the name of Eusebius or Hegesippus, and Louis XVI by the name of Saint Peter; throw the whole process back seventeen hundred years; and your sceptical historian realises that he has to treat those 'late' or 'early' writers, also, with respect. People who live in great cities do not, I think, sufficiently realise how longlived and how accurate verbal tradition can be in simpler communities. We know, from experience, in Ireland, for example, that the traditional memory can go back with accuracy to the events of the Rebellion of 1798.[1] For my part I would not refuse belief to any otherwise plausible tradition whose origin can be traced to within two hundred years of the event it commemorates.

As I pored over the question during those hot Roman afternoons, when I ought to have been drinking Frascati or loafing in the Campagna, I found that I had to choose between the traditionalists and the documentarians. I had to choose between the stout faith of a man like Cardinal Manning who once said that 'the appeal to antiquity (i.e. to history) is both a treason and a heresy', and a scholar like Merrill,[2] sympathetic, not

---

[1] See, for an illustration, *The Last Invasion of Ireland,* by Richard Hayes (Dublin, 1937); it is based, largely, on local traditions, checked and supported by documents. The supplementary documents of the 'early' Christian writers are, it is true, lost, so that this check is not available in their case. This does not mean that earlier documents did not exist.

[2] *Essays in Early Church History,* Edward T. Merrill (London, 1934). Merrill was Professor of Latin at Chicago, an Anglican, and I believe utterly objective. Compare *Petrus und Paulus in Rom,* by Hans Lietzmann (Berlin, 1927); an historian, a non-Catholic, objective, giving full weight to the tradition.

GENOA: PALAZZO DURAZZO. '*Superb staircases of palaces on the Garibaldi . . .*'

EX VOTO PAINTINGS

Above: *Shipwrecked sailors saved by the Virgin.*

Below: *A woman rolled-over but miraculously unhurt.*

CAMOGLI

'Gaudy, glittering, golden . . .'

FLORENCE: THE CAMPANILE. '*Coloured like a morning-cloud and chased like a sea-shell . .*'

THE CATHEDRAL,
SIENA

'The wedding of
Gothic and
Byzantine . . .'

ROME: SANTA MARIA IN COSMEDIN, '*A delicate campanile . . .*'

VENICE:
EARLY MORNING
'Let's take the
penny ferry across
Canalazzo . . .'

TORCELLO. *'A vast and dimly-glittering mosaic of the Last Judgment . . .'*

questioning any tenet of the Catholic Faith—not indeed in the least concerned with it, for it does not arise—yet resolutely sceptical as a historian discussing historical documents. To Merrill the whole tradition of Saint Peter's movements in Rome is not even a tradition: it is an example of how myths develop. Step by step he traces each mile of the tradition, or the myth, weighing each document's reliability, the New Testament—and even the most loyal Catholics, such as Monsignor Barnes,[1] do not suggest that there is any evidence there for Peter's burial in Rome—Ignatius, Clement, Dionysius, Hegesippus, Irenaeus, Tertullian, Origen and Jerome, and on finding that they are all 'too late' or that any of them borrows from a predecessor, withholds belief. For such scholars the question 'Where is Saint Peter?' is thus not only a fascinating unsolved problem, but until a tomb is found, of undeniable date, bearing an undeniable *Hic Jacet,* a problem that can never be solved. Such scholars do not solve many problems.

The Evidence

STILL I persisted; in my own microscopic way following the path of many others for whom Rome has spread these alluring nets of speculation. Suppose, I said to myself, suppose we leave out of the discussion altogether whether Peter came to Rome while he lived, and concentrate on the problem of where he is buried. That problem may be briefly defined in this way. The first note of certainty is not struck until the fourth century. Constantine the Great certainly believed that he then reinterred Saint Peter's body in old Saint Peter's. What is, or was, the guarantee that he was not mistaken as to the body he interred? In other words, is there a sound and verifiable deposit of historical information account-

[1] See *St. Peter in Rome,* by Arthur Stapylton Barnes (London, 1900).

ing for the bestowal of the saint's body, from its first burial,
wherever that may have been, in the first century, to Constantine's reinterment four hundred years later? Once again, as
far as documentation goes, there is not.

How near, then, can we get by means of documents to the
death of Peter? We can get quite near; within about one hundred and fifty years. The earliest statement which may refer
to a tomb of Saint Peter in Rome is one made by Gaius, a Roman Presbyter, about the years A.D. 200–210. (This is recorded by Eusebius,[1] who died about A.D. 350, and whose history of the early Church contains many such statements by
writers whose works are no longer extant.) Gaius made his
assertion in answer to a heretic named Proclus, who claimed
that the graves of Philip and his prophesying daughters were
to be seen in the Holy City of Hierapolis in Asia Minor, where
Saint Paul had founded a Christian church. Proclus, in saying
this, was attempting to argue that his doctrines were in continuity with the times and persons of the apostles. (A non-
sequitur.) 'Come to Rome,' Gaius retorted, "and I will show you
the τρόπαια of the Apostles, Peter's on the Vatican Hill and
Paul's on the Ostian Way.' But what did Gaius mean by the
τρόπαια? Does it mean a tomb? It might mean a memorial. Gibbon, for example, takes it to mean a trophy, writing:
'One hundred and fifty years after the glorious deaths of St.
Peter and St. Paul, the Vatican and the Ostian Road were distinguished by the tombs, or rather by the trophies, of those
spiritual heroes.' And, indeed, the argument of Gaius could
have been advanced on the existence of mere trophies or memorials, though not so impressively as on the existence of tombs.
Is the probability that he meant tombs?

Observe the shift that has now imperceptibly taken place in
our researches. We have gone over from documents to things,
from history to archaeology, out of the study to the sunning
lizards on the crumbling walls of the Appian Way. For it is
there, along the silent pavements of the old Appian road out

[1] Vide *Historia Ecclesiastica*, II, 25.

of Rome, that the enquiring pilgrim comes on the crux of the problem. He will pause at or pass the little church which marks the place where Peter, flying from persecution, is said to have met Christ, entering Rome for another martyrdom, with the famous question, 'Domine Quo Vadis?' He will pass on to the catacombs of Saint Calixtus and the Church of Saint Sebastian, the Roman centurion who was martyred by having arrows shot into him; a figure familiar to us all from many paintings. He is the hero of Wiseman's novel *Fabiola*. Here, to the rear of the main altar, he will see, underground, the curious *bisoma*—a grave containing two bodies was a *bisomum;* three a *trisomum*—with the inscription indicating in the third or fourth century that it was 'inhabited' by the Apostles Peter and Paul. This is the inscription of Pope Damasus, well known to archaeologists and students of early Church history, beginning:

> *Hic habitasse prius sanctos cognoscere debes,*
> *Nomina quisque Petri pariter Paulique requiris. . . .*

> *'Here you should know that saints have dwelt,*
> *Their names, if you ask, were Peter and Paul. . . .'*

Was Saint Peter, then, interred here? And why? And when? Or does it mean that when in Rome he lived in a villa nearby? One tradition says that some Orientals tried to steal the two bodies from the Vatican and the Ostian Way back to their birth-place, and were followed and caught by pious Romans, who interred the bodies here in the crypt of Lucina and later took them back to their original tombs.[1] Another tradition holds that under Heliogabalus they were again removed for safety to these catacombs. Both traditions believe that the bodies were finally restored to their burial-places on the Vatican and the Ostian Way. It is inconceivable that Pope Damasus invented the whole thing.

[1] The latest scholarly book on the subject maintains this thesis. See *Le tombe Apostoliche nell' eta paleocristina,* by Giulio Belvederi. Published by the Pontifico Instituto di Archeologia Christiana, 1948.

The Excavations

At this point I found myself
dining one night with a very pleasant, if rather mysterious,
Italian army officer to whom I bore an introduction from an
American friend. I had made contact with him through the
First Secretary in the Foreign Office, who had said: 'We will try
to find *il capitano* for you, but you see—he comes and goes. If
we do find him he will, no doubt, telephone you at your hotel.'
And any time I wished to meet him afterwards it was always
like that. The words Secret Service naturally leaped to my
mind, for it is one of the commonest characteristics of Secret
Service people that they like to conceal the profession with bla-
tant publicity. We met, and over *scampi* and Frascati we talked
contentedly of a great many things that would have warmed
the cockles of the heart of Mr. Lubbock's Deering; 'real' things,
such as current Roman politics, the present careers of certain
former Italian generals, the poetry, life and fate of Ezra Pound,
the romantic story of that picturesque Scarlet Pimpernel, Monsignor O'Flaherty of the Irish College, who planned the escape
of so many wanted men under the German Occupation; always
under bonds of secrecy that I still respect, although I cannot
help thinking now, if I may judge by the one which concerns
Saint Peter, that they were all so many *secrets de polichinelle*.
I do not recall how Peter cropped up—I probably could not
keep him out of the conversation—but *il capitano* at once put
his finger to his nose, dropped his voice, leaned over the table
and revealed to me that the most secret excavations had been
going on all during the German Occupation under the floor of
Saint Peter's, by direct order of the Holy Pontiff. The archaeologists were, he assured me, at that moment within a few feet of
finding the veritable grave of the Apostle. And when it was
found Protestantism would not survive for a generation! But,

of course, it was still an official secret; although he understood that certain very private publications were already passing among a few of the top-ranking Roman archaeologists. . . .

I do not know how the rest of the night passed. Apart from my serious interest in the problem of Saint Peter's history the Sunday-newspaper journalist who is buried in every highbrow writer trembled in me like a setter who sniffs game. 'Secrecy be damned!' I said to myself as I walked home to my hotel in the Via Veneto. There must be some tactful way of getting a glimpse at those 'very private publications'. For days I nosed about, wishing I had an introduction to a Roman Cardinal; or even a Monsignor; and at last I came upon a sympathetic young English archaeologist who promised to help me. Within six hours he rang me up. He was laughing as he spoke my name.

'You can help me?' I cried.

'No trouble at all,' he laughed. 'You will find excellent articles on these diggings, with pictures, in *The Illustrated London News* of March 9th and September 7th, 1946. Enrico Josi has described them fully, with more photographs, in the London *Times* of February 27th, 1946. You might also consult *The American Journal of Archaeology,* volumes fifty and fifty-one. And you might look up the *Communications to the Pontifical Roman Academy of Archaeology,* by Fathers Ferrua and Kirschbaum, in 1947. And I think you should have a glance at. . . .'

When you enter Saint Peter's and stand by the Confessio under the glittering baldachino and look down the stairs at the tomb which may, after all, be the tomb of Saint Peter, you are looking down towards the crypts. If you go down into those plain, white-painted crypts where the popes are buried, you find that some of their ceilings are rather low and that some have recently been made more lofty by the lowering of the floors. That was how the most recent diggings under Saint Peter's began during the Occupation; partly to lower the floors and partly to enlarge the area for the tombs of later popes. As the archaeologists dug they discovered a complete Roman cemetery with pagan and early (second to third century) Christian graves, and realised that the entire area occupied by the church and the slope beneath it had been a burial-ground. This discovery has modified previous assumptions as to the site of the Circus where the Apostle was believed to have been martyred, for no sign of the Circus was found, although one of the new tombs, that of a man named C. Popilius Heracla, carries an inscription over the entrance recording the dead man's wish to be buried 'in the Vatican, near the Circus'.

Il capitano was wrong also about what the diggings have revealed. The dating of the Christian tombs proves only that Christians were buried in times of persecution on the Vatican Hill, within a stone's throw of the Circus of Nero and Caligula; and that nothing would be more natural than that Peter, if executed in the Circus, would be buried where Constantine believed he did in fact reinter his body. So far they prove no more. The diggings have for the moment ceased, having teased the mind with the thought that, perhaps only a few more feet away, the final proof awaits the ring of the spade. For the denials of the anti-traditionalists exist in a void and have the impressiveness only of a void. They do not assert; all they can say is, 'I do not know.' Six words of an inscription would turn all their words to dust. They have not yet come to light. The problem remains unsolved.

The voice of Faith meanwhile declares unfalteringly that Saint Peter lies under that high altar, beneath that blazing baldachino, amongst those endlessly burning candles, behind those golden gates. The tomb has never been opened. It probably never will. Where would be the use? If it were, the most we could expect to find would be a collection of relics, of which the most we could expect the scientific man to say would be a willing, but indifferent, agreement that they are 'bones of a male person, not impossibly belonging to the first century A.D.'

Only the darkest sceptic, or somebody without a blossom of poetry in his heart, would say, 'What does it all matter?' Perhaps earlier in the world's course it would have mattered to more men, when the possession of apostolic relics was felt as proof of the possession of Apostolic doctrine. Those days are gone. Nevertheless the emotion with which men heard of the discovery of the true cross, or of the tomb of Christ, could hardly be much greater than their emotion if they heard that, beyond yea or nay, rather than on the weight of probabilities, the Apostle Peter lies beneath the heart of Rome. For we deal here with things that humiliate reason. One coin, one heart-broken message from the hand of Judas; a lock of the Magdalen's tumbling hair; some scrap of an actual letter that Saint Joseph might have left on the bench for Mary, would have more power to bring Christ before us than all the debates of all the Biblical exegetists that ever were. The cult of relics is not just a simple or vulgar curiosity. It is an effort to come close to the saintly or the divine.

Much too Much Past

BUT I was through. I had had by this more than enough of the uncertain pleasures of speculation. I was finished once for all with the shadowy and shining past. I turned from the sacred to the profane one evening, at the very portico of Saint Peter's, stepping into a carrozza and driving to dinner in the Piazza Colonna with a friend from one of the legations; and after dinner we went on to hear *Faust* under the warm summer stars at the Terme di Caracalla; a wonderful and fantastic performance, a heaving hunk of histrionics, on a floodlit stage as wide as the Colosseum, with full ballet, horses galloping before the footlights, winding processions of villagers, bandsmen and soldiers, as big a caste as a Hollywood movie, so that one half of Rome seemed to be on the stage and the other half in the auditorium. It is a splendid setting for any opera. It is perfect for *Aida*. How Italians love the panoply and the emotion of it! Beside their full-blooded way of singing opera an English performance is the piping of a school-miss. Italian opera alone deserves the adjective Grand; big voices, big castes, big stages, big orchestras; the modern counterpart of the big circus of ancient Rome.

But I found, that same night, that no man can ever wholly leave ancient or sacred Rome behind him completely or for long. After the opera our cabby was waiting to drive us to a night-club restaurant beyond the Porta San Sebastiano. It was a drive that reminded me impressively, yet once more, that the ancient awe of Rome is but a hand's breadth from the modern pleasure, and when the next night I drove alone along that Appian Way I knew it even more assuredly. It was of all my Roman nights the most exciting and chastening; jolting along that ancient, narrow road, in the midnight silence, between high walls and crumbled mounds and invisible ruins, with only a rare light from a street lamp, or a villa blinking unexpectedly out of the blackness, and the mind never free of the thought that, beneath the earth, are miles of catacombs, warrens of death. It was the old jumble all over again; here the catacombs; there the Ardeatine Caves, where hundreds of Italians were murdered by the Germans; beyond, a night-club; here, a modern villa; there Cardinal Wiseman's little church looming against the sky, while the ancient cypresses whispered and a prowling police car hummed out under the arch where one of Mussolini's aces had lived, almost as famous for his loves as D'Annunzio: and across the mounds the dim campagna spreading wide under the stars.

My Friend Cipolla

ONE morning in the great piazza of Saint Peter's I found that one may cross the chasm with a glance. I have thought of writing a story about that glance. It would be based on a chance encounter with a little humped man who caught my eye as I lowered it from what I took to be the outline of the roof of the Appartamento Borgia: a passing revival of my old interest in Savonarola, who, as we all know, was the Borgia's great enemy in Florence. I might easily have snubbed this strange-looking figure, but God had sent him, and it was not to be. I answered his polite query truthfully. He said, throwing out his fly on my stream of consciousness: 'You know Michelangelo's portrait of Savonarola?' In surprise I said that I did not. When he offered to show it to me, saying it was in the Sistine Chapel, I knew he was an unofficial guide, and unjustly decided that he was a fraud as well, for I knew, or I thought I did, that there is no portrait in the Sistine Chapel. It turned out that he was quite right. There is a little *ritratto* of Savonarola tucked away in the bottom left-hand corner of the Last Judgement.

Having nothing better to do, and glad to talk to somebody, and willing to look at the Sistine ceiling again, I let him lead me away around the streets, as one must now do, to the Vatican Museum. In two minutes I realised that he was as mad as a March hare. His name was Cipolla. He was not in the least interested in the Sistine Chapel nor did he afterwards once mention it. I think now it must have been he who put into my head the fancy, which I have already thrown out, of the scholar who visits Rome for a holiday and is lost for ever down its catacombs of history and archaeology. (Have I mentioned that if all the passages of the catacombs were put end to end they would reach from Venice to Sicily? Cipolla had reached about as far as Calabria.) His pet theory was that the cradle of Aryan Adam is not where men usually place it, somewhere about buried Samarkand, north of the Hindu Kush, but in Asia Minor among the Galatians; a theory much to my taste, since the Galatians were Celts. On this he talked volubly. Of the Sistine Chapel he talked not at all. The result was that our perambulation paused three times at pubs, where he traced with a dirty finger in spilt beer the vagrant growth of Western civilisation. In my fiction we should have gone arguing from pub to pub until nightfall—I would call the story 'Why I never saw the Sistine Chapel'—and under the moon put an end to all wars in the Common Fatherhood of Man: his phrase. Or was it his? For, though I shall not be believed, I had earlier met another Italian who believed that all Europe sprang from a common Ligurian source. I can give this man's name also, Tombolini; he has written a large book on our Ligurian origins, and been decorated for it by King Umberto. And only last week I read a learned article about the secret sales of pottery made to archaeologists in Pisa by peasants from Montepulciano. The theme of that writer was the Etruscan origin of all Western civilisation.

Now and again, in between the Galatians and Civilisation, my dear lunatic talked also of the vast wealth of the Vatican with the inevitable cynicism of all Italians no matter what the subject, and most of all inevitable when the Church is in question.

'But,' I said, 'surely the Church must be poor nowadays? With all those countries that have been overrun by war or absorbed by Communism?'

He spread his hands, and gazed at me as if it were I who was mad.

'Consider,' he reminded me, 'the amount of food and money the Church is distributing in relief. Relief sent from all over the world. It is largesse. The poor have become more than ever dependent on the Church.'

'Yes,' I remembered with pride. 'We in Ireland sent what we could. Sugar, I believe. And wheat.'

'The Vatican makes a good profit on all that,' he smiled, making the curious Italian gesture of placing the left of the thumb of the right hand to the right side of his temple and drawing it slowly downward with a cunning smile.

'Profit!' I cried. 'But it was sent gratis!'

'Aha! Gratis! Yes! But there are certain *expenses* attached to distribution!'

I shrugged. He enlarged, annoyed by my incredulity.

'But I assure you that the Vatican is *very* rich. It has investments in businesses all over the world. Religious Orders and the faithful all over the world invest in the Vatican Bank—which pays a fine dividend—indirectly, through these businesses. Oh!' he forestalled my objections, 'the Church does not go into business directly, you may be sure! It gets wealthy business-men in Belgium or America to work for it. It never takes on a whole business. Perhaps half, perhaps a quarter. These people'—waving his hands madly towards the Vatican, and evoking a picture of rows and rows of cardinals bent over ancient ledgers, large as the Domesday Book, fat as the Borgias—'are *splendid* business-men! They are at it *all day long!* They are *excellent* men of affairs. What would you expect? They've been at it for nearly two thousand years! Ah!' he groaned, back to his Galatians, 'if I only had a few thousand lire to complete my studies! I need so little! A few hundred thousand lire! But would *they* give it to me? If I could undertake a *scavazione* in Hierapolis . . .'

For a while I listened, deeply puzzled. Then I interrupted him. He was at the moment in the middle of an attack on Communism.

'You *are* a Catholic?' I asked.

He looked at me, a little coldly.

'Naturalmente!' He resumed: 'These *scum,* who are destroying Christianity . . .'

As I listened to him a great glow of joy spread through me. It was as if the heavens had parted and a voice had come from a soft heart of light, rosy-coloured and mothering, to explain to me something whose obduracy had troubled me all my life, without my knowing, indeed, what it was that so long oppressed me. The Voice said: 'Now thou knowest why so many Catholics are such tiresome people.' This man was a Catholic, and he was not at all tiresome. He was most engaging. But he was a sort of Catholic I had never met before. He was the first Catholic I had ever talked to about religion who eluded Gibbon's theory for the Roman toleration of the Jews as contrasted with their persecution of the Christians: namely, that the Jews were a *nation* and therefore entitled to their own odd religious beliefs, but the Christians, being Romans, could only be regarded as a *sect*. Signor Cipolla escaped the impeachment completely. So, I realise, do most Italians. The discovery was to alter my whole life.

Elsewhere—I will qualify this presently for Ireland—it is the misery of Catholics to be still regarded as the ancient Romans regarded the early Christians, a body of people who can never be entirely trusted, since their higher loyalties, as with Communists, pass the bounds of country; as, indeed, they do and should do. This breeds in Catholics outside Italy a defensive or 'on guard' mentality which prevents their religion from being as unselfconscious as their nationality. Whereas, in Italy, if faith and fatherland are not absolutely identical they come as close to it as is humanly possible. This dear dotty Signor Cipolla was the first Catholic I had talked to who had not the outlook of a sectarian. That he was a little dotty added to the wonder of the discovery in the amazement of his liberty: a man whose intellect (such as it was) had sold itself neither to his race nor to his religion, as his Asiatic theory on the one hand and his anticlericalism on the other showed. He was an Italian and a Roman and a Catholic and a sceptic and a citizen of the world, and yet he was unaware of any of these things, being all of them simultaneously and instinctively. In no other one of the three countries in which I have lived for any length of time, Ireland,

England or America, have I found religion so limber and so light-hearted. I had never conceived that it could be so. I fell in love with it on the spot. I desired to possess it immediately; so much so that had Signor Cipolla been a handsome young woman instead of a crochety old man of seventy my desires might have wandered somewhat from their true object.

One might imagine that I would have met many Signor Cipollas in Ireland; and Ireland should, one might also think, being a nation mainly composed of Catholics, be as free of sectarianism as Italy, and one day I trust she will be. Unhappily the hang-over from the centuries when Catholicism was a persecuted sect—something as alien to the British Empire as Christianity was to the Roman Empire—keeps the defensive sectarian mind alive amongst us long after what bred it has passed; just as the oppression of our nationalism has made that, too, nervy and sensitive. The result is that intellectual liberty is still almost unknown in Ireland. In England things are a little better. There Catholics are in a minority, and that minority has been politically suspect since the days of Queen Elizabeth, but they are given every liberty by the majority, if only for the same reason that Christians in the provinces of the Roman empire often had an easy time under some tolerant proconsul like Gallio: they might kick nobody in the belly, but nobody might kick them in the belly either. Gallio was tolerant to Saint Paul because he did not care. But minorities naturally form cliques, and cliques, inevitably, lay tremendous stress on loyalties, and loyalists are inevitably touchy about criticism. There are no Catholic anti-clericals in Britain. And nobody can be a sound Catholic who cannot be, if he wants to be, a sound anti-clerical. It is his self-assurance of an inmost and unassailable core of Faith. All the Catholics I had hitherto known or known of in Ireland or England had either had a chip on the shoulder (Mr. Evelyn Waugh), developed complexes (Mr. Graham Greene), been controversialists (Mr. Arnold Lunn), been terrified rigorists (the type illustrated by our Irish Censorship), or lived in a hallucinatory blue funk (anti-Communists in Connemara).

The one type I had not met in these Saxon or Celtic countries was the type who, like old Cipolla, took his Catholicism as mildly and naturally as breathing.

Dear Signor Cipolla, I salute you. You are as legion as your race. And, yet, I had never known you existed until we sat in that pub under the Vatican walls, which you both defended and assailed with so much gusto, and with your finger wandering in the beer-stains all unknowingly drew my line of fate.

He was still talking when we sat in the benches of the Sistine Chapel. But, gradually, the old man's voice became drowsy and when he said, 'Lean back and look up' (as all the other tourists were doing) he leaned back and fell sound asleep. I saw, then, not so much Michelangelo's God the Father sending the electricity of life along his finger into Adam as a vast procession of men, not all Italians, for whom Christianity was less a creed than the colour of life itself, inconceivable in any other colouring, and as completely unlimited, untrammelled and unaware as a wave, or the wind, or a tree.

Cipolla slept on. I pushed a thousand-lire note into his pocket and stole away. It was still not noon; one begins one's sightseeing early in Rome to avoid the great heat of the zenith. I motored back to Saint Peter's, for I was by now in a fever of haste. That great village, for it is more like a village or a small town than a church, was conducting its usual variety of affairs in its various market-places. A long file of Calabrian pilgrims were entering its hollow halls, their wailing voices rising and falling in a strange, unearthly, flesh-creeping hymn that went echoing about the dome like a banshee. A stout cardinal led them to a side-altar to pray, stoutly, in shouting unison. Tourists wandered to and fro. The usual guides ushered the usual groups in the aisles. Americans looked up from their Baedekers or Murrays in secular curiosity or clicked cameras behind pillars. Friends chatted. A mass was being said in one of the transepts. In the same transept a dozen confessionals were busy, each indicating, on a plaque outside, the language in which one could confess—French, English, Polish, Hungarian,

German, Italian, Czechoslovakian, all the tongues of Babel. Outside each confessional a slim wand is fixed like a little fishing-rod and as each penitent emerges he, or she, kneels outside the priest's compartment, a hand comes out, lifts the rod from its fixture and taps the forgiven sinner on the shoulder.

I thought with emotion of my dear anti-clerical friend, now sleeping softly in the Sistine. My one wish was to become one with him in Christ. But it was more years than I cared to count since I had been to confession, and how could I ever explain to a confessor the reason why. A French priest, an Italian, indeed any priest of these hidden confessors, with conched hand to ear, would understand all the usual stories, be bored to yawning by them. Women? That would cause no trouble to either of us. It would be so normal as to be almost a relief. Theft? I would be asked how much and bade make restitution. The sin of Simon Magus? Since the sinner was returned that would thereby be all over. These things would pass lightly. They were the worn coins of sin. But mine? I looked longingly at the Czechoslovakian confessional and wished I knew the language. He would understand. A Hungarian priest would understand. Best of all a Spaniard; even an Italian would do, and under pretence of reading a prayer-book I covertly consulted my dictionary. *Ragione politica?* But he might think I was an anarchist or a communist. . . . Regretfully I decided that my Italian was not good enough. An English priest?

'You see—' I rehearsed, while the Calabrians howled the responses a quarter of a mile away, and the bell tinkled on the altar, a band of sun crept down from miles high, and the penitents came and went, a girl grinning back at her lover, a boy coming out with a smile of contentment—'you see Father, when we took up arms to defend the Republic the Church pronounced us virtually excommunicate.'

The good priest, possibly from Bury-Saint-Edmunds, perhaps a convert Wykehamist, probably a mild paleographer, would peer at me in astonishment. He might think hastily of the Spanish Civil War; or it might occur to him that I am a

Mosleyite. For what could he possibly know about the intricacies of Irish revolutionary politics? The whole thing suddenly seemed silly and embarrassing. Suppose he said, 'What Republic?' how could I explain that there wasn't really any Republic at all; it was something Mr. de Valera had thought up with a lot of distinctions about *de jure* and *de facto*. No Englishman could sympathise with nonsense like that. And yet, if only in sheer courtesy, I must give some explanation. I wondered had he ever heard of the Fenians? I wished that even my grandfather had been a Fenian, but all I knew about him was that he drank himself out of a farm in County Limerick. Impulsively, I shoved myself by main force into the empty compartment, deciding to talk in broken English like a foreigner.

He drew the slide. As soon as his voice whispered to me I knew I was sunk. It was rich with the buttermilk of County Limerick. The sweat broke out on me. This man would know *all* about the Republic. He would take the side of the Bishops, as in duty bound. Or else he would say something like:

'Yerrah, for goodness' sake? And what Brigade was that now? The First Cork? Sure, don't I know Tommy Barry as well as I know me own hand?'

And we would become so pally that I would sweat again with shame to have to tell him my tale. What he actually said, in a rapid, soft and gentle voice, was this:

'Well, now, I suppose all the usual sins since then? Women and drink and no mass and bad language and dirty stories and all the rest of it? Ah, well! My poor child! God has been very patient with you. Say three Hail Marys now. And God bless you.'

And I was hardly through the Contrition before his hand lifted in the Absolvo te . . . and the slide drew. I came out of the confessional trembling with fury. Three miserable, miserly, paltry Hail Marys! After years of defiance! The thing was fantastic! I fumed at the humiliation of it! Under the vast dome, in that great town of Saint Peter's, I felt as minute as a

Lilliputian. And then I realised the infinite kindness of the man and I was overcome with emotion.

The bell tinkled. A woman kneeling on the marble beside me fluttered her fan under her face and breathed out a loving 'O Vivo pan del Ciel.' Out of the corner of my eye I saw the girl whom I had seen grinning back at her lover when she entered the box. She was looking at the altar with dilated eyes. In those seconds I knew that I was caught, and caught for ever. I was lost or saved, according as you happen to look at it. People approached the altar. The Light of the World became flesh of their flesh, I was present at the greatest drama in all the world, in all eternity. *Ecce Agnus Dei* . . .

As I stood in the too-great heat and brilliance of noon on the steps before the portico I looked about me for Signor Cipolla—it was he who had done this to me—with a simultaneous desire to embrace him and to put my toe under his behind. The little dark figures made the piazza into a plain. He was a grain of sand. He was a drop of rain. I would never see him again. I shall always remember him with affection. The obelisk cast no shadow. From a pedlar I bought a rosary. A carozza was unburthening itself of three American soldiers. I took it and bade the cabby drive to the Janiculum. As we passed the Garibaldi monument he lifted his whip.

'See,' he grinned, 'he looks always defiantly towards the Vatican!'

I looked up at the old bearded guerrilla in his roundy hat glaring sideways at Saint Peter's. Then I looked at the cabby.

'You are a Catholic?' I asked him.

He seemed aggrieved at the question.

'Naturalmente!'

We climbed out and leaned over the balustrade and surveyed the roofs of Rome over which the heated air formed a quivering mirage like steam or water. The cabby started to talk. I did not listen. As I looked I was murmuring under my breath the words 'Civis Romanus sum'. By degrees I gathered that the voice beside me was simultaneously glorifying Garibaldi, talk-

ing of the wealth of the Vatican and denouncing the Communists. Below us in the valley a bell tolled softly. Then another. The deep notes and the little notes tolled out the
Angelus. The cabby paused in his flow. I glanced sidewards at
him. A far-off look passed over his eyes like a cloud and I knew
that he was murmuring a prayer.

'But,' he resumed like a torrent, 'they make *millions* of lire!
I, myself, I have a cousin who knows, for a fact, that . . .'

I threw in an occasional 'Si! Si!' for politeness sake. The
scene spread far beyond the pallid hills; far over Italy and far
beyond it; as far as thought can reach. To myself I said: 'I have
left a nation and joined an empire.' As to what kind of empire . . . I thought of John Henry Newman's—'a vast and
ever-growing imperial Church great enough to make flaws and
imperfections of no account'. A bit strong, that; a bit too off-
the-earth; a little bit too philosophical. Poor old Savonarola
would have frothed at this bland reference to 'flaws and imperfections'. Yet, Newman was essentially right. Imperfect in
an imperfect world. Should it not be said honestly, though,
when the imperfections showed? Bloy, Péguy and Bernanos
would say so. J. H. N. could not: the convert with his back to
the wall. I spread my hands. The cabby thought I was being
sceptical.

'But my own cousin told me,' he cried. . . .

'I once met a bishop in a railway train,' I said, 'who believed
that the three marks of the Church should be that she be poor,
unprivileged and free. I disagree. She should be immune; an
immunitas—Lord Acton's word; privileged on every count
and exempt on every count; an enclave recognised by all men
as something separated from this fleshly world. She should
therefore be celestial; that is she should have to do only with
the heavenly order, and though she must, since this is the
world and not the otherworld, have to do with temporal things
she should employ no temporal weapons. Whenever she does
she is in danger of becoming a tyrant and a bully. She should be
rich, the richest of all mortal institutions, so that she should be

able to influence the thoughts of men by all these same things, and more, with which the universities of the world influence civilised men. In fact, as universities should be immune, rich and profane she should differ only by being immune, rich and sacred, so that the world should be content to judge her by two worldly tests—that she did not meddle with temporal things and was never vulgar. As to her celestial work nobody could judge that but herself and heaven. People would say to that, of course, that her wealth would corrupt her. Wealth is less corrupting, by far, than poverty, and less, too, than power; and what has ever corrupted the Church but power? Make her celestial, immune and rich and she will have no power but the power of heaven and of the intelligence.'

The cabby looked at me miserably. He naturally did not know what I was talking about. I said:

'Let's have a beer.'

He understood that.

Venice

Travellers of the classical age, 'the olden days of travelling now to return no more', when one made the slow approach to Venice by gondola, were wont to sympathise with us of a later generation ejected summarily into a railway terminus. Towards the beginning of the second volume of *Stones of Venice* there is a splendid description of this gradual entry; as fine a piece of prose as Ruskin ever compiled. If anybody were strong-minded enough he could, doubtless, still arrange to be met by gondola at Mestre; or deflect from Padua to Chioggia or Fusina, and so enter Venice by water. It would be a rather deliberate and self-conscious entrance. There is, however, another way, unknown to Ruskin . . .

Somewhere about Ravenna the Adriatic appears far below

like a blur of smoke. Beyond the swampy lagoons of Comacchio, where Garibaldi hid from his hunters, and his wife Anita died, we pass over the meandering mouths of the Po; and then over the mouth of the Adige; and then the headland of Chioggia crops out into the sea. The man at my side said, 'Ecco Venezia!' We were thrumming in over the long razor-shell of the island of Palestrina towards the lean breakwater of the Lido—the whole string of sandy breakwaters are a *lido,* or bank—and my heart thumped on all six cylinders as I recognised the Venetian lagoons. There were the islets, small as boats, which I was soon to know as Poveglia and Santo Spirito and La Grazia and San Clemente, rowing among which, at night, I was so often to feel alone in the world under that deep behind deep of tinted air which men so weakly call the blue Venetian night. There were the larger islands flattening out to the north, Murano and Burano and Mazzorbo and Torcello. In between lay the great island of Venezia herself; although, anatomically, Venice consists of about a hundred islets sewn together by threads of bridges into one patchwork mass. I saw no canals. They were buried deep between the houses.

Before landing on the Lido airfield the plane circled. I saw a cluster of opals set in a crescent lagoon backed by the Euganean Hills, and the heights of Vicenza and the valleys of Cadore that rose to tiers of haze that must have been the foothills of the Julian Alps. Then the world whirled its mirror and the landing-strip came sloping up to meet us in gushes of bumping heat. After that, the final approach across the warm yet balmy lagoon was as gentle as a folding wing, as drugged as a falling eyelid, more quiet than a floating leaf. It was a slow fading into a Castle of Indolence.

For the beginning and the end of Venice is that immediately you step into your first gondola the amiable pirate in browning straw hat with red ribbons, rowing behind your back, who lives in three rooms of Number 1576, Torreselle, two twists off the Grand Canal, with his wife, mother-in-law, sister and six water-rats, is not a gondolier, but the child of Circe and Silence; that he will hush you in his arms away from this mortal world as softly as the boat glides from the pier; that it will be well with you if you can ever return to it; or if you do, ever bear to live in it again. People say that anybody who travels in Japan is never the same person after. I once knew of a man who had made love to an Indian priestess and after that Western women meant nothing to him. Browning's fish went from cool to warm water and was never after happy in either. One's first visit to Venice is a climb to a Mount of Revelation. It unseats the reason.

My reason told me that men and women in Venice have to pay the grocer's bills, go to the movies, suffer toothaches, have trouble with the kid's school reports, the maid, the stove and the choked drains, but though my reason told me all this, it did so over a flying shoulder. When next I met the poor thing it had a shivering hand and bloodshot eye. It never quite recovered from the hunted life it had been leading in the meantime.

On going Corvo

BEFORE setting foot in Venice one book which every traveller should read is Corvo's *The Desire and Pursuit of the Whole*. It is a very bad novel. It is the most beautiful tribute to Circe ever written, and the truest. This is what happens to people who go to live, and to many who had intended to stay only for a little while, in Venice. They go Corvo. Corvo was taken to Venice for a brief holiday; refused to leave it; piled up debts; was reduced to pauperdom; thrown out of his hotel; rejected by his friends; tramped around his beloved city in the winter night like a homeless cat; got pneumonia; recovered; died and left this, his last, wonderful tribute to the Circe who had killed him. There are Venetian vitals, curable by charcoal. There is Venetian vertigo for which the pharmacist provides no herb of mercurial moly. Talk not of the isles of Aeaea and the Southern Seas. This is the Island of Hallucination.

Venice has, none need tell us, its commonplaces. Who sees them? Did Corvo? Read again that sad and lovely description of his homeless walks at night—and we who tire after two hours of walking will sit, exhausted, at the end of our perusal of these marathons. He saw the falling haze, wrapped in his old blue boat-cloak, from under the portico of Santagnese, dream-lost; or standing in the small hours on the lonely length of the Zattere, gazing across at Giudecca, which he insisted on calling by its old name of Spinalunga, or else, Venetian-wise, Zuecca (for no name ever passed his lips that one finds on map or in guide; any more than a Parisian Ulysses would dream of referring to the Boulevard Saint Michel), but what his ravished soul really saw on those miserable nights were the lights of heaven along the far shore of Zuecca, fluttering 'like little pale daffodils in a night mist coloured like the bloom on the fruit of the vine'. Or, when the long bone-aching night comes to an end and he has walked from the Accademia eastward around by the Gardens and around Sanzanipolo and by millions of little back alleys and the long solitary quay through the Ghetto, past Santachiara and Sanraffael, around and around to the long, dark, rat-haunted Fondamente—one has to walk but a sixth of the distance, say in and out and up and down and back and forth from the Piazza to the station, to know what that perambulation means—his soul, still unbroken, saw only that the dawn was 'misty, pink and glittering-grey like salmon-flesh and scales'; and so he slept at last, steaming in the sun, before the Bucintoro, sated, still grateful, happy although he had not eaten for three days. You and I, pallid tourists, not fit to be mentioned beside this heroic genius and lunatic, would not endure that even for Venice. But do we, either, ever see it commonplace? Does anyone? Even a Venetian realistic novelist?

The city's swarm is hardly to be escaped; the city's smells;

the fleshiness and foulness of the parishes of San Canciano or
San Cristoforo; the rich fish, flesh and fowl of the markets that
soon dispel any idea that Venetians are pure spirits; the sad
hospices; the many banks; the hospitals; the asylum; the pri-
sons; the cigar-brown skins under the rags; the glowing thighs
and biceps, polenta-fed; the vermin; the *merceria's* mobs of
black-marketeers, bright-eyed, keen-nosed, gaily vulpine; the
gangings around the Campo San Bartolomeo, beyond the
Goldoni monument, where, and not on the Rialto, a modern
might spit on a Jewish gaberdine; the kids plunging in the
lukewarm canals where American high-speed launches must
have churned-up dogs and doges by the thousand; the in-
defatigable marble-chippers; the needlework sweat-shops; the
Burano slums; the trattoria where the journalists of the
Gazzettina gossip like any journalists in the world; the five-and-
ten; the blonde English A.T.S. always alone in the Blue-Moon
Coffee Shoppe; the nursemaid always devouring the latest pas-
sion-story from *Assisi* in the Giardino Reale; the exhausted
barcajuolo sleeping in his gùndola (not *gond-óhla,* Corvo
would have moaned; and anyway preferred a *pupparin*); the
one crowded Rio that is just like another crowded Rio except
that each new one seems more crowded. . . . We see. But
'What do we see?' is answered by 'What remains in the memory?' And what remains? Admit it; or am I abnormal; but for
the Grace of God etc. We first remember our friends. 'Charles
was so gay in Venice that year. . . . I was there with Lisel and
Enriqueta in '38. . . .' We recall, after, a dream floating on a
dream, and we floating and walking through it for ever, as
blissful as hashish-eaters, believing while we are there in all we
see; persuaded by the charm of the people; finding the fullest
persuasion of reality in the magnificent food that like genii
they lay before us; lost in admiration before fantasies of marble
and colour and carving; we remember velvet moons, torrid
suns, thunder over Zuecca, rain-pocked canals. And as we remember we do not question if we have been here. But *were*
we?

Venice has no more reality than a film which has stopped dead; all those vivid, gesticulating creatures suddenly arrested, with mouths open and eyes staring. There was once a city called Venice, a city palpitating with creative life. The crowds, the buildings and the art remain; a vast and exquisite work of art; probably blown out for us in the glass-works of Murano. She is like the Virgins that the Italian men carry on their shoulders on feast-days, to be gazed at, but never possessed. One might well feel that if somebody tied a hawser to the foot of the campanile of San Marco and towed the whole raft of bobbing logs away to the Pacific or into the middle of the Indian Ocean it would all go on just the same as before, an ingenious lovely toy. And this is not either fancy or ignorance. We know too much, so much that we have the sense to refuse to remember anything but the beauty before our eyes.

Venetian Water

IN our hearts we know that Venice came to a stop as slowly and as imperceptibly as ebbs her slight tide that made her great and then played her false. This city that once 'held the gorgeous East in fee', the clearing-house of all Europe in its traffic with the Orient, the millionaire of the spice trade, never recovered from the shock of the news brought to the Great Council one terrible day in the year 1497, that a Portuguese sailor named da Gama had rounded the Cape to India. It was that year, and none of Ruskin's picturesque dividing-lines, that first slowed up the film. The Turkish wars that robbed her piecemeal of her empire turned her into slow-motion. By the eighteenth century she was stopped dead. And no statistic can explain what this lovely city —now packed to suppuration; a flat on the Grand Canal to-day costs about 200,000 lire a month—has been living on ever since, apart from polenta and its past. It is absurd to think that so numerous a population can live on such feeble industries as tapestries and tourists, glassware and jewellery. Even its shipping, which is its mainstay, must be minute in comparison with Genoa. Marseilles clears ten times as many ships with only twice the population. What keeps Venice from vanishing into thin air is an unsolved mystery.

The first result is that we meet here the most bewildering contradictions of ancient dynamism and present somnambulism, deathless beauty and melancholy gaiety, endless contrivance, gallant persistence and final ineffectuality. The second result is that anybody with a grain of wisdom presented with so lovely a city at once forgets everything about it but its loveliness; with the third and final result that although one may read the greater part of everything that has ever been written about Venice since its hey-day, from Goldoni to Corvo, one will never get any other feeling but that this exquisite and magnificent, this solid and squalid city conjured out of the wraiths of the sea is, for them all, still sea-wraithed, still sea-veiled as with the iridescent spray and the spume of the goddess-mouth that blew it from her conch. None of us who write of it can stop ourselves from so glorifying this creation of the past that its dawns, its days and its nights become intimations of immortality. It is a confession, whether we know it or not, that Venice is an inviolate work of art, a projection of the Schopenhauerian will, a timeless essence, one of the greatest achievements of the whole cosmic movement of human desire for its insatiable satisfaction.

Reason, by this time flying distraught from me, perhaps to the island of San Lazzaro to study Armenian with the Mechitarists, or to study lunacy in the islet of San Servolo where the mad are housed, snarls at me over its shoulder: 'I suppose you know, dotty, what all this comes from? Water! Merely water!' And Reason is quite right and, as it so often is, it is also very silly. Merely water? One might as well say merely history. Everything Venetian has been dictated by the sea: her origin, her power, her architecture, the temper of her people, her ruin and her final transfiguration into an object of delight.

To illustrate this let us think of one thing only—what water has done for the face of Venice. It enabled her alone of all countries west of the Adriatic to keep her bond with the East when the Franks were binding Europe to Rome. 'This detachment of Venice from the other nationalities of Europe is reflected in her architecture, which from first to last has a character of its own distinct from the rest of Italy.'[1] The results are evident to the merest glance in their medley of the Lombard, the Roman and the Byzantine traditions. In more literal language, water has modulated Venetian architecture in a score of ways. It has sent every façade plumb as a cliff to the canal, sans gardens, pavements, areas, paths, approaches, or other intermediaries of any kind. It has lifted others of its buildings on great flights of steps high over the quays, like the church of the Redentore or the church of San Simeone Piccolo, and this not for mere theatrical effect, but because the spring tides and the east winds sometimes lift the sea ten feet and flood the piazzas. It is water that invites colonnades below, balconies above (the balcony is a feature of Venice as of its vassal Verona), magnificent doorways, skins of marble or mosaic to resist the salt air, and set lavish carvings and decorations on the one and only façade which can be seen. For this ground-floor concentration of décor and carving is more lavish in Venice than anywhere else in Italy, this being of all cities of the world the most constantly close up to the eye and therefore the most fit for miniscule work. And when the buildings are up, how the water shimmers the façades for those outside, and the ceilings for those inside, making them palpitate with a constant flicker of second sky, so that nothing is ever static. The sculptures seem to sway. The very under-arches of the commonest bridges are made of shot-silk. For us, as we pass, these buildings are doubled in the trembling mirror of the canal; for those who live in

---

[1] Thomas Graham Jackson, *Byzantine Architecture and Decoration*, Vol. I, p. 229 (Cambridge, 1913).

them we also are double; an unlikely, coloured bouncing to-and-fro such as no asphalt street could ever provide. I suppose the two most beautiful city highways in the world are the long straight line from the Arc de Triomphe to the Louvre and the serpentine Canalazzo. Water has compressed life on the narrow fondamente so that it, too, seems doubled. Water has created thousands of bizarre corners. Water has made every sound in the narrow alleys as hollow as in a wood. It has put a finger on the lips of noise so that, except where the steamers churn or hoot in warning, the only sound that traffic makes is the flip-flop of shoes, the tamed sea's whisper or the lonely cry of the gondolier, *à-oel,* echoing like a melancholy owl as he approaches a corner.[1] *Merely* water!

As Ruskin shrewdly remarked, many of these buildings which would pass unnoticed on Pall Mall are charming in their unique setting; and he remarks, too, how well the variety of the styles set each other off, as we must readily agree if we recall, say, how much more fantastical the old Cà d'Oro seems by contrast with the Renaissance dignity of the Palazzo Miani-Coletti next door to it.

If the sea has modulated the mind of Holland how much more so the mind of Venice: this odd amphibian circumstance which makes every man in Venice swim since brathood like a dog, gives him the body of a god, and puts the sea's horizons into his eye; and yet, since most of them must live on terra firma, must have helped to make them unusually inventive and adaptable, creative and ingenious, with bifocal sight and dual-purpose hands, both delicate and strong, as fit for fine gold-work and glass-work as for the building of those adamantine dams and dykes whose engineering has kept the island open to the ebb and flow of the tides and safe from the malarias of a *laguna morta.* If you are interested in such things, take a steamer some day to Brondolo, below Chioggia, and admire the daring and the power with which the Venetians have de-flected their river, the Brenta, twenty miles off its natural course,

---

[1] Corvo describes it as a 'clanging, bell-like *'É-oe!'*

and then threaded those dead lagoons hidden behind the live lagoons with profitable and purifying canals. This enormous ingenuity, characteristically Italian, must be supremely Venetian. Venetians have told me—I do not know if it is true—that all the canals have been planned cunningly to ensure a steady if imperceptible flow. One must admire a people who have brought great ships through sand, built railways over mud, and brought water under water. If it had not been for this endless fight against alluvial silt Venice would now be what Ravenna is, or Bruges, or Aigues-Mortes or ancient Adria, a village now some twenty miles inland, which gave its name to the Adriatic. It is hardly for a foreigner and a passing traveller to do more than guess at this mixture of dynamism and conservatism which must have finally emerged from the domination of the sea; a governing mind at home; a wide, adventurous seafarer's mind abroad; bold, ruthless, curious, arrogant, aloof; and yet under the surface emotional; not unaffected, surely, by the barbaric imagination of the Orient, whose mark is all over the art of Venice, in the brilliance of San Marco, a church that would be at home in Constantinople, in the lavish canvasses of Veronese —Verona a city of the Republic—of Tiepolo or Tintoretto. The seer would not agree that the cluttered splendour of Venetian Baroque is also eloquent of the Venetian character, but in this we must ignore him; he was so wicked as to speak of San Moisé's 'frightful façade' and 'insolent atheism'. It is hard to forgive a man who cannot love stone that still strains and palpitates with the emotion that first transformed it merely because the emotion was slightly insane.

By this time reason is simply gnashing its dog's teeth at me with rage. 'I knew,' he barks, 'what would happen to you once I abandoned you! Fantasising! All *this* out of water? And, at that, *salt* water! Gah!' And he doubles around a *calle* and sticks his tongue out at me between the legs of a stone lion. Let us throw him a sop or two to stop his horrid noise. Water has narrowed every lane and made them all smelly and dark; it is a shock to romance to see a woman coming to her door to thread a needle up against the sky. Water has produced a saturnine melancholy among these amphibians. A doctor friend, having moved to Rome after several years in Venice, once told me that most deaths from violence in Rome are from passion, in Venice from suicide. The winters can be morose; though I would have adored the sight of snow deep on the piazzas, hooding the gondolas, and clustering into every coign and crevice of San Moisé during the white winter of '47. Water has made Venice overcrowded. Water brings a terrible damp heat in August. It deprives us of trees and lawns. Too much water has made bathing in Venice impossible; and on the Lido one endures the least attractive bathing in the world, unless you happen to like to bathe *en masse* like Indians in the Ganges; and I still feel on my footsoles the burning sand of Sottomarina, across from Chioggia, and the burning sun, and the people trudging out with little poles and bits of calico to make shade to lie in; though I remember, too, as sensuously as if the warm water were still lapping me about, the hours lolling there in the shallow Adriatic, with those barbarically painted sails of the fishing-vessels—blues and crimsons and ochres—triangled like Eastern dhows against a sky and sea too bleached with heat to have any horizon other than a pallid haze swooning into infinity.

Nor is this all, dear horrid Reason, that your 'merely water' has done to Venice. When, at last, she ceased to be the doorway to the East, when she lost her empire with her trade and her monopolies with both, when she should have turned her hand to other devices—there was the water and the mud, once her slave and now her jailer. She is not a Manhattan on whose rock skyscrapers may climb. Nowhere can she expand. The Queen of the Adriatic has become the captive of the lagoons. Sometimes, in the dead quiet of the night, it is said that you may hear the mud tremble under the sea: the faint sleepy shrug of the Lion outside the cage reminding Saint Mark that he is within it.

Dissolving Antinomies

VENICE is thus full of apparently irreconcilable antinomies. There is not a ramo, nor a calle, not an hour of the day that one does not meet their dissolution. One recalls them by the hundred. . . . This torrid morning I am passing out of the dimness of San Moisé, idly wondering if it was the Oriental influence that sanctified Moses as I look back again at the carnal clusters on the façade that threw Ruskin into such a spluttering rage. I lean over a humped bridge beneath whose shade a gondolier lies fast asleep in his gondola. I pass on and pause by an entirely modern chemist's window packed with nostrums, glittering with feminine war-tackle. Then I stroll a few feet beyond and come on one of those eloquent obituaries that Italian piety pastes on dead walls, or hangs in shop-windows, or inserts in the newspapers to show the world that dead friends are not forgotten. They always have the formality of a traditional style, they suggest the fluency of a paid scribe, and they testify to the innocence of a warm heart. Under an emphatic black crucifix this one declares that the mother, father, wife, little daughter (*figlioletta*), uncles Fernando and Angelo, or some such names, and all the cognates, male and female, of the beloved Giulio Bonatelli are still *straziati* (lacerated?) by the most cruel, by the most immature deathblow that reft their Giulio from them at the hour of seven o'clock in the morning one August four years ago. *Nella sua breve e pur feconda esistenza.* . . . 'In his short and yet fruitful existence he was ever inspired by the most scrupulous rectitude; was ever prodigal of the high and serene gifts of his noble soul, his rare intelligence and his boundless culture alike to his family, his profession and his fatherland, so that now he leaves behind him a gaping void which his relatives and his friends can never hope to fill . . .' As I read this pious memorial, behind me are the chaffering black-marketeers, offering tobacco, scents, foreign money. The crowds float past unheeding. I can just see the feet of the sleeping gondolier, sticking out into the sun that burns his soles. In the flickering miasma of the heat the statues on the church seem to sway. A canal-steamer hoots peremptorily and a gondolier shouts back angrily.

Is there any other way of reconciling this eager, greedy order of common existence and this traditional order of thought that secretly melts it in life and sadly relinquishes it to the grave otherwise than by thinking that everything here is a parable rather than a reality: a parable dissolving the reality; or a reality that is but an image of the parable. 'Nothing,' says Santayana, 'that is given exists.' From the moment in which we are born we are dying. Life is, by anticipation, its own ghost. And I am sure that even the black-marketeer selling me lire at a swindler's rate, or the chemist who yesterday sold me an electric razor of an unfeasible wattage, would, if pressed, agree. They all know it. They have lived too long. They have seen worlds die. Nor would I, for one moment, believe any Venetian who disagreed—my padrone for one, who is probably at this moment concocting yet another letter to the *Gazzettina* to complain about the smoke on the Grand Canal; a violently assertive agnostic—for I have no least assurance but that even he, on his deathbed, will howl for his priest, and afterwards there will be his photograph and a bit about 'in sua breve e pur feconda esistenza' in the chemist's window, under a crucifix as big and as black as . . . well, as the smoke on the Grand Canal —which is, itself, but a parable of impermanence.

Mornings in Venice

THIS drunken city has degrees of sobriety. By night she is a siren and a bawd and should be trusted less. At night, unless you stuff your ears with cotton-wool and lash yourself to the mast of common use and wont, you may wake up to hear yourself squealing like a happy little piggy. In the early morning she is as innocent and persuasive as Eve. One does well, indeed, to look at her before she has fully awakened; very early, as early as the morning Angelus; those hours when the sweetness of morning sleep softens every face and at the end of night has cleansed every soul of the impurities of the fleshly day. . . .

It is morning. Anywhere in Venice. Where? Let's take the penny ferry at the foot of the Calle Vallaresso (just beside the Hotel Monaco, a stroll from the Piazzetta) across Canalazzo to the gold-orbed Dogano or Custom House, near the church of Santa Maria della Salute. (Pay no heed to Ruskin if you happen to have read him on this church; he disliked the volutes, moralised over the dome, and was irritated because a church to the Virgin should be larger and grander than the church on Zuecca to the Redeemer.) We wander past it, cross the little bridge to the right, and after that,—well it doesn't much matter where we go. It is too early to ring the bell in the alley beyond the bridge to see the beautiful little cloisters of San Gregorio. They are private, but one is never denied the pleasure of entering them at a reasonable hour. Perhaps it is best to follow, roughly, the line of the Canal; or follow the man in front of you; if there is a man in front of you at six in the morning. As you stroll you begin to leave the parish of the Gesuati—three hundred years older than the Gesuiti; and per-haps a more charitable if less cultivated body—and enter the parish of San Trovaso. You may not find this church. That will not greatly matter either. You will merely miss another Tintoretto, and the city swarms with them, and you may, in any case, irreverently if not inexcusably, feel that the ripple of living sun on canal-water, the slashed shadows, the in and out of lanes and bridges is far more lovely than all the Tintorettos that were ever forged in the garrets of Venice or elsewhere; anyway, if you keep on past the Campo Santa Margherita and the Church of the Frari you will find in the Scuola of San Rocco, before noon, as many Tintorettos as any eye can absorb in a week.

In my weeks of loafing about the alleys of Venice I found that I came to love best—I do not know why, unless it simply was that I came to know best—these five or six western parishes between Santa Maria della Salute and the Rialto bridge. Had I lived three hundred years ago I should therefore have been of the faction of the Nicolotti. For the church of San Trovaso divides western from eastern Venice; and as the eastern faction were called the Castellani, after the church of San Pietro di Castello down at the lagoon beyond the Arsenal, so the westerners were called the Nicolotti after the church of San Nicolo dei Mendicoli away off in front of us by the docks. It was, roughly, Right Bank against Left; and the older bank against the later, in so much as the Rialto was the seed of Venice. To make an Irish bull this right bank of Venice is its Rive Gauche. It is, at any rate, the more bohemian bank, what between the art-school, the Academy, the Archives, the markets, the sailors, the docks and the prison. At night when the tourists sit in the Piazza of Saint Mark the *popolazzo* sits along the Zattere, under the strung beads of electric lights in the sailors' cafés, Nico's or Negrini's; watching a great tanker throb out to Alexandria or end its five thousand miles from Galveston; and then all the boats will sway under the light wash, lighters and yachts, and old heavy tubs, and barques, and the ferry pontoons rise and sink, and there seems for a moment much more liveliness all over the whole wide channel across to the lights of Zuecca and the fading dome of the Redentore than there ever is along the Molo. Corvo lived on this side, after he was thrown out of the hotel in the Piazza; and Zelda lodged on the Rio di San Trovaso; and Ruskin had the wit to live in the Albergo della Calcina. If you want to find it, turn left along the canal when you come to the lovely little Campo San Vio and keep on until you come to the very end on the Zattere. It must have been a charming place to lodge then when ships were still mainly sails. Even yet there are houses with gardens here, a rare luxury, just across the bridge. Their foliage and their creepers are vivid and cool over the old brick walls and in the water beneath.

If I do wander this way I will loaf for a while in one of those pubs by the Gesuati and then turn back the Rioterra beside them—a *rioterra* is a canal that has been filled up—or else, for Zelda's sake persist to the San Trovaso Canal and back towards Canalazzo. That way I shall miss the Accademia. The Lord knows I shan't mind much, for it is full of rubbish.

I wish all books including this one could be manufactured with a little music-box embedded in the back-cover so that, from time to time, the reader could, at a given sentence, press a spring and read to accompaniment. I do not see why the cinema alone should have this adventitious aid to mood and sentiment. If this book had its music-box it would now be sighing softly as a thousand images pass before me.

I am crossing the Campo San Barnaba. . . .

But if I have a music-box why cannot I also have a microscopic film? In a little shaded cowl at the front of the book, where you would see the shadowy sunshot square, the crumbling stucco, the old dusky church. You see me entering San Barnaba, in whose undistinguished dusk an early mass is being offered up before a few worshippers. I have bought a bag of cherries at a stall on the way and I munch them still, which, if you are a northerner you will think irreverent and if you are an Italian think very sensible and natural. But I cannot finish them and I leave them on the seat when mass ends, hoping some thirsty brat from the lanes will find them. When I come out into the sun again I stop at the Ponte dei Pugni for the view down the Canal at the pink campanile of the church of the Carmini. It is famous for having been straightened in a most ingenious way. Woodblocks were put into the three sides opposite the leaning side, at different levels from the ground, and then they soaked the wood in acid until it gradually crumbled away and the tower settled down and became perpendicular once more. That was the theory. I swear it still leans crookedly. With the help of my filmetta please test my eyesight. I swear half the campaniles of Venice are off the straight. There is another curiosity here. On the bridge the reverent Nicolottan will notice four footmarks inset in white stone, toes aggressively directed towards toes. In those footmarks the leaders of the fight placed their right feet and awaited the signal to let fly. Now there is a parapet to the bridge. In the good old hammer-and-tongs days they fought on bridges sans parapets, and what splashing and ducking there must have been as mob pressed howling against mob.

How embarrassingly kind Italians are! This little girl rushing after me is waving my bag of cherries. 'By your favour, sior, you have forgotten your cherries?' So I loaf on, munching again.

The Gondola

LIFE is stirring now; thrusting away the bedclothes, stretching its limbs, staring in surprise at the sun. On every little canal boats come stealing by. They are not gondolas; too small, and without the steel prow, or ferro. Perhaps they are pupparini? (Only the devotee knows all the different sorts of boats of Venice; topi, valesane, cavalline, barchette.) Seen from above, as from a bridgehead, they have at least the essentials of the gondola, and it is from above that one may note them. The marks of the gondola are chiefly three;

that the rower does not, as with us, sit with two oars and his back to the way he is going, but stands and faces and presses forward with all his body on a single oar; that the rowlock is not a fork, though called a *forcole,* but a free arm-bend of walnut—the oar is of beech—along which the oar moves fluently at will; and that the vessel has a delicate gumboil leftward twist or malformation towards the prow to balance the weight of the *barcajuolo* on the right of the poop.

It is these three things that have given rise to his three cries: the warning hoot; the *Prèmi* and the *Stáli*. These cries are quite easy to understand if we remember that a gondola, or pupparin, is propelled by a double stroke, the main stroke and the return. The main stroke pushes the boat onward, but since it is on the righthand side it naturally slews the head around to the left, and the *barcajuolo* corrects this with his return stroke, *under water*. When he presses he is responding to *Prèmi;* when he is returning the stroke he is responding to *Stáli;* that is to say, when he presses he is moving the prow leftwards and when he is pulling he is urging the prow to the right. But, of course, when he shouts he is not ordering himself, he is ordering whoever may be coming towards him around the next corner; and that means that he shouts to make the other fellow do the opposite of whatever he himself is doing so that they may pass free of each other. In short, Prèmi means, 'Go left of yourself (because I'm going to the left of myself).' And Stáli means, 'Go right (because I'm going to the right of myself).' The diagram makes it clear. The man below is the one who shouts.

And he himself is going left or right because he likes the wide sweep. Of course, he can only claim this right if he gets his shout in first. When both shout together there is likely to be a flood of good old Venetian obscenity; but no blows. Italians love to row, with terrific passion, but it is one of the charms of their nature that they blow it all off quickly and when it is done it is done and laughter shines as gaily as before.

So the gondolas steal up the little canals, laden to the gunwale with produce from the markets by the Rialto. They keep on gently appearing from under the crescent bridges or stealing around corners of sea-green water like silent raiders. Their baskets of green grapes, of purple aubergines, scarlet Italian tomatoes (shaped like a plum, deeper red than ours), peppers,

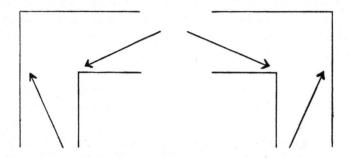

plums, pumpkins, pink-speckled sugar peas, or those Adriatic fish that gleam with every colour in the rainbow, are unloaded by little *calles* on to stalls set in shadowy corners. Or a pair of ragged boys, brown as negroes, dressed only in canvas shorts, will pull up their old barque by a trafficked bridge and cry: 'Oh! Che bell' uva! Tutto, tutto, tutto, bello! Oh! bella, bella frutta!', as if apostrophising their own wares.

A Lavish City

As we wander on through these *calles,* in and out of those little *campos,* coming every fifty yards on a tall campanile seen along the perspective of a canal, pink as a mignonette against the sky, the natural freshness of the morning is sweetened by those stalls of pears, plums, peaches, greens and brilliant fish; the canals look cool and clean; the narrow lanes seem almost airy: the sun is still kind, and not, as it will become at noon, pitiless, grilling, incandescent, choking, warming the breezes from the lagoon into breaths of hot air. Then, moment by moment, the noon heat thickens; a babel rises; the clotted smells stand at bay, thick as gruel; the dead centuries steam through the flagstones and creep out of the ancient crumbling walls. This is the hour to take refuge in the church of the Frari or the Scuola di San Rocco which is from floor to ceiling (and even on the ceiling—and what gleaming, golden, glittering ceilings!) packed with lavish Tintorettos. In these cool retreats, away from the markets' babel and the palpitating heat, though even here one avoids the slanting stabs of sunlight from the high windows, we realise that the Venetian craftsmen were as devoted as monks. Outside, life is suppurating. Here the toil is minuscule. Here, before the exquisite detail of a gold ciborium or an intricately hammered altar-gate, amazing in its virtuosity, of baroque wood-carving or marble inlay, we understand how the emotion of the Italian nature tamed itself to create with infinite pains the undying beauty which in turn produced a further lust to create more beauty and more. In the same way the traveller tames himself to look not so much at Venice as into Venice, into every stone and corner, invoking each individual hand and mind that tapped and gouged, moment by moment, inch by inch—even as the gold mosaics were laid piece by piece with delicate skill, to catch the light, on the walls of San Marco Cathedral—until at last Patience achieved the suffusion of its triumph. I am not thinking of palaces and churches. There are more carved stones in Venice, each line exquisite, each leaf or twig a work of art, which are never looked at at all, or at most by none but a casual passer-by, idly craning his neck, than would make another city envied for its wealth and famous for its beauty: a Madonna casually set in a niche, a piece of stonework as irrelevant as if the mason had merely done it to while away an evening, a lavishly carved door, for which a museum director would give his ears, rotting away in a passage frequented only by house-cats or scavengers, or Ruskin. I remember one day taking a wrong turning, near the Campo Santa Margherita. I should not now be able to find it if my life hung on it. I found myself in a *calle* that ended up in a dead end, a tiny *corte,* and was about to turn back when my eye fell on an old carved block of Verona marble through which a wall has been built in the most cavalier indifference to the craftsman's art. I now know it to be of Verona marble, and an ancient well-head, because I have found out since that, as one might expect, the tireless John—he who knew all, saw all, and told all—also found it in his day, when searching for the land-entrance on the Rio San Pantalon to the house whose Byzantine arches he had spotted from the Ca Foscari. I cannot believe that one out of ten thousand visitors, or for that matter Venetians, has ever laid eyes on that old Verona well-head.

That morning another kind person kept watching over me, a photographer on the Campo. I had had a long chat with him about photographs that I saw in his window and desired to possess. They had been taken by a British officer and the good chap went to endless trouble to find me his name and address in Scotland. Seeing me go astray down that *calle,* he chased after me. Seeing me on my right road, he chased after me again with some new suggestion about how to get in touch with 'his' Major. They are, one says it over and over, the kindest people.

There is no 'end' to this crapulous and lovely labyrinth. On a lazy day I may give up at the Frari or surrender at the near-by steamer station. On a less lazy day I may wander on to San Toma, and San Polo, and from there walk to the ferry of the Madonnetta; a better idea, since from the opposite side of Canalazzo I can walk (past the Teatro Rossini and the Teatro la Fenice) for lunch at the very best restaurant in Venice—the Taverna della Fenice. If I am a little less lazy still and there is a gondola for hire at the ferry I will, before lunch, again 'look into rather than at' some of the most interesting architecture in Venice; for hereabouts, in a cluster, are a half-dozen of its few remaining Byzantine palaces.[1] Hard by the ferry are the Madonetta House and the Braided House, to use Ruskin's names; just beyond the Rio dei Meloni is the Palazzo Businello; on this side of the steamer station of San Silvestro; and diagonally across the canal is the Palazzo Loredan, the intervals of whose arches, you remember, sent Ruskin mad with delight because they vary by the subtle difference of two inches. But if once we get involved in Byzantine architecture it will be more than five minutes before we get free again. It may be wiser to be even less lazy still and round out the morning's strolling by emerging into the babble and brilliance of the markets of the Rialto, the fish-market, the vegetable-market, and the market-for-everything-eatable-on-earth beside the little homely church of Giacometta. And then, quite exhausted, you and I will disappear into a side alley near the Rialto Bridge— anybody will tell us the way—to lunch at the Graspa d'Ua, which would be as excellent as the Taverna della Fenice if only one could eat in the open air.

When we emerge, paunch-tight, we find that the sun is now focused, as through a heavenly magnifying-glass, directly and with special solicitude on our individual polls. The Canal blinds us. The houses are radiators. The market's smells, the steamers' smoke, the lane-smells, bloom like a jungle. The only people who seem to have any sense are those reclining under a gondola's awning whose fringes do not as much as sway in the airless heat. At that hour we either agree that it is folly and high lunacy to travel in Italy in the heat of midsummer; or we feel that there is in this very excess of blinding glare and ruthless heat, in this high season of flesh and fish and fruit, a proper metaphor of the nature of Italy itself, so exuberant, so excitingly prodigal, so running-over, so lavish, so unrestrained.

---

[1] *The Stones of Venice* is what Americans call 'required reading' for visitors to Venice. But the books of Thomas Graham Jackson and J. Arnott Hamilton on the Byzantine influence are much more objective and clear. Adrian Stokes' *Venice* is extravagantly ingenious, but suggestive and contains wonderful photographs.

Torcello

So I find it. Day after day, all that summer, the sun had burned tirelessly. Day after day it rose with new vigour. It had been hot in Turin, and I had said with satisfaction: 'This is the Italian sun I dreamed of.' But it was still hotter in Genoa. It had been as hot as the hobs of hell in Florence. In Rome I had to get a new suit of clothes, because by this time I had lost half a stone and my trousers were lapping across my middle. I remember how the tailor near the Fontana dei Trevi groaned *'Niente pancia!'* as every trousers he produced swayed around me like a sail in full wind. But in Venice that August people cursed the heat. They said, *'E esagerato!'*—and the padrone of my hotel, who was a Roman and should have been used to heat, declared every day that if the much longed-for and long looked-for storm did not come to-morrow he would pack up and go off to the hills and abandon us all to blazes. All day long and every day I could feel the sweat tickling down my ribs, and the men's shirts were dark across the shoulder-blades. I browned like a cigar. My siestas became prolonged. My nights became my days. Every morning the naked lady with the shield on the little gold orb of the Dogano showed that the air—I cannot say wind—was still puffing from the direction of Damascus. It was the moist heat of the scirocco. As I write of it now, amid rain and fog, I think of it with a longing that is as painful as a lust.

Those afternoons if you went out on the Piazza after lunch it was as deserted as an architect's drawing. You saw nothing on it but the black-hooded tripod of the photographer in the centre of the square and the pigeons pecking. The hundreds of tables in front of Florian's and Quadri's were deserted. At that hour you crept behind the awnings under the arches and drank spremutas, and sweated them out again.

There are, fortunately, a few refuges from this absurdity. The best are the small islands; the dearest, Torcello. There you have, at least, natural grass to lie on; the one thing you miss in Venice. When I say this to my friend Freilich, who supplies ships and yachts with stores, he laughs: 'In Venice you buy grass. If you like I'll sell you some?'—and when I still protested he sent me down by the Arsenal, where I saw some horrible, balding, dusty, moth-eaten stuff misnamed grass, and I remembered how Corvo, that unfortunate child of genius and misery, had played snowballs there one winter with his boy-girl Zelda. There is another attraction about Torcello. You can lunch and dine there as well as in the best Venetian restaurants.

I am thinking of the day I shivered. I was sitting in the Piazza with a young American officer. They were billeted on the Lido that summer. He was an intelligent young Southerner who hardly ever talked, a good companion for Venice. I called him Ginger.

'Freddo?' he asked in astonishment.

'Just a sweat creeping down my belly.'

'Even the Lido is better than this,' he grunted, but I made a face.

'Torcello?' I suggested.

The waiter brought us a time-table. There would be a steamer in forty minutes.

The barometer on the campanile showed thirty-five (Centigrade), which in Venice is worse than forty in Rome. Underneath it a dog lay stretched as if dead, in brief shadow. A country priest appeared beside us, one hand fanning himself with his black beaver hat, the other wiping his neck with a blue handkerchief. He had just been showing the Basilica d'Oro to his flock of peasants. They were strewn now on the stone benches under the arches of the Ducal Palace. Their fat, cork shoes were kicked off; their big, veined feet cooling on the stone; their dark bundles pillowing their white heads. I said: 'Your people are all old?' He smiled and said, longingly: 'The young ones are gone swimming to the Lido.' He waved his blue handkerchief towards the dog 'The animals are wise; they don't stir.' But where in Venice can you lie like a dog? At this hour the Lido swarms. And if you go there later than nine in the morning you cannot hire a frontline box. If I went back to the hotel and lay naked in bed, behind closed shutters, panting like the priest's dog, the sheets would warm under my body and the canal outside would smell like a goat.

To get the steamer for Torcello you either go by vaporetto along the Grand Canal to the Ca d'Oro, and then walk by the Rio di San Felice to the Fondamenta Nuova; or you go all the way by gondola; or you can go by gondola from the Rialto for the joy of passing San Giovanni e Paolo and Bartolomeo Colleone[1] again and yet again; with the Campo San Vio it is the most attractive campo in Venice; or, in spite of the heat, you may find it more rewarding to walk. So we walk, pausing twice for a beer, through the thousand lanes that lie between the Rio dei Gesuiti and the Ospedale Civile, whose canal is supposed to waft you the best smells in the city. We walk and we walk, and we get lost, and Ginger droops (it is his forte), and trails his right leg, which I think must be a millimetre longer than the left—a bullet in Normandy—and the winding stews get more and more narrow, and more and more stinking and stifling, and it seems to us that we have gone astray until we begin to pass little workshops with men chipping away at histrionic angels in white marble, and then we know we are all right. Sure enough, we now pass the office of the Cemetery Board; sunlight appears at the end of the *calle;* we see blue water; and at last the long brick wall of the cemetery island of San Michele stands on its own reflection out on the lagoon. Or not 'stands', sways rather in its own miasma.

Across the still water at the end of the quay there is a tumble-down house called the Casa degli Spiriti. The line of mainland, far away, on the horizon, is a blur of haze. The lagoon is un-breathed. Its surface is unbroken except for a pile here and a pile there. I had long ago seen, in an old blue book on a book-

---

[1] 'I do not believe that there is a more glorious work of sculpture existing in the world.' *Stones of Venice* (1898), iii, 14.

stall, a dim photograph, pale as if over-exposed, of this casa lying on the water like a raft, the world's end of Venice to the north, and I had wanted to see it more than I had even wanted to see San Marco—this crapulous, neglected, uttermost tip and relic of Venetian high-life dreaming out its senile days into the Adriatic. I do not know now why it was so evocative on that second-hand bookstall in Dublin. I have forgotten all my pre-notions of Venice; except that if I close my eyes now I can re-call how I had imaged a special palazzo, plonk on the water's edge, with an entry from a gondola at dusk, down a dream-labyrinth of canals, and once its doors clanged I would be de-tached from the world, alone, isolated, lost, unrecorded. There are, unfortunately, no such palazzi. Am I a romantic, happiest only when things, places and people swim in my own or some-body else's imagination? A couple of days ago I saw San Gior-gio Maggiore in a mirror of the hotel reflected through the open window and said: 'It looks even more lovely in the mir-ror.' Ginger, sprawled in an arm-chair, had mocked in his sanely sardonic way, 'That is because you have removed it one degree from reality.' Perhaps one should have no pre-notions about anything, such as mine of this wreck haunted by the laughter of sixteenth-century *mascherati,* for its rooms were clearly meant for receptions and gambling; and how they would row here at night, swan-moving, with every gondola's nosetip lit like a glowworm; though its name may have come from something much less romantic, such as the chance winds that could carry voices, hollowly, from the chattering fonda-mente. My old blue book said that it was then, nearly fifty years ago, used as a studio by a painter named Mr. Humphreys John-ston. Pure Henry James. Though he preferred Florence and Rome. At night now one would hear a constant squeaking under the rotted boards.[1]

[1] Just as I write this I find that my old blue book is not so very old. It was first published in 1907 and was later reprinted. It is invaluable for those who like to wan-der alone. *Venice on Foot* by Hugh Douglas. (Methuen: London.) Much of its in-formation is out-of-date, but what on earth does that matter? All Venice is out-of-date.

Things age in Venice without dying, and in this northern quarter, once, as somebody said, the aqueous 'Park' of Venice, thronged with idling gondolas, things have frayed like old lace; yet not at all dismally. "Age cannot wither . . .' It can; but beautifully. If the palaces persist only in name, by the score, by the hundred, they persist, older in their civility than the oldest northern homes, except the castles and the timbered houses, out of centuries when this shore facing the northern sea was supposed to be free from pestilence. The superstition must have been universal and persistent. I recall that even so far away as Dublin all the best eighteenth-century houses face north. Ambassadors and visiting royalty honoured the same superstition here. But then they would have had their myrtle gardens down to the sea, so that if I dive down a few calles and ramos and cortes to see where Titian lived—quite near the steamer for Burano—I will be reminded, in this hot heart of a modern slummery, that he had his famous 'View' across the lagoon.

This pallid and pink consuming San Michele, cut in two by the funnel, would not then have been a cemetery, with its thousands of dead packed in rows like a card-index system; including Corvo. Every church then had its own graveyard; its Campo Santo. And is there not a Campiello dei Morti somewhere? It was Napoleon who changed San Cristoforo della Pace into San Michele (dei Morti), quite sensibly and rationally, and as usual with all rational ideas, with a progressive comicality and bestiality so that all modern, that is nineteenth-century, Italian cemeteries have an air of rational horror. Slide 'em in and shut 'em up. Number three thousand four hundred and sixty-two. Safe as houses. Unless a bomb falls within a quarter of a mile and, as I saw happened at Camogli, all the boxes and bones fall out.

I suppose the people who own this quarter now do not give a damn about the proximity of Death. They have enough pagan zest for life to keep death far from their thoughts, and enough Catholicism to sublimate it when they have to meet it. To them death is part of life in so far as everything is midway between an emotion and a fantasy. Which, no doubt, is why they wail and clutch one another so magnificently at funerals, make death part of the whole drama of life, as they make a meeting or a parting. A friend saw two men parting yesterday; they kissed and kissed, they shook hands, they groaned, they waved to one another, and as they drew apart one said to the other, '*A domani!*'

What is Death? See you (in Paradise) to-morrow.

The First Venice

In the steamer we sit behind an old Franciscan priest, sweating in his ponderous brown frock. Each grey hair on the back of his neck is beaded. His robes are a vapour-bath. He has been shopping in Venice and hugs a great basket with a hinged wooden lid locked by a key fit for a cathedral door. The steel roof of the steamer holds the sun. We stick our heads out of the windows to get air and watch a funeral floating by to the cemetery, the mourners hooded, the gondolas hooded, the favourite pink gladioli strewn lavishly on the coffin, the relatives clutching each other in their happy grief; and then big barges pole patiently or row, inch by inch, to Murano, and the little sandbanks float by, covered with a bloom like a grape, the lovely lavender-coloured weed they call *Roscani di palude,* and tiny islands that still look like the lazaretti they certainly once were, or powder magazines, or jails, or a fisherman's tiny kingdom, and to the north coral Constanziaca piled with the bones they exhume from San Michele, and islets that are only homes for sea-crabs, like San Pietro and Ammiano, and to the south San Francesco nel Deserto, whose black cypresses against the smudge of the Lido still farther south suggest the deepest, coolest shade. I ask the Franciscan if it really is deserted, and he smiles back and nods.

'Nobody lives there?'

'Nessuno.'

'Nobody at all?'

He grins. 'Le lucertole.' (The lizards.)

It seems, indeed, not only deserted by man, but disjoined from the very sea itself, from this world, from life, a Fata Morgana whose self and inverted self is less real than all this space and spread of light through which we hiss hushingly towards that even more unlikely cube of a cathedral campanile in the distance, towering from an islet that we know to have been crumbling into a like desert condition for a thousand years.

The steamer noses into a vacant channel of mud through a marshland that suggests bayous and a delta.

And what, in fact, are all these sunlit lagoons and pinnacled islands but the effect of the invisible juncture of rivers and waves on a vast spread of mud washed over aeons from the Alps and the Apennines—an intricate, reticulated juncture well known to every gondolier, pilots of the hidden channels, revealed to others only when the fallen tides reveal, between more and more islets, the submarine streams? Some hot night let the water tempt you to drop over the side of a gondola five, six or seven miles from the mainland, and you will stand ankle-deep on the softly powdered Apennines.

One may nicely measure this flatness by following with the eye a string of telegraph wires stretched as level as a builder's twine across the marshes towards Mestre and the haze of the hills of Arquà, and see why the Venetian tides, so vastly spread, like the last wavelets on a sandy beach, sink and rise so lightly as to be unobserved.

At the wooden jetty only we two get out. The steamer circles and hisses away. The heat descends. There is not a speck of shadow. We see a vineyard, a canal, a grassy path beside it, and an old man with a *sandalo*—a pinnace shaped like a crude sandal, not fit to be called a gondola—willing to row us anywhere. But where is there to row to?

Even on the most unbearable days there is a little breeze on

Torcello; imperceptible; still, a motion of the air. Or is this, too, an illusion of light and space? For the mauve tamarisk droops heavily and the clustering *mignone* has not enough breath to blow its purple trumpets. Yet, the walnut leaves crinkle and the water of the channels is not smooth, although when one slips into it, for it is too uninvitingly muddy to dive, the water is not cool and the mud into which the foot sinks is warm as at a spa. It reminds me that the rivers of northern Italy are muddy all the way back into Lombardy. But sometimes the breeze does fan, as to-day it fans, cool and steady; and then it is heaven to lie and snooze in the shadowed grass under the immensely tall tower of Santa Maria Assunta; or, at least, it seems immensely tall when the pink stalk floats over one's head into the blue sky among the whirling swallows, or up towards tiny clouds whose faint motion makes the tower lean slowly over to one side.

Torcello—everyone says it, I have no option but to say it again—was the mother of Venice. The phrase is inevitable but inaccurate. Torcello preceded Rialto (which preceded Venice) that is all it means. The people who settled on the actual island of modern Venice came from Aquileia, a place of lagoons near Grado near the Gulf of Trieste. It was probably this which induced Corvo to call Torcello the grandmother of Venice, which is as pedantic and correct as his way of spelling it Torxello. The thing is that when Venice was a swamp Torcello was a big town. It is now not even a *ville morte;* not even a *village mort.* Just plain dead. It contains little but its two empty churches, Santa Maria and Santa Fosca; a thousand years old and almost a thousand years disused. Even we, walking along this grassy path, are hushed by time and feel lapped into the same incongruity of history. For there are three other buildings here worth calling buildings, and though they are centuries apart, Torcello's timeless clock makes them all contemporaneous. They are the two little palaces where the Archivist once lived and the Council met (there must also have been a palace for the Podestà to live in, but where is it now?), and an ex-

quisite and silent restaurant called 'Locanda', owned by a clever gentleman who has another and noisy restaurant in Venice which he calls 'Harry's Bar'. Otherwise, about this mudbank, a few vineyards, a few small orchards, a few hollow meadows salvaged from the sea, two or three farmhouses, and up the winding channels, half hidden in the muddy reeds, one may come on a fisherman's home toppling over the tide. Anything else? A boat under a shelter. In the wrack at your feet a rusty tin can without top or bottom through which a lizard darts. If you stare over the marshes you guess at a seagull. The island peters out in the usual lavender haze. It is silent.

It is silent as it was when Attila burned Altino off to the west, south of Treviso—if it were night the lizards would have been transfixed by the glow—and the mainlanders took to their boats and nosed into this Nuovo Altino, a miserable refuge. 'But, after all,' they would have said to each other, looking out under their wattle roofs at dawn, hearing the waves hiss into the reeds and the mournful cries of the gulls, 'it's only for a while.' Later, as more and more refugees, over the months, the years, the generations, came to the islands about and staked them up and dug themselves in,[1] it seemed that it would be for ever, and that Torcello would be the capital of a great new settlement. They brought stones from the mainland, they brought their martyrs' bones; a tradition says they brought a crude stone chair on which Attila had sat; they built their cathedral as they flourished. But the bigger island won, the highest bank and the steepest channel, the Rivus Altus or Rio Alta, or Rialto, five miles away, and last of all Venice, out on the southern shore facing her dominion—the sea.

We ordered dinner at the 'Locanda'—*prosciutto con fichi, risotto al pomodoro,* and a cool Soave Bertani, to be followed by peaches and coffee—and wandered off to swim. Ruskin would not have done this. He would have crawled about humbly and devotedly on his hands and knees with a measuring-

[1] Cassiodorus says they squatted and nested like sea-fowl.

tape in the cathedral. But E. M. Forster is honest about travel
in Italy, in a sentence that every book of Italian travel might
quote on its title page. After mentioning a tangle of traffic in
Florence, composed of a tram, some white bullocks, and
marching soldiers accompanied by some small boys turning
somersaults in time with the band he says, 'Over such triviali-
ties as these many a valuable hour may slip away, and the
traveller who has gone to Italy to study the tactile values of
Giotto, or the corruption of the Papacy, may return remembering nothing but the blue sky and the men and women who
live under it.' So, to-day there could be no choice between a
swim and finding out if Ruskin was right in his joyous discovery that the pillars of Santa Maria dwindle in girth up the
nave to increase the illusion of perspective.

Santa Maria Assunta

ONCE again, how can one recall,
let alone record, the aimless hours of these summer days? We
wandered by the dumb attraction of the few almost indeci-
pherable paths about, as indifferent to our destination as if we
were straying fowl. An ancient peasant working in a hollow
field, where there were fig-trees and some withered corn-
stalks and not much more, so that I could not see at what he
was working, led us, with the inexhaustible kindness of the
Italian, to the best bathing-place. It seemed to us the worst
bathing-place, all dried, cracked mud, and wrack, and moist
mud, and a strongly flowing current, which was something I
have seen nowhere else among those stagnant waters of the
lagoons. We swam, and then wandered back, as aimless, again,
as two pecking hens, and found ourselves beside the cathedral.
   The cool shadows of its bricks are crumbling homes for ants.
Its dignity is bare. But bareness and nakedness are the marks of

both this great church and its strangely Oriental neighbour, the rotondo of Santa Fosca. Here again—I say 'again', thinking of Murano and San Marco and the Fondaco dei Turchi—is the art of the Bosphorus floating on the lagoons: a Greek cross plan with tiers of typical byzantine squinches in the angles and detached columns for a dome that, alas, never soared over Torcello's flats; instead, there is a wooden roof and low drum.[1] But Saint Fosca has at least slim pillars of Greek marble outside, while the façade of Santa Maria has only one carved crumbling architrave, and inside it is a tomb.

Italian churches are generally such a dazzling cluster of paintings and carvings and gildings and statues and candles and hangings and votive offerings and pious prints, with every century, and every kind of taste, exquisite and monstrous, all jumbled together, that this nakedness of Santa Maria is frightening. In a northern or Protestant country one might be prepared for it, perhaps expect it, even be soothed by it. Here one could only think that before their island began to crumble beneath their feet the creators of Santa Maria Assunta had not the leisure to cover their cathedral with marble and mosaic and jasper and porphyry and alabaster and gilded and tinted carvings as no doubt they, like the builders of other longlived churches over in Venice, hoped and planned. As we stood in the lightsome, hollow nave, so little frequented and so rarely open as to be smelly and sweaty this August day, all we could see that they had had time to achieve was the chaste pulpit, the little chancel-screen with beautifully fantastic carvings of birds and beasts, and the carvings on the marble capitals of the pillars. The altar is unadorned. The tiers that rise like plain stairs behind it in the circle of the apse, for the priests and their bishop, are so crude that one can hardly be certain of their purpose. We had seen, outside, that the very shutters are rough stone flags, about four inches thick, hung on iron staples—the

[1] 'Here though we have a Greek inspiration it is pretty clear there were no Greek builders; and had the dome ever been finished it would probably have fallen.' Thomas Graham Jackson, op. cit. Vol I. 237.

Syrian builders in the timberless Haouran desert had to impro-
vise in just this way, using stone for every purpose. As we
looked, we felt, or at least I felt, as embarrassed as if we had
intruded on somebody's secret poverty.

Then we turned to look behind us, and gasped. There on the
great expanse of the western wall, covering all its height and
width, is a vast and dimly glittering Byzantine mosaic of the
Last Judgement, a sign of what the men of Torcello might
have achieved if time had not put a stop to their ambition.
It was like a sudden peal of trumpets. I felt as if a human spirit
had risen from underneath the ground and said: 'We wor-
shipped here. All the ritual of the Christian Church made this
nave fume and burn with the incense of our praise and the
passion of our adoration, glow with the hope of salvation and
tremble with the terror of eternal hell. Whether this old familiar heat stifled us, or the winds fingered the roof-tiles and the
spume sprayed across the flats and the candles slanted, *that*
image was there in the dusk. Poor? Naked? We who might
pass in for one moment to touch the feet of the Crucified felt
our nakedness before the nakedness of our God, our poverty as
we passed out under the eyes of our Judge. But empty? How
could this church be empty whose imagery was one of the first
things our children saw and the last thing our dying would
remember?'

'Not much to see there now,' Ginger said as we came out into
the heat and the sun.

'The gods have left their house,' I said, as we wandered to
the rear of the apse and lay drowsily in welcome shade on the
long grass under the tower. 'There was no sanctuary lamp.'
And I explain what that means: an empty tabernacle.

'But I thought in your religion God is everywhere?'

'When people say that God is everywhere they usually mean
that God is nowhere. If they really meant it they would as soon
go down on their knees to pray in a cocktail bar as in a church.
I could no more pray there than I could in Harry's Bar or Saint
Paul's. It is not a church now. It is just a building.'

'Surely, Saint Paul's,' he bridled, 'is a great work of art?'

'A great work of art?' I sighed. 'Art? Artful? Artless?' I once looked up the word *art* in that repository of confusion Roget's Thesaurus, and found among the list of synonyms, 'Ulysses, Machiavelli, sly-boots, fox, Yorkshireman, Scotchman, Jew, Yankee and intriguer.' There were references to *toilette* and to tailpiece. To gems, architecture, shoulder-knots, epaulets and *comme-il-faut*. The cathedral of San Marco and a lady's face. A church is what old Ruskin called a Book of Common Prayer.'

'That,' he remarked sleepily, 'no doubt explains why Italian churches are empty—except for gaping tourists?'

Still, it *was* their church, their work, built, admired, thought of in hours of distress. As every traghetto in Venice has its Madonna, sooty, with a tiny electric bulb, withered flowers, neglected, but never quite forgotten. I said so. Ginger gazed at me for a moment and then made that expressive Italian gesture which opens the palm level with the face and shivers it upwards to Heaven in exasperation. Then he went to sleep.

I woke up to find him gone, I redozed. His toe woke me up again. He had found a better place to swim; near the ferry; two old greasy steps that are all the remain of the quayside of a once-busy piazza. By now the water of the channel was a little cooler, the shadows a little longer. We returned for dinner on the open loggia. It was a perfect meal. We gossiped. . . . Our cigarette ends began to glow.

As we strolled back along the path to the landing-stage the west was also beginning to glow. The day died by inches. The Venetian sunset is best from any of these islands, or from the northern fondamenta, or from the Lido facing back to Venice where Maddalo saw

the flood
Which lay between the city and the shore
Paved with the image of the sky.

That evening it was never more lovely, with the Euganean

hills drinking rosy death and a saffron curtain rising slowly from the breathless water as if the lagoons were on fire. Only once before had it been as wonderful; one evening when dining on the Lido, at the Belvedere. Oh! the *fegatini alla Veneziana,* and the *mozzarella,* which is a cheese like Roman *provatura* made from the milk of the little blue Campagna buffaloes, spread with chopped anchovies, ending with *zabaione* as gold as the evening star above Santa Maria. That Lido evening, as the sky became a deeper red and a still deeper red behind the city's towers, the lights began to twinkle on the water, and presently Venice ceased to exist. This evening we watched its death from the flowing steamer whose wake burned in long shining eels of light. The lamps from the other islands were daggers of swaying fire. These reflected lights of Murano and Burano and the gathering dark suggested a depth of lagoon that does not exist. The islets were shadows on the sea.

As we were too lazy and too full of wine and food to walk back from the Fondamente through the slums, a gondola took us by the Rio dei Mendicanti, where the full moon fluttered in the canal, past the darkening head of Bartolommeo Colleoni, out at last to the lighted Molo. There we could hear, above the babble of quays, the distant throbbing of a band playing the Marcia Funebre from 'The Twilight of the Gods'. We sat in the Piazza to listen. It was a tribute of the *banda cittadina,* the waiter told us, 'per onorare il Maestro Direttore recentemente deceduto'. We drank americanos in the satisfying joy of being still alive and sober enough to know it.

What we may have talked of, if we did talk, I cannot, naturally, be expected to remember. The band would have played on for the dead musician. The moon would have risen over the cathedral. The steamers must have hooted from the landing-stages. And nobody in the babbling Piazza would have heard more than the loudest notes of the horns and the heaviest wallops of the funeral drum. . . .

The music stopped. The band broke up. The floodlighting died. The two little mechanical statues over the clock-tower hit their great bell eleven times and Ginger said he must go. A launch from the noisy cluttered Molo took him away to his billet, and I was alone.

Night on the Lagoons

I TAKE a gondola and go out on the southern lagoon, to my golden goddess, as I have done every night since I came.

Then she was frail and slight as a virgin; to-night she is breasted like a mother, but still I do not know whether it is I who am trembling or she, like lovers when the long marriage-day is at last done. When I think of her now I sigh, an exquisitely hopeless, exquisitely happy sigh, at the silence, the translucence, the velvet sheen. But I lose even the strength to sigh when I think of the spaciousness, the boundlessness, the calm infinity of the Venetian night. For here the moon is not, as with us, a thin wafer pasted on a level sky, or at most an orb flitting through it, cloud-chased, and not much more than cloud-high. It is a complete globe surrounded by air, centred in air, a divinity so inconceivably remote as to seem far nearer, if such a measurement were possible, to the void behind it than to us beneath it on the still waters. And this vastness above affects everything below, as if the spread of the waters must match the spread of the sky; so that although we know well that these little seaweed blobs of La Grazia and San Clemente, Santo Spirito and Poveglia, Saint George of the Seaweed and Saint Angelo in the Dust, are quite near to Venice, we seem under this moon to have come to them from a great distance and they as remote in the darkness as Pacific atolls. Nor do the specks of light we have left behind us, along the Molo and flickering the Piazzetta, dwindle this spaciousness about us; nor the lights downfalling on the white three-legged posts marking the channel northward to the Lido; nor the faint multitudes that cloud Giudecca. They are dwindled to nothing by the supreme nakedness of midnight. Nothing human prevails against this limitless space. Indeed, it expands all the more if we pass by a rare wandering gondola like our own, with its firefly *fanale* doubled from its prow in the water beneath. We see only one immense pulsing track along whose path, in delicate feeling for the wonder of it, the gondolier steers us to the moon's shore. If, now and again, we lift our eyes from the quiver of the water we find that in spite of all this radiance the things of world, though touched by it, remain dark. The distant bell-tower of San Giorgio Maggiore is a stalk of blackness that at once invokes the bright immensity above and surrenders to the dark immediately below. The shipping in the Giudecca channel shows a line of brass or the curve of a funnel, yet it all remains an indistinguishable hulk of clotted shadows. The moon drills holes into wharves and boat-sheds; it flecks the cypresses of a garden; it enters a gaping doorway; it creeps on the wavelets' edges along an island's shore; it suggests a thousand things; it defines none. Always the only positive light is that fluttering path before us; the only sound is the whispering and lapping of the water, the oar turning in its *forcole,* and the patient breathing of the gondolier. The only positive darkness is the prow of the gondola, rising and sinking, always rising and sinking, always nosing silently southward to the stubbed outline of some nameless dot jet against the radiance behind it. Has this summer night no end? Or shall we float farther and still farther south towards the eelmouths of Palestrina and Chioggia; and out between the forts south and south-west into the open Gulf, to the horizon of the Adriatic, to the thousand miles south and west to the Cyclades; and as far again; always south and west; until the moon grows pale at the doorway of the Orient where even now the waters are beginning to feel the chill of dawn?

Talk of the Devil

THE days passed, one by one, for weeks, and I had never been so content, never so much at ease, never so purely animal. I had let the surf of sensation roll me over and over on its sands. I had basked like a seal on the rocks of Nepenthe. The things I most enjoyed are the things least communicable; slivers of sunlight on water; a gondola passing; a white sail; a blissful sense, less sensual than a sense, a half-awareness of a pleasing ambience that can never now be defined, since I was only half aware of it and did not question it; odd things like the great noise at half-past nine each evening, when all the blessed bells in the Piazza rang together, why I do not know, and the demons with the raffle under the Ducal Palace—they didn't care about ART—roared through their loud-speaker, and Florian's and Quadri's played their Austrian tunes in disunison. (What could they play of Italian music but, perhaps, bits from *Rigoletto* or *La Bohème?* It was always this Austrian or German nonsense such as one might hear in any little café in Vienna.) Altogether a wonderful medley of noise such as went, I make no doubt, right to the heart of every Italian present. Or I enjoyed the talk of a stone-cutter about the various stones used in Venice; enjoyed *pesce di spada al pomodoro con piselli;* and the little squashy purple figs with the ham; and the thick cream in chocolate with creamy cakes; and enjoyed comparing *peperonati* and *zucchini* and *melenzane* and never getting them clear; and going one by one through the countless kinds of fish; and hearing the padrone curse the municipal authorities because they let the clergy stop them from having a casino in the Palazzo Dandolo where Casanova once gambled, although, he cried, Venice used to be full of these gaming-clubs, and as Londoners cool off in the dawn at Covent Garden's coffee-stalls, and Parisians at Les

Halles, the Venetians used to relax at the Vegetable Market; or I enjoyed the old waiter we called Pop who looked like a dreadful Hun and was a perfect baby. I enjoyed all the odds and ends that every traveller enjoys, adds up, remembers and forgets.

Then, one night, under that very moon of the lagoon, I found the old, old Devil tempting me. I caught myself asking myself, 'Why don't they write about all this? I do not mean about the Past. That has been over-written. I mean that there has this last thirty years, even in poor Ireland, been more good drama, poetry and fiction about the life of to-day than in all Italy about herself of *to-day*. Why does . . .'

But I just caught the Devil in time. For with temptation there is only one thing to do. If once the Devil gets inside the keyhole of the mind, one is all but lost. If once he gets a leg on the floor of the mind, one is quite lost. I wailed: 'I am beginning to have regrets! I am beginning to *think!*' The very next morning, before I could spoil the perfection of it all, I fled.

For wherever else in Italy one may be permitted to think, one must simply never think in Venice. To think in Venice is to be as lunatic as Mrs. Shandy, who, of all moments of the day and night and of all her life, chose the one supremely unsuitable moment of Tristram's history to ask Mr. Shandy if he had wound the clock and put out the dog.

Venice is the supreme test of a traveller's capacity for absorbing and enjoying the unfamiliar without question. Can there have been, for instance, a man who, on looking for the first time at Saint Mark's, did not feel within him the rumbles of the struggle for innocence? Possibly, if he has come from the East; for to the Oriental everything in Venice will seem natural because familiar. 'One may perhaps,' says one of the few reliable experts on Byzantine architecture, 'without being too fanciful trace an Oriental feeling in Venetian architecture from first to last; in the ogee arches of the windows and doors; in the strange Arabian-looking tester over the pulpit at Grado; in the picturesque decoration with inlaid plaques of the Palazzo Dario, built in the early days of the Renaissance. These are all

features peculiar to Venice and the countries over which she
ruled, and seem to show that she always looked east rather than
west.' But even when we recognise that we are in a western-
eastern city, and know enough about Saint Mark's to be prepared for that adjustment—know that it is said according to
tradition to be a copy of the vanished Church of the Holy
Apostles at Constantinople; observe the Greek plan; recognise the Byzantine style of the capitals, with their deep-cut
traceries and the pulvino or impost-block reduced to a firm
abacus; note the few animals or human forms, in accordance
with the old Byzantine iconoclastic tradition, almost as strict in
that as Islam; even though we may anticipate the colour and
glow of the mosaics, laid on piece by piece, cunningly, to catch
the light; or may remember that never a ship came into the
lagoons from the south and east without some gift to decorate
this lavish church; or be reminded that no domes rose in Italy
after Saint Mark's until the time of Brunelleschi . . . even
when we know all this and expect all this there must still be a
war in us between habit and novelty which will cloud the eye
and interpose questioning thought this side of joyful sensation.
What *are* those four horses *doing* up there over the central
porch? Why *is* that window behind them so glum, like a railway station? What is all this rocketing crocketing doing on the
gables? I must repeat what I have written about the Giotto
campanile in Florence. If we have only seen Saint Mark's in
pictures such questions will appear impertinent and silly. Face
to face with Saint Mark's itself the senses do not stir immediately and spontaneously. But who, fascinated by any beautiful
painting of any beautiful woman, by Titian's Flora, the Mona
Lisa or the Fornarina, seeing her in the flesh, might not well
fail to be attracted? I will confess that there were days when I
thought that San Marco would make a good entrance for a fun-
fair.

In Venice there are only two ways to complete enjoyment.
Either we come there with the eyes of innocence, and continue
to enjoy it in innocence; often, as a result, enjoying things that

the experts may believe we have no business to enjoy; or we must come there with expert knowledge, often, as a result denying ourselves much natural enjoyment, as Ruskin did: for there is, in the end, no such thing as completely expert knowledge, and experts are liable to be at the mercy of their own theories. After all, is it not Innocence but Knowledge that growls at those crockets on Saint Mark's, or that refuses to be enchanted by the Baroque statues of San Moisé cavorting in mid-air?

The experts need not froth at me for saying this. I would not say it so resolutely of any other Italian city but Venice alone. I make a special case of Venice. Elsewhere—in Pisa or Florence or Rome, cities where the intellect was powerfully and deliberately at work—one must bring knowledge to bear on what knowledge made. The carefully planned Pisan front is something that it is well to understand, not only to feel. But here so much has come from spontaneity and instinct that if we cannot respond with spontaneity and instinct then there is no half-way house to the specialists.

If then, as I did, you find yourself asking too many questions in Venice, know that the time has come to fly; unless, to be sure, you are prepared to fly farther—to Istanbul and to Antioch; with the Comte de Vogüé to the lost cities of Syria; with Choisy to the British Museum and Egyptian texts in search of the embryonic dome; with Jackson and Strzygowski to Dalmatia; from Mycenae and Thebes and Ctesiphon to Limoges and Périgueux and Angoulême, step by step along the forgotten tracks of Europe's childhood from Bagdad to Britain. For myself, I know that I am neither innocent nor expert, neither spontaneous nor specialist. I either gape and enjoy, or I muddle things out and muddle things up—usually up—until I find an expert to 'explain it all'; in other words to stop me from muddling with a sort of sleeping-draught of that real knowledge which is the stolid husbandman of instinct.

In Venice I had no expert by me. When I found myself starting to think, or to do what I call think, I knew it was time to run fast from Beelzebub. I took a ticket for the first place that occurred to me, which was Verona, there to swim, and lounge, and sunbathe, and never think about anything at all. And there, at the bombed railway station, stood Beelzebub, awaiting me with a smile, fat as a fool, accompanied by seven other little Beelzebubs all in gold-braided caps, with clever books under their arms, all smiling as benevolently as Japanese. We all got into a carozza, a little crowded, I admit, and chatting as sweetly as only old enemies can chat, we drove off to our appointment at Samarra, each of us wondering, behind his smile, by whom exactly this appointment had been so obligingly arranged for what was to prove the last weeks of my Italian summer.

Verona

I SHALL always remember Verona as I first saw it, in the dusk of a magnificent storm, looking across the muddy flow of the Adige at houses, mountains and sky through a film of rain that swiftly became a downpour. I had thrown open the casement windows and was watching the hissing drops pockmark the river beneath my windows. The dusk thickened as the thunder began to rumble among the Brescian Alps; an unceasing cannonade, an aerial bombardment that crashed and echoed as if buckets of noise were being tumbled out of a hole in the sky down the iron valleys. The houses on the far bank kept advancing and retiring, greenily, in explosions of beautiful lightning. The river gurgled. Along the horizons witches' fingers kept gesticulating bonily and phosphorescently. The bells of the Angelus were ringing gently in several tones all over the little city.

The room behind me kept sinking and rising out of a submarine dimness whenever the lightning flashed and fell. In one corner Beelzebub sat in an old plush armchair, smiling at me speculatively, his fat thighs crossed, one hand tapping his knee. Over the whisper of the rain in the river he said, in the lull of a rumble, as if in professional approval of Jehovah's wrath: 'Not a bad show?'

I had chosen the hotel because it was on the river. I chose it from my very old Baedeker—old and, by now, rather tattered, for I had formed the habit of tearing out pages and maps every day for easier reference according to my itinerary. It had recommended this place some thirty or forty years ago, and here it still was, pleasantly proposing to me that I and Italy were both in the year 1908. I was the only guest. A new proprietor had recently taken over the hotel, and even now workmen and boys were sticking up thin marble slabs in the foyer downstairs, and upstairs the painters were scratching the outside of my door. It was not very cosy, you may imagine, with all those ladders and paint-pots, but I do not hesitate to recommend it: the Grand Hotel Riva San Lorenzo. Pay no attention to the grandiose name. It cost L 450 a day, for room alone, which was about five shillings.

When my Doppelgänger spoke I turned, and by the glare of a sudden flash, followed by a prolonged echoing explosion, I examined him. I had never seen him so clearly before, though I had, of course, frequently talked to him—that is to myself, which comes to the same thing. (It is, as the reader knows, my secretest vice to have long arguments with him.) He looked like an Oxford don, with a soft full beard that reminded me of A. E. or William Morris or John Ruskin. He had the benignant blebby eyes of an old nanny, thick eyebrows, a falcon nose, and a sedentary paunch. All in all, he looked what you might call a nice old boy; and he looked damned intelligent.

The light flashed again. A million billiard-balls fell down an iron staircase. The bells rang on, undisturbed.

'This town,' I said, 'would make a wonderful setting for a film. And I know the title. "The Bells of Verona." With Bing Crosby.'

He sniffed.

'We underrate ourselves. Having been absurdly sentimental in Venice, we now wish to suggest that we are being cynical in Verona. What we are really doing is trying to hide our emotion.'

I raised my eyebrows loftily and returned to the glory of the storm. When the lightning hit the flood it was a river of golden snakes. In Venice my padrone would be rubbing his hands and gazing at the fretted lagoon with relief and pleasure. Rain brings up the fresh smells of dust. Does it bring out the bouquet of the canals?

'Now,' the cultured voice resumed, 'we must recall the associations of Verona. Dante. He was exiled here. We mustn't forget that. At the Court of the Can Grande. The Big Dog. Son of the Mastone. The Mastiff. Nice bunch of scoundrels those Scaligers. We must see their wonderful monuments, of course. Oh, yes, they must be examined *very* carefully. Then, what else? "Two Gentlemen of . . ." By Mr. Fletcher and Mr. Shakespeare. "Romeo and Juliet", by Mr. Shakespeare alone. Though Italians are better acquainted with the version of Signor Verdi. We shall see Juliet's tomb, though, I need hardly say, it will be empty. Naturally she never was in it . . .'

I whirled on him. He looked at me enquiringly.

'Yes?'

'We've had quite enough in Rome,' I snapped, 'about tombs. I shan't forget the chase you led me there after Saint Peter.'

The epicurean hands fluttered weakly.

'You can't deny it was interesting?'

'And futile. However,' I chuckled, 'I paid you off for that in Saint Peter's.'

A shadow passed over the humane countenance.

'There is,' he hurried on, 'a Roman amphitheatre in the Piazza Brà, where,' he smiled, currying favour, 'they have been having *more* open-air Grand Opera.'

'I refuse to be sarcastic about Grand Opera in ancient ruins. I like it.'

He shrugged faintly, as a don might to any barbarian; and

evaded discussion, also as a don would, with anybody, barbarian or not.

'Perhaps there is something to be said for the idea,' he agreed diffidently, no more meaning it than a don would. 'But, of course,' and he leaned forward eagerly, really interested this time, 'the great thing to see just now are the pictures in the Castel Vecchio. All School of Verona. Oh, probably a bit of a mixumgatherum. Provincial stuff in some ways. But *most* interesting.' He rubbed his fiend's hands. 'We shall have a *lot* to say about those pictures. Oh, quite a lot!'

I have always noticed that the one thing which brings even a pale glow of warmth, as of a consumptive, into his tea-rose cheeks is the mention of painting or sculpture or indeed any form of art. He loves everything inanimate.

'What I am looking forward to,' I said, with malice, 'is the swimming-pool. I hear Verona has a first-class swimming-pool.'

I hurt him that time.

'A swimming-pool? In this weather!'

The rain was already diminishing, the thunder fading back into the Tyrol.

'This is only a summer storm. In an hour it will be as bright and warm as ever. To-morrow morning the sun will be burnishing the whole land.' I laughed at his disapproving face. I was enjoying myself now. 'And there is something else I am looking forward to. On Monday there will be a horse-fair in town! An Italian horse-fair should be fun.'

That knocked him right out. He could not speak for a minute. He rose, more than ever like a wounded don or a shocked nanny.

'Have we come to Italy,' he demanded, 'to see *horses?*'

'And horse-copers,' I assured him. 'If we are humanists we are presumably interested in humanity. Unless we are of that awful tribe known as inhuman humanists?'

He looked at me for a second or two. I was so pleased with myself—I confess it in shame—that I did not see, and am only now presuming, guessing back at it, his eyelash peer. Oh, a most cunning Devil! He sat down again.

'So we are interested in horse-fairs?' he said softly.

'Most!' I cried, triumphantly.

'More than in art?' he smiled, as to a wilful child.

'Far more!' I cried, also rather like a wilful child.

The fingers of one hand fondled and gathered up the flaccid pink skin on the back of the other.

'Very well,' he murmured. 'Do not let us deter ourselves.'

A pale ray of sun stole between two dark wine-bags of cloud. The only noise now was the whispering race of the Adige. The Angelus had stopped.

'And now I'm going out,' I said saucily. 'Coming?'

He shook his head.

'We are not, frankly, much interested in these provincial towns. Pleasant little places enough. But thoughtless . . . thoughtless.'

'My cup of tea,' I smiled, bowed to him, and bumped my way out past the painters and the terrazzo workers in the foyer.

The old boy, who himself looked at that moment very like Ruskin, called after me:

'Ruskin said of Verona: "*That* is a city to be proud of indeed." You might ask the padrone if he agrees. He's a Milanese. It might start an interesting discussion with him.'

But I was too cute to be caught that way, ignored the padrone and stepped out into the Corso.

A Small-scale Florence

THE rain had stopped. The streets gleamed. The dusk was now miraculously reversed into an evening of bright and delightful coolness. The grass and the flowers in the gardens of the Piazza Brà were spring-fresh as I dined under the awning of the Löwenbräu and watched the evening crowds. The amphitheatre of Diocletian rose sombre to my left, too perfect to persuade, but with enough reverend brickwork to impress; on my right an old fourteenth-century gateway; beyond it the old guardhouse. Little to disturb but the usual bore in the centre of the gardens—Victor Emanuele II on horseback waving Italy to victory.

After the fervid excitements of Venice, that *femme fatale* of Italy, so beautiful, so seductive, and the bewildering tumult of Rome, this was exactly what I wanted: a pleasant country town living its own perfectly natural and normal provincial life, yet with enough of history and enough beautiful things to occupy the mind and delight the eye. One gets weary of an excess of loveliness. Even Siena had been too picturesque. I think it was Robert Byron who once said that you can only enjoy Italy when the monuments are off your conscience. There is sufficient antiquity in Verona for distinction without exhaustion. In an hour or two one may glance at most of its monuments, though it takes weeks to absorb their detail. After dinner I strolled about aimlessly, and before night fell I was at home with the geography of the little place.

There are, I found, only two main, busy streets in Verona. The Corso Cavour, with the Castel Vecchio at one end, magnificently poised over the river, lined by Michele San Michele's lovely palaces, passes through a Roman arch to the northern end of the Piazza Erbe, one of the liveliest and loveliest and most happy market-squares I know, bright with the awnings and umbrellas of the market-women, prattling at all hours. And parallel to the Corso is this busy side of the big city square, called by everybody the Brà (from pratum, a meadow) and by nobody the Piazza Vittorio Emanuele, dwindling into the thin lane of the Via Mazzini, which is as jostling as any Genovese sailors' quarter. That ends up at the southern end of the Piazza Erbe. The rest of Verona, apart from a few side streets, or the Via Pallone on market-days, is almost sleepy. For anybody entering Italy from the north, Verona is therefore a good place to rest after the journey, and ideal to fall at one's ease

into the rhythm of Italy. I could spend a summer here quite
contentedly, exploring the valleys that lead north to the foothills of the Tyrol—Verona is not more than thirty-five miles
from the former Austrian frontier—using it as a centre for
such towns as Mantua and Vicenza; and it is only twenty miles
from Lake Garda. I foresee that the next time I go to Venice I
shall, if coming this way, from the north, go through Verona
to Padua and pause there, and then instead of going on by the
railway through Mestre go by *tranvia* through Fusina, and so
across the lagoons.

There may be another reason besides the unassuming quiet
of Verona why I so quickly felt at ease in it. As I have said, it
is quite near the frontier of what up to 1919 was the old Austrian Tyrol; the Trentino. Due north, in the districts called the
Thirteen Parishes, and north-east in the Seven Parishes, there
are the descendants of Bavarian colonists, in whose dialect, so
an Italian scholar tells me, scraps of Middle High German may
yet be heard. I mean, we are pretty far north here, and the
architecture is northern, and though the famous Lombard energy may now be a thing of history (declined—who suggested
it?—with the decrease of wild-flesh in the forests and the increase of tame vegetables in the gardens), there is a something
in the air that is not of the soft south wind. I can well believe
the Ruskin was right when he found in Verona the master-
school of the Gothic of Venice, there, indeed, to be elaborated
under Byzantine influence into something far more rich and
strange, if also more stiff and languorous, less vigorous, less defined, less bold.

Is it, I wondered, not merely the Teutonic tradition that I
feel, but that the climate is less relaxing than on the lagoons;
and in spite of the warmth, and the innumerable balconies—
for which Verona is famous—that testify to it, I began to
wonder that the roofs were not more steeply pent to throw off
snow. The river's force I can see. All its banks are now walled
in, and when I cross the river to the lovely Giusti gardens,
where one could dream away many a morning, I tread a street

called Interrato dell Acqua Morta. The name tells me of swamps and islands and a filled-in branch of the Adige whose fierce sweep once cut into the land like a spear. Looking down into the rain-swollen river, and thinking of the muddy Arno, I decided that there is more than a touch of the force of Florence in Verona. The Guelph and Ghibelline factions, as we all know from the 'Montagues' and the 'Capulets' (Montecchi and Capuleti) raged here, too; the Scaligers repeated the ruthlessness and bloodiness, as well as the patronage of the Medicis; made their money, like them, out of common trade. Their name means that they began life as ladder-manufacturers. The strong houses in the Corso, like the great Castel Vecchio of Can Grande, are not only palaces, but forts. It is probably a fair comparison. A small-scale Florence, though far more charming than Florence; with the Pinacoteca to match the Pitti, the Giardino Giusti to match the Boboli, a toy-scale Piazza dei Signori, churches as striking as many in Florence, the old walls, the northern hills for summer-residence, and native painters and sculptors. And just as Florence, for all its wealth in art, gives out a strong human smell, so I felt in Verona most of all the presence of its people.

I am recalling the day of the funeral. Some children on holidays by the sea had been drowned while boating. Their coffins came from Milan by train, smothered in flowers, in open wagons where soldiers stood on guard with fixed bayonets. When the train arrived at the station there were scenes of the wildest emotion. I saw one mother, howling like a wild beast, so hysterical with misery that she had to be lifted on the shoulders of four men as if a corpse herself; but a screaming corpse; for as she lay rigid on their shoulders with arms extended as if crucified she still screamed to the sky. The procession winding across the big Piazza was immense. It took a half-hour to pass. Every institution in Verona was represented, convent children, the schoolboys, confraternities, friars, priests, military, police, civic officers; and as each coffin came into view, and then each group of mourners laden with im-

mense wreaths crossed by printed ribbons, and then the sob-
bing relatives, murmurs and moans rose and fell like the waves
that had washed the little bodies ashore. That noon the whole
city shut its shops. From noon to five in the evening all life
stopped.

That day I got an intense feeling about this small city that
whirled me back to the intimacy and compactness of Limerick
or Cork or Galway. The *Corriere's* full-page reports, with big
black-banded photos of the 'lutto cittadino' was like an issue
of *The Cork Examiner* or *The Galway Democrat,* only much
more sensitively done. No Irish journalist would have the art
to speak of the drowned children as *un fioretto di bambini,*
seeing them as a lost bunch of flowers. But the imagination
had been captured and the communal heart stirred in exactly
the same way, and I realised that everybody in that town must
know everybody else. Indeed, to see that it is so all you have
to do is to dine any evening on the Piazza. It is a public
audience, with friends detaching themselves from the Corso
to come to a table for a chat, eyes following faces with evident
familiarity, salutes passing, whispers following. Oh! A scan-
dalous little city, ideal for a storyteller.

Not for one moment would I compare Venice and Verona.
Verona was a subject-town of Venice and remains its vassal;
and even if it did give the Gothic hint to Venice it was only as
the vineyard gives the grape to the winepress. The comparison
suggests itself: Verona is to Venice what Beaujolais is to
Champagne. (Would that I had a flask of Beaujolais beside
me at this moment.) Still, Verona has one great pleasure that
Venice has not. It is a pleasure, while you are being delighted
by some Scaliger tomb, erected for a ruffian and fit for a god, to
know that what I must keep on calling a natural, normal life is
going on about you. It destroys the museum-feeling. I think of
Torcello. It was a perfect day. Its exquisiteness lay in its desolation, its loneliness, its intimations of mortality, and immortality. I returned to the Marcia Funebre, and spent the midnight hours in a swoon of ecstasy on the moonshot lagoons.

But I had to fly from the lagoons when I began to think that what Torcello was Venice might yet become; that the neglected palaces will, in perhaps another hundred years, begin to feel the piles beneath them crumble away. Here as one sat sipping a cinzano under Dante's statue it was an assurance to hear the markets daily babble through the Volto Barbaro; or as one left the Duomo to see the countrymen with red kerchiefs under their throats and bits of sticks in their fists come trotting in on their high-slung pony-traps to the fair-green, as their like had done since Pliny and Catullus walked these streets.

Art and Reality

ON market-day I deliberately sipped the naturalness of Verona like a wine-taster. I went to and fro between the fair-green and the Castel Vecchio; early in the morning, then after lunch, and again in the afternoon, tiring now of painting and sculpture, now of beasts and men, yet refreshed by each for each, feeling each time an almost insensate delight in the identification of art and life, the exaltation of the people of the campo by the artists of the castle.

What I was enjoying chiefly was the fundamental realism of the pictures. For this underlying realism of Italian painting is a thing that, over several months, I had only come to recognise fully by seeing it in its own surroundings. Those faces of madonnas that we find so unearthly when we look at them in London or Paris seem so because our habit of regarding all religious painting as unearthly in its subject prevents us from seeing that it is entirely earthly in its models; even as we may think that their mountains and lakes and limpid skies, and their backgrounds of castellated walls and arched perspectives are unlikely, even fairy-like, not only because they are formally drawn, but because we are unfamiliar with their actuality. The same unfamiliarity must come between us and all foreign art, such as Chinese painting or Indian sculpture, and would probably disappear likewise if we could go to China and India and be able to say of them as of these Italian paintings that these faces and towns are real faces and actual towns fancifully sweetened or heightened. I shall never forget the shock of joy I experienced when I casually turned that day from a landscape in the Castel Vecchio to another landscape which, for a second, seemed no less and no more beautiful, no less and no more real, and suddenly realised that I was looking through the frame of a deeply-embrasured window at the sunny perspective of the Adige. The gap between art and life in Italian pictures is, in short, much smaller when we see them in Italy than when we see them out of it. This, I have no doubt, has always been obvious to everybody but myself.

It made it all the more delightful for me to discover it for myself. You may know, for instance, Pisanello's picture in the Church of Santa Anastasia of Saint George liberating the Princess of Trebizond; a painting that is, when first seen, an hallucination of fantastic towers, campaniles and domes, richly-caparisoned horses, a collared hound, a dragon, a lion, a crouched ram, criminals swaying on a gibbet, men-at-arms, all, though now much *guasto,* in a blaze of a hundred colours. We no longer see such caparisons (or dragons), but when one has spent a few months, indeed a few weeks, in Italy that medley of pinnacles, domes, towers and turrets, immediately recognisable as Venetian and Florentine Gothic, holds no surprise; just as that lovely, pensive, heavy-lidded face of the princess may merely recall a girl seen at the swimming-pool. The background of Antonio Badile's *Madonna of the Piazza* is almost a photograph of a corner of Verona. Domenico Morone's *Madonna of the Fan* is a type straight from a coffee-shop. Bartolomeo Montagna's *Saint Giuliana and a Franciscan Martyr* came bowling in to-day to the fair-green.

So it is with a great many of those pictures, from the very

earliest. From the delightfully innocent thirteenth-century popular fresco called *Madonna Allattante,* showing the Virgin holding her breast in the greedy mouth of her baby, to the Mantegnas and Moros, what kept on impressing and pleasing me was their indubitable veracity. They are another argument for those of us who believe that writers should write and painters should paint only what they know, taking models only from nature, never from another writer or painter, another country or age. I am quite sure a great, if not the greater, part of the pleasure these pictures gave to the people who first saw them was on the lines of 'Will ye look at Beppo in an angel's wings! The dead spit of him!' This is not to deny all idealisation. I am equally sure it was not the 'dead spit' of Beppo. It was Beppo as he either is, now, in angel's wings, or as he was then, in moments when he heard wings whir like a swallow's in the passing breeze.

Soon after I came back from Italy I went into the National Gallery in London to look at the Italian pictures and test this again. The first picture I looked at was Verrocchio's *Tobias and the Angel.* Its charm is in great part its intimacy of detail. There are tiny figures on the bridge; the fish is held by what looks like a black bootlace; so intimate is the observation that Verrocchio has crossed the third and fourth toes of the angel; the dog is not much less realistic than Jan van Eyck's in *The Burgher and His Wife.* I next stood before Piero de Cosimo's *Battle of the Centaurs.* Here is realism in its most modern connotation; that which, for some reason, thinks low or brutal or sordid life more real than life which is refined and subtilised. You may remember the fierce group on the left where a Lapith is biting a centaur's nose, and he in turn grips an agonised Lapith apparently by the testicles and a third drags the victim away, and all four are streaming with blood; and, yet, there is tender and exquisite feeling, too, as in the whiteness of the mare with the pointed ears and the rich blackness of the stallion. Botticelli's *Miracle of Saint Zenobius* blends a like realism—as in the contorted face of the mother—with a formalism of concept and colour that may well distract us from the reality of the painting if we do not deliberately look for it. The same is true all around, even of the most idealised picture, like Filippino Lippi's *Virgin and Child*. If we could remove the virgin's face to another context she could be, as she probably was, a little street-girl. But this realism is gone now. People have forgotten or refuse to bother to understand that Realism is merely a convention whereby you take a bit of physical fact and play tricks with it. Realism implies Magic. You take a simple wench and, lo, by magic she is changed into a Madonna. It is the same as changing a billiard-ball into a flower. A fountain of gold leaps from a top-hat. If you cannot be a magician you must stop trying to be a realist; for if you cannot wave the wand the billiard-ball remains and the wench remains and the top-hat remains, ball, wench and hat; which is not funny. To-day, Realism has become one of the most silly, beastly and degraded words in the language. They talk of surrealism. There is no such thing. What is the *Madonna della Sedia* but reality surmounted? What they should talk of is subrealism, for that is what most of their nonsense is.

I have a young friend, younger at any rate than I am, a sculptor, who after studying in Paris resolutely returned to work in the little city of Cork, where no sculptor has ever worked before—apart from 'monumental' sculptors carving pretty figures for tombstones in the base commercial Italian fashion. He works in an old yard, near a tannery, in a near-slum, where somebody breeds greyhounds; alone; with nobody to talk to about sculpting but old stonemasons, 'Sons of the Dust', as they call themselves in their trade. His models are servant-girls. His Madonnas sell fish or scrub floors. He is at present carving a Virgin and twelve Apostles for a church in San Francisco. When they will look up, in 'Frisco, at those figures, to which he imparts by formalising them a degree of hieratic dignity, they will not think of a Cork servant-girl or of Cork fishermen, any more than we, looking at Morone's *Madonna with the Fan,* think of a Veronese servant-maid. Yet without their realism, however idealised, these sculptures would not hold anybody's eye.

Fair-Day

VERONA was, by no means, the first place in Italy in which I had been pleased, in snatches, by this sense of the oneness of art and life, but it had never before given me such intense satisfaction as on that crowded fair-day when I wandered to and from between the two extremities of the town: from the castle by the northern sweep of the river along under the towering rose-red walls of the Via Pallone to where the river swept to the south below the campo.

'Even in those old walls,' I said to myself, 'what a bond there is between the design of art and the needs of life'; and I remembered that skilful Veronese arch to which Ruskin draws our eyes, where the mason so nicely mingled bricks and stones, gradually drawing the redness of the brick into the white cut-stone voussoirs; and as I walked I noted the Veronese trick of mingling courses of brick with courses of rounded pebbles, a simple but delightful touch of popular craft; and when I saw an old ironwork railing to a balcony and heard a farrier's anvil clang near by I thought how to this day the tradition of the ironworker's skill must still live on. In all this I was making that bridge, which every artist longs for, between the loneliness of his private dreams and the gaiety of the public square.

In the campo I might have been on a fair-field in Tipperary. In that hot dusty market-place under the walls of the mediae-val town, glowing like a rose in the sunlight, as I stood watching a group of farmers dispose of an ox, dignified of countenance as an ox in a Greek frieze, I noted that they made every single one of the gestures that accompany the selling of a cow at an Irish fair: the middle-man dragging purchaser and seller together, clasping their hands, beating his palm on the joined fists, splitting the difference, cajoling, abusing, mocking, appealing and triumphing. There were the same passion, the same humour, the same leisurely sense of timelessness. The horses were trotted up and down in the same way; the cows poked at belittlingly, the dealers abused and abusing; the stalls sold similar goods; the inns offered the same bargain-lodgings for the night. There was the same pleasant smell of dung. And after the great midday heat the cafés filled and heavy meals of risotto or macaroni were ladled into the maws of red faces and washed down with local beer or red wine with the same gusto that Theigue or Pat will ladle in his bacon and cabbage and draught porter. Though, to be sure, with what a difference in the background! Instead of our monotonous, endlessly-same Irish country pubs, shops and cement houses, which one seems to remember most vividly under a drizzling rain, and I do not mind saying, even remembers with a foolish affection, here is the sunlit heritage of centuries.

Is the Bridge Down?

AND then the Tempter pulled the lasso that he had been for days playing about my unfortunate head. I asked the question I had dodged in Venice. For I had suddenly thought of Somerville and Ross—for that matter I might have thought of Jorrocks—and all my pleasure had gone cold.

'You mean?' said the cultured voice at my side.

'I mean—' I said, hardly turning to look at the full beard, sad eyes and falcon nose of Herr Doppelgänger—'I mean—where is the expression of all this in Italian art to-day?'

'In painting?

'I mean in novels and plays. It's in painting all right! It is in . . .'

I stopped.

'Yes?' he prompted. 'We are thinking that that *was* rather a long time ago, aren't we? Come, let's stroll out of this noisy place. It's impossible to think with all this mooing and bellowing.'

Deep in thought (Oh! up to the neck in it!), we went slowly towards the river, heads down, seeing nothing any longer, not even the glorious church of San Fermo,[1] nor the sun on the Adige as we crossed over to the Left Bank, Veronetta as they affectionately called it, and so to the Giusti gardens, whose five-hundred-year-old cypresses were smoking magnificently to the blue sky, perhaps the finest and oldest cypresses in all Italy.

Here I must ask my reader to observe how truthful I am. No self-exculpation? Nothing here about wrestling with temptation? But it just does not happen that way. Preachers say, 'When the Tempter says to you *Do this,* or *Do that,* say to him . . . etc.' But the Tempter is never such an ass as to say anything of the sort. He does not put the apple into your hand, saying, *Eat this.* He just puts the apple into your hand, and you wake up to find that you are absentmindedly eating it. Surely it must have been at some time or another everybody's experience to become suddenly aware that he is absentmindedly kissing a lady whom he had no business to be kissing? 'Of course—' the preacher will go on, implying that he knows all about this (as he does not or should not)—'of course, you cannot be blamed for an unconscious lapse, but when you do wake up, *then* is the time to wrestle.' I am not excusing myself. But has anybody really ever wrestled with an apple? Which he has, in any case, already half-eaten? My intent at that moment

[1] 'The whole of the architecture of this church may be characterised as exhibiting the maxima of simplicity in construction and perfection in workmanship' (Ruskin). It is in this church, on the outer arcade, of stone and inlaid brick that he discovered the arch-type of Venetian Gothic.

was simply to take this old argufying Beelzebub by the neck
and show him what a fool he was. We would have it out once
and for all! And after that—never again; not one other word of
argument ever again about *anything*. I admit I had said this
about six thousand times before. Firm purpose of amendment
and all that. I am a sinner. I confess it. Hopeless! When it
comes to sinning the Russians and myself are like crossed
fingers.

'The thing is inescapable,' Beelzebub went on, deftly treading
on a snail. 'There are two clocks in Italy, the Then and the
Now. The beauty is partly Then and partly Now. Now, in so far
as the sun and the cypresses and the vineyards are unsoilable;
and the monuments are all but immortal; and there are so
many of them that even the restorers and the dealers have not
been able entirely to spoil their glory. Now, too, in so far as the
people are the most charming people in the world. Then in so
far as they have added little to what they have inherited. We
can't evade it! The people are the axle of the whole question.
The first time we see Italy we are too charmed by the pure
picturesqueness of it to think or ask beyond it. Then imperceptibly we begin to get interested in the people, and at last
we end . . .' (here he smiled at me like a kindly old father-
confessor, pinching my arm affectionately) '. . . we end up
at a horse-fair, asking ourselves questions.'

'That reminds me,' I said. 'Where have you been these last
few days?'

'You missed me?' he asked with a hopeful smile. 'Here and
there. Here and there. Even in Verona there are one or two
intelligent people with whom it is pleasant to have a little
thoughtful discussion. But we must not lose track of our ideas.
What a fine piece of stonework that is,' he deflected, looking at
a fountain-base. 'Sixteenth century, of course. They do
nothing so good nowadays. And it needs to be repaired. Yes,
yes,' he sighed, and we began to climb towards the grotto, 'it
all so often reminds me of the old Spanish proverb. "In Spain

everything decays except the race." Coming from Ireland, we can appreciate that!'

I knitted my brows fiercely.

'And, yet, somehow,' I grumbled, 'I thought I had settled this once for all in Siena. Italy makes Italians—Italians make Italy—nation and man have become one. Being and not doing, and so on.'

'There is no such thing in Italy as one nation, not in our sense. Look!'

We had climbed high enough to be able to see, across the roofs, the Apennine peaks beyond Lago di Garda and above Lago d'Iseo. He was pointing down among the roofs with his graceful flabby hand, on which a signet ring flashed in the sunlight, towards the outline of the Roman amphitheatre.

'There is one Italy. Rome. Latium. Your vast and long "perspective of history". Too vast. Too long. Too rich.'

'Too rich?' I asked.

'Too rich! And too old and too dead and yet too powerful in its influence on the Italian mind. They can never forget they were once the greatest empire in the world. It is like being born poor of rich parents and not being able to forget it. A sort of "Tess of the d'Urbervilles" situation. The very first minute we landed in Turin that hot morning, and saw the arcades and the Grand Opera monuments, and the next day that absurdly immense Piazza by the river, with chamber-pots hanging from the pillars, we realised that it was a colossal anachronism. The Italian *folie de grandeur* began with United Italy. Even before then Garibaldi had it. Mazzini had it. Mussolini had it—badly. They just cannot and will not cut their cloth according to their measure. United Italy,' he went on, 'was the curse of Italy. It killed all the old local familiar life and folk-ways. It did not weld. It merely centralised and rolled-out. Cavour merely gave them an illusion of power, unlike Bismarck, who gave Germany real power. They didn't want power, because power means responsibility, obedience, submission, ruthlessness, work, and ultimately war.'

Art and the Populace

'BLESS their hearts,' I said fervently; and then, 'Are we trying to blame Garibaldi? I mean for handing over Italy to the King instead of founding a modest Republic? But what is a Republic?' I sighed. 'I know all about these Republics. We are supposed to have one in Eire, and it is enough to make any man echo Carducci's "La nostra patria e vile". The Republic becomes the tail that wags the dog. There is another Spanish proverb. *Raza de perro malo por el rabo se conoce.* You know the breed of a bad dog by his tail. There are only two Republics in the world to-day, Russia and America. And they are both empires.'

He shrugged. We were now sitting in the lofty look-out and did not look out, though to our right was the old Roman theatre where once Theodoric sat on a bronze horse so large that birds flew in and out of its nostrils to nest in its belly, and below us the panorama of the Apennines over the cypress-tips and the roof-sea of Verona. He said:

'It is a large question if the republican idea suits them. Did it ever? You know we talk loosely of the mediaeval republics of Italy; but they never existed. Florence was never a republic. It was a makeshift, hand-to-mouth balance of power, a constant squabble between one set of privileges and another. The Medicis were geniuses in the art of remaining private citizens within the framework of the republican institution while being secretly masters of the State—simply by seeing to it that nobody but their own crowd ever got power.[1] Only once did Florence have anything like a democratic constitution; when Savonarola got it for her; and they soon got rid of him. Or, rather, the Papacy did. There is no denying it: the idea of the State, even the true City State, not to speak of the National

[1] See Villari. *The Two First Centuries of Florentine History* (London 1905, p. 487).

State, never really took root in Italy. The nobles and the merchants didn't want it. The terrific individualism of the Italian nature resented the thought of obedience even when they most needed alliances. And the Papacy did not encourage it. There is a famous comment of Machiavelli about that. He says the Popes "always feared everyone who rose to great power in Italy, albeit his power was exercised in favour of the Church. And insomuch as the Popes sought to lower that power frequent tumults would arise and frequent changes of power, since fear of a tyrant led to the exaltation of some feeble personage, and then as his power became increased he in turn was feared, and being feared, his overthrow was desired." And, mind you, it is hard to blame the Church—if we once grant it the right to be a temporal power—with the old Empire in the north always threatening it, and who could trust the French, and who could trust any one of the city states not to combine at any moment with one or the other for its own ends? The reason Savonarola was burned was not because he was a heretic—it has long since been conceded that he was not —but that he encouraged the French King to invade Italy, and because he defied the Papal League formed against him.'

'And yet the great flourishing period of Italian art——'

'Exactly. When Arnolfo di Cambio was planning the Baptistery of Florence was it the *popolazzo* or the *popolo grasso,* the wealthy and the noble or the masses, who commissioned him? The point is that great art is not created by great masses of people. It is the creation of the few. The very few.'

'We shall fall foul of Ruskin over this, you know?'

Beelzebub petulantly stamped his patent-leather foot and cried:

'Ruskin was a genius. He had a mind packed with knowledge. He wrote divine English. He had X-ray eyes. Nobody but the dogs of the lanes knew more about Venice than he. He was a giant. By all means let us go down on our knees before his exposition of Gothic and Byzantine, as he literally went on his knees, with note-book and ruler, before them. Nobody has ever done it better; probably nobody ever will surpass him. We have to admire the man who sketched, with meticulous accuracy, the details of Venetian palaces while hanging over the Grand Canal—doubtless to the astonishment of the natives —with one arm about a pillar and his sketch-book propped between his tummy and the wall, or who went crawling with a candle into the vaults under the canal at the risk of getting malaria and of being bitten by the rats. But we must also re- member that the man had two manias. He believed that the essence of architecture is ornament, and that all modern build- ings should slavishly follow the style of six hundred and fifty years ago.[1] And that was because he loathed Renaissance art and admired Gothic and Byzantine; not just that he had a preference for the one and an antipathy to the other. And that came from the fact that he loved everything that idealised reality. Byzantine formalisations and Gothic idealisations were right up *his* street. And all that probably came from the fact that he was a mild, lymphatic, shy poor chap, with no least capacity for human friendship; or, as we know, for love. In other words his criticism is an amazing mixture of objective and subjective. Naturally he was antipathetic to Renaissance vigour and arrogance. He abused it like a fish-hag. Its atheism, its deadness, its want of variety, the envy of its artists, its sen- suality, its vanity, its paganism, its boastful pomp, its infidelity, its immorality, its appeal to base feelings, its ugliness, its aris- tocratic and unbending spirit—they are all his own words and

[1] 'The rigid formulas of the classic school were ridiculed by the neo-Goth, but he in his turn promptly put himself into fetters of his own forging. We were taught to analyse old work "as a German grammarian classes the powers of a preposition; and under this absolute irrefragable authority we are to begin to work, admitting not so much as an alteration in the depth of a cavetto, or the breadth of a fillet". And on this principle the new school worked during the greater part of the last century, producing a vast output of work imitating more or less well, or more or less badly, the architecture of the Middle Ages, and in a few cases, it must be confessed, rivalling if not surpassing the model in every respect but that of originality. But if there is one lesson more than another which archaeology teaches us it is this: that art to be worth anything must be modern, and express its own age and no other. It has always been so in the past. . . .' T. G. Jackson. *Byzantine and Romanesque Architecture,* Cambridge 1913, Vol. I, Introduction; quoting Ruskin from *The Seven Lamps of Architecture,* 1849, p. 190.

phrases. If, with that, mind you, he had had any real human warmth—and, mark you, pity for poor people who can't have Art is no sign of warmth; the poor don't want Art, they want affection—we should think that behind this Gothic fury of his there lay some possible, some attainable, desirable concept of life. But had he any such concept? The man who believed the Italians were much better off under the Austrians?[1] Who had a lot to say in Venice about man (in the abstract), but not a word about Manin, that great Venetian who less than a year before had stood at bay among the lagoons through the long agony of the siege of the Venetian Republic? The man whose only comment on that siege is that a cannon-ball tore a hole through a Tintoretto and that nobody had yet mended it? The man who spoke of the poor of Venice only once, so far as I know, and then to say sarcastically that they have three festas a week and work far less than an English labourer?'

Here Beelzebub glanced wickedly at me, as he quoted an earlier taunt of my own at himself:

'We all know the inhuman Humanist. The inhuman Mediae-valist should share beds with him. Whistler was a perky vulgar little devil, but beside him Ruskin was a pompous, ungenerous, parsonical ass. I have no patience with the sort of criticism which uses the Middle Ages, or the Renaissance, or anything else to play the taws on one's own rump. Anyway, I believe there was just as much arrogance and envy among the mediae-val artists as there was among the later men. Think of the fierce squabbles over the building of the campanile in Florence, for example. And how could buildings like the cathedrals of Siena, Pisa, or Florence be built other than by individual minds con-structing as deliberately as an engineer constructs a bridge? I just do not believe that art, anywhere, at any time, can be created in any other way. Though, of course, I freely admit that

[1] 'There is, indeed, much true distress occasioned by the measures which the Government is sometimes compelled to take to repress sedition, but the blame of this lies with those whose occupation is the excitement of sedition.' *Stones of Venice,* Vol. III (London 1898, p. 221).

every such individual is indebted in some degree to a tradition
and cannot create entirely outside a tradition! As for Ruskin's
idea that there was a decay in art because there was a decay in
religion after 1500 that is another subjective idea, born of the
fact that he was born of a Protestant father and mother who
believed that Rome was Sodom, Gomorrah and Babylon
rolled into one. Naturally all art had to be bad in Italy after
Luther pinned his ninety-five propositions to the door at
Wittenberg! I believe that all art, in a word, partakes in some
degree of the aristocratic spirit.'

'Hold hard now!' I cried. 'We are contradicting ourselves,
First we say the Italians have a *folie de grandeur*. Then we say
they did their best work in the very times and circumstances
that, if anything did after the Roman empire, would justify a
feeling of pride in the grandeur of Italy's genius and destiny?
Which do we want for Italy? Modesty or arrogance?'

Herr Doppelgänger raised his delicate hand and let it fall
with resignation.

'Arrogance is justified when it justifies itself. When it doesn't
it isn't. Why it does at one time and does not at another is not
for us to say. We describe what happened. It is for Italians to
explain. Ultimately it is probably a question of traditions help-
ing or not. Some do. Some don't. Switching on arrogance
doesn't produce art; nor switching on humility either.'

'Are we getting lost?' I asked. 'Let's remember that in all
this what we are talking about is *modern* Italy. Our real question is whether the old traditions carry over into the present;
whether our friends the cattle-drovers down there in the
Campo have any mortal connection with the painting in the
Castello or the architecture in the Corso.'

'Well, then, if we are talking of modern Italy let us certainly
leave Ruskin out of it. Whatever Ruskin was he was not modern, he was certainly not a man of his own day.'

I mused. An Angelus bell began to ring beneath us. Was it, I
wondered, a question of distinguishing between natural great-

ness and that pretentiousness which *is* a *folie*. But whence this folly? Doesn't it come from some sort of evasiveness? Then I said:

' "Too rich?" That was your word. I wonder . . . Suppose I were, for example, a Veronese and "owned" Verona, or better, a Venetian and "owned" Venice as I might "own" Dublin by birth and habit. Suppose the Piazza San Marco was mine day after day and night after night? I would have everything that the eyes and the heart desires of beauty. Colour, marble, gold mosaics, towers, pinnacles, bells, pigeons fluttering, the Ducal Palace, the towering campanile, the colonnades and arcades, the blue sky, the hot sun, the wine, the lagoons. I could lean casually against the noblest bronzes, scrape my match on a Byzantine pillar, look in no direction without plangent pleasure, never wander ten yards without wishing to pause and drink in some new satisfaction, as exciting as it would be soothing, even if it were only the sun leaping on a patch of water reflecting the black and gold of a flotilla of gondolas. . . . Suppose I had all that, would I be urged to ask for more? Or to put it another way, has the soul of Italy created itself to satiety while our poorer life constantly demands more and more imaginative compensations?'

'Paris is rich. It is not silent, and it has consistently produced the greatest painting in Europe since the seventeenth century.'

The cypresses in the gardens were darker than they had been. The Apennines were growing more and more clear as the sun drew its warm light closer and closer to their serrated lines. I thought I observed a delicate September quality of coolness in the evening air.

'I think the truth of it is,' said my other-half, 'that the time is gone since countries could live on their own fat. The old momentums grow weary. They are an old people.'

'A lovely people,' I insisted. 'I will not have a word said against them.'

The hand lifting weakly, neither in assent nor dissent, was pinker than ever in the new softness of the light.

'You don't mind their evasiveness?' he asked politely.

I laughed.

'I don't even mind their lies, and I think they lie even more ardently and often than we Irish do. In Dublin I bought an English detective-story. I only started to read it last night. The victim was an Irishman. One witness in describing him to the Inspector said: "He interested me. To me he became a living symbol of what we used to call the Irish problem. He had the wit, the versatility, the charm and the good looks of the real southern Irishman, and he had the illogical, rebellious, thriftless, lying habits of the type. . . . He couldn't go straight, because he was by nature devious. . . . He always lied. I knew that he lied. He knew that I knew that he lied. On that basis of mutual understanding, Inspector, I studied the Irish Problem." [1] A few nights before I was reading a novel by F. Marion Crawford, an American writer, who was writing about Italians. He said this: "The Italian is apt to share the opinion of the ostrich, who ducks his head and believes his whole body is hidden. Foreigners use strong language concerning the Italian lie, but this only proves how transparent the deception is. It is a singular fact, but one which may often be observed, that Italians who lie systematically will frequently believe each other to their own ruin, with a childlike faith rarely found North of the Alps. This seems to me to prove that their dishonesty has outgrown their indolent intelligence . . ." [2] I expect both statements are to the same degree true, false and irrelevant. But why did you ask me if I minded Italian evasiveness?'

'Haven't we answered it just now? "Their indolent intelligence." They evade the facts. Or, as I was saying, a race cannot live on its fat. It has to keep on using its intelligence. Patriotism is not enough. Nor tradition. Tradition is a tree that needs pruning, grafting. Even forests fall. What sort of tradition is it that could put up a thing like the Victor Emanuele monument

---

[1] *Murder by Matchlight*, by E. C. R. Lorac.
[2] *Sant' Ilario*. F. Marion Crawford.

in Rome, right under the shadows of the Capitol? They need realists to keep on stirring them awake.'

'In Florence I felt that the human tradition is alive. In Siena I felt that the patriotic tradition is alive. In Rome I felt . . .' I slowed down cautiously and then went on '. . . that the religious tradition is alive.'

'These things are the ground-swell,' he murmured. 'That always heaves.'

'We must do them full justice,' I insisted. 'When it comes to politics they are not ostriches, as Crawford suggested. Talk to any Italian about politics and he will deride his own politics. They are as politically sceptical as the Greeks. They refuse to deceive themselves about politics'.

'That at least the House of Savoy taught them—by being a failure. They found that whether they were a centralised kingdom or a series of disparate duchies the poor remained poor and the rich remained rich.'

'They got more personal liberty!' I cried.

'What good is liberty without spaghetti?' he asked.

'They were always just as short of food.'

'They were never any more short of happiness. And if they *are* sceptical about politics,' he went on angrily, 'why are they so damn sentimental about everything else? Why aren't they sceptical about art? Or at least critical? Look at the way the French take their own art to pieces. Always questioning it, analysing it, fighting like furies over it. It is the great weakness of English art that they are too damn' polite about it. "Quite good old chap. Perhaps, if one may say so, always, of course, deferring to your opinion, might it not conceivably be possible. . . ." Do you know where all the vigour and intelligence of Italy has gone to? Into engineering and sport.'

I laughed at a pleasant memory.

'I remember one night in the Piazza della Republica, in Florence, a terrific row started among the waiters. You know the way Italians argue. They nearly came to blows. They completely abandoned their clients. They screamed at one an-

other. It was all about the bicycle race in France. The Tour de
France. A Frenchman had won it, and Italians came second,
third and fourth, and a Frenchman fifth. I have forgotten what
exactly was the point. Very like us Irish. The only things that
excite us, too, are sport and politics.'

His face glowed in the sunset. His whole body was a hellish
pink.

'It all comes back to the realism of the Castel Vecchio. I
would call it not Realism but Modernism. As we observed,
they used to paint the facts of their own day, devotedly, with
absorption, you might say with obsession. Where is all *that*
"realism" gone to-day?'

'Dear heavens, the realism is the basis—I agree to that—but it
is—I made that quite clear—*only* a basis, heightened, softened,
anything you like, idealised. . . . And why do you call them
sentimental? They are a naturally romantic people. As a romantic myself——'

Beelzebub drew his soft cow's tail from under him and
gently brushed the dust from his shoe-tip, and slyly smiled
sideways at me.

'Have we forgotten that we once wrote something rather
good about that? About the difference between being romantic
and being sentimental? Shall we quote it? "When the will of
the world, now barely hanging on by its finger-nails, becomes
intense again romance will warm life all over the globe. For
romance is not made of pretty things. As a movement it began
in France out of dissatisfaction and despair; it was heralded in
England by a poet who wanted to speak the language of simple
men and describe the most common and actual things. Romance comes out of blood and tears and sweat

> *A mound of refuse or the sweepings of a street,*
> *Old kettles, old bottles, and a broken can,*
> *Old iron, old bones, old rags, that raving slut*
> *Who keeps the till . . .*

Yeats created his lovely and idealistic play *The Countess*

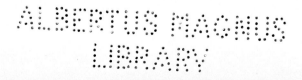

Cathleen out of his puzzlement at a real woman whose soul was being destroyed by fanaticism and hate. Baudelaire's flowers were made of evil. Villon's songs were made of rags. Chocolate-box colleens are made of money. Sentimental Ireland—or shall we say Sentimental Italy—is made of currency notes. The essence of both is pretence and escapism. Countess Cathleen ni Houlihan as a pin-up girl. If we want the romantic Ireland—or shall we say Italy—to come again it will not be by the closing of eyes but by the opening of them; indeed by following Yeats's epitaph, cut on the limestone flag over his grave under Ben Bulben:

> *Cast a cold eye*
> *On life, on death.*
> *Horseman, pass by!'*[1]

He rose.

'You were right,' he went on. 'Romance is made out of cold reality. If you get away from reality—and it is *so* easy—you get something which is such an evasion of all experience that we call it sentimentality. You say, for example, that the religious tradition lives. Does it? Or if it does, how does it? We are in Verona. Take a carrozza to-morrow and go out to the chapel of the Little Flower which they call the Santuario Basilica di Santa Teresa del Bambino Gesù. There is modern Italian religious art at its unbeatable worst, its most deplorably hideous, its most nauseatingly sentimental. Angels in white marble, one playing a marble harp, complete with marble strings, one pointing upward, one pointing downward, Teresa in coloured wax, fully clothed, in real clothes, behind plate-glass, the Virgin toppling above, all of them in different sizes, amid a dazzle of tiles, reliefs of Popes, cute carvings, cunning whatnots, a mountain of vulgarity, the sort of slush with which your Irish churches are packed, ordered from shops by the foot or by the piece, the counterpart of the thousand *devotionettes* that corrupt the innocent soul as gauds lure innocence to be a

---

[1] *The Bell.* Edited by O'Faolain, Dublin (August 1945).

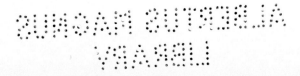

harlot, and all forgiven because, forsooth, "It is so *innocent!*"
The world wasn't made for innocents! Nor am I,' he leered,
'to be defeated by innocence.'

'It's better than materialism,' I said, feebly.

'Is that the best you can say for it?'

He sniffed the evening breeze.

"I must be going. I have another appointment," he murmured, 'and I must leave you. There is a young man in Athens
in sore need of me. I shall have to fly all night. Wish me a
happy landing.'

And with a benign smile and a nod he strolled down the
path between the cypresses, his soft tail swaying behind his
heels, and the sunset over the mountains glowing on his horned
curls. A good devil? A bad devil? Or just a devil? All I know
is that I had not defeated him and that he had answered nothing. But he had broken the spell.

Vale!

AFTER a while I followed
through the twilight. A fountain tinkled drops of light. I dined
for the last time in the Löwenbräu and had a last drink in the
shadowy Piazza Dante, where a fresh poster on the base uttered some political catch-cry. The Piazza Erbe was lighted-
up and prattling. The corso on the Via Mazzini was as thick as
usual. The river whispered me to sleep.

In the morning I took the train for Milan. The green of the
rice-fields was as vivid as a wet Irish field, and the water of the
irrigation ditches gleamed. Near Pavia—I went as I came via
Turin—the clouds based on the horizon stood in the blue air
like arrested explosions. Once again, and for the last time, the
clear sky was a revelation of the purity of vision of this Italian

atmosphere. A campanile stood with clear rose edges, as in Fra Angelico or a Sienese fresco. I saw in that moment with the eyes of many painters, and saw why and how they saw with such translucent eyes into the soul of things.

All night I went through France, on to Paris and to the Irish plane, and the next afternoon we were over the motionless corrugation of the Irish sea. Then the brown-green foothills of the Wicklow mountains, and the velvet softness of the Irish fields floated through the steam of the Irish clouds. As I drove into Dublin the grass was up to the udders of the cows. In a Dublin hotel I dined on a chicken that had been a good and kind chicken, and had had a good and kind hen-wife; and on bacon that had been a good and kind pig. The cook would have been lynched in Italy. There were bands playing in the street outside. They had been celebrating something called 'Ninety-Eight. The houses were hideous. The people were friendly and courteous. As I ate I was thinking of the Löwenbräu and the blue transparent sky and I was thinking . . .

'Grand weather, sir,' said the waiter. 'A great bit of heat, thank God.'

I looked out at the pallid sunlight. Absently I said 'Yes?'

. . . I was thinking that when next I go to Italy I will not think at all.

DI